Laugh & Learn
Cartoon Features

Laugh & Learn Cartoon Features

For Church Publications

Eddie Eddings

BAKER BOOK HOUSE
Grand Rapids, Michigan 49516

Copyright 1991 by
Baker Book House Company

ISBN: 0-8010-3211-3

Printed in the United States of America

To
my loving wife, **Mary**, who has had to live with an
"animated cartoon" for twenty-one years

And to my super-talented children:
David, **Jenny**, **Tammy**, and **Amy**

And to
Dr. J. William F. Miles, my beloved mentor

Contents

Introduction

I love facts. They enlighten and entertain the mind. They are God's arguments.

I love laughter. It can help overcome resistance and dissolve tension.

I love God's Word. It always challenges the reader to go deeper into its truth and encourages the believer to appropriate its principles. No one can read the Bible and remain the same.

I love to stimulate people to reverence God. An apprehension of God's sovereign grace is the best way I know to humble the human heart and glorify God.

My prayer is that you will find this book both challenging and fun!

Eddie Eddings

Cartoons

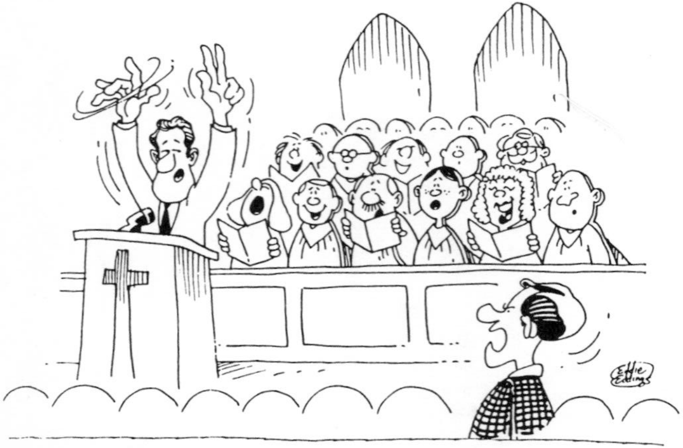
Eddie Eddings

"YOU CAN'T FOOL ME! HALF OF THOSE CHOIR MEMBERS ARE NOTHING BUT CARDBOARD CUT-OUTS!"

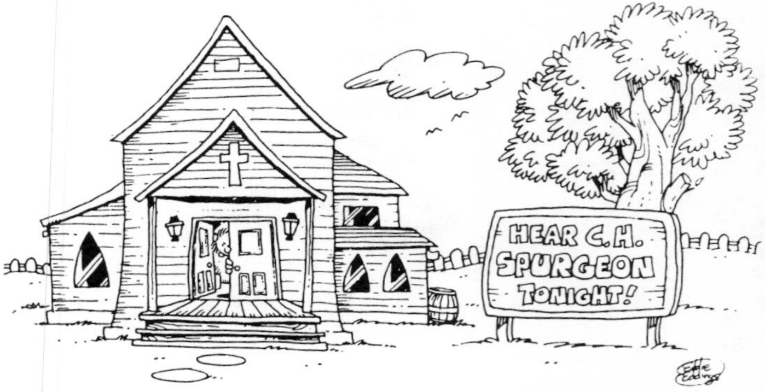
HEAR C.H.
SPURGEON
TONIGHT!
Eddie Eddings

IN AN ATTEMPT TO BOOST ATTENDANCE, REV. "BUBBA" BROWN LEGALLY CHANGED HIS NAME TO CHARLES HADDON SPURGEON.

[redacted]

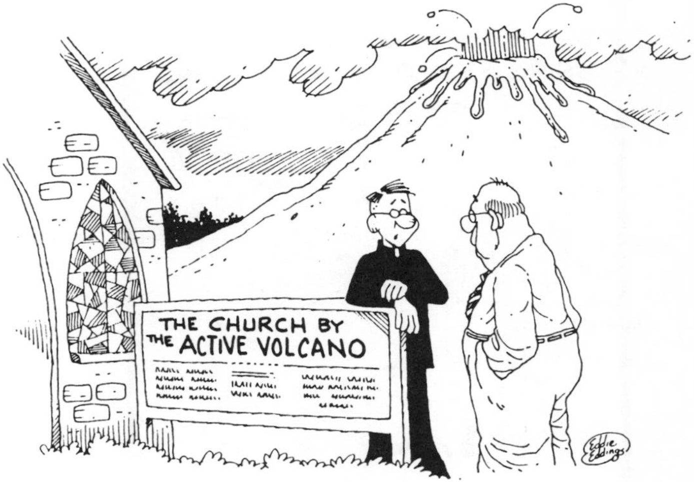
THE CHURCH BY THE ACTIVE VOLCANO
Eddie Eddings

"I'M THINKING . . . A NEW LOCATION MIGHT HELP ATTENDANCE . . ."

DOBSON
FILM
[redacted]

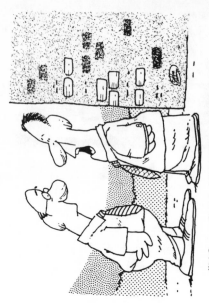

"THEY ARE HAVING THEIR WEEKLY DISCUSSION ON THE DOCTRINE OF ELECTION!"

"NO . . . I'M A SIX-POINT CALVINIST . . .
I BELIEVE IN BURNING HERETICS."

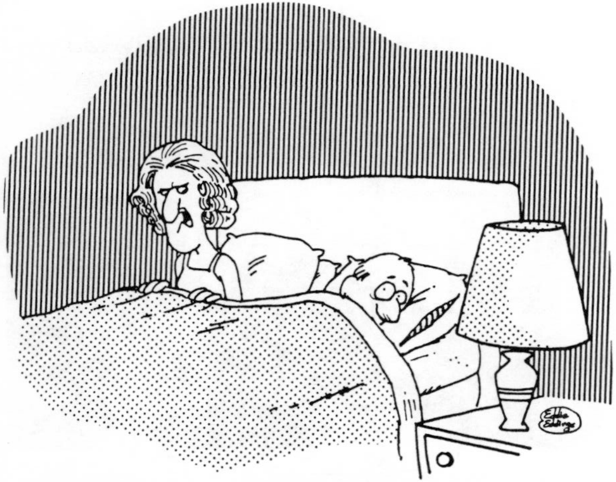

"HOW CAN YOU JUST LIE THERE AND *ACCEPT* SUPRALAPSARIANISM?"

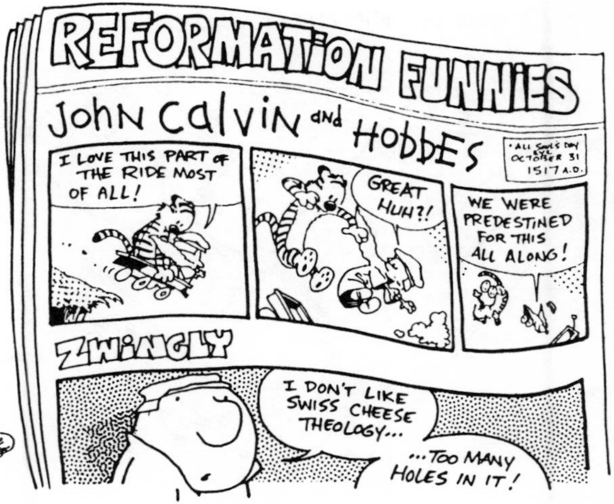
REFORMATION FUNNIES
JOHN CALVIN AND HOBBES
ALL SOULS DAY
OCTOBER 31
1517 A.D.
I LOVE THIS PART OF THE RIDE MOST OF ALL!
GREAT HUH?!
WE WERE PREDESTINED FOR THIS ALL ALONG!
ZWINGLY
I DON'T LIKE SWISS CHEESE THEOLOGY...
...TOO MANY HOLES IN IT!

Eddie Eddings

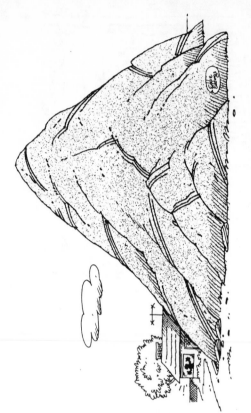

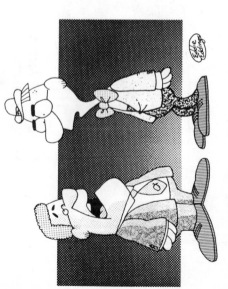

"WE WERE SO BLESSED BY THE VISITING PREACHER THAT WE GAVE HIM A STANDING DONATION."

Eddie Eddings

SOMEONE, SOMEWHERE, HAD BY FAITH MOVED A MOUNTAIN IN FRONT OF REV. RUMLOE'S PARSONAGE.

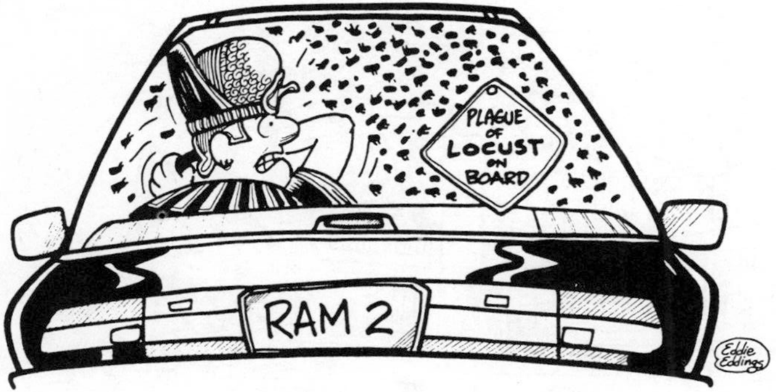
PLAGUE OF LOCUST ON BOARD
RAM 2
Eddie Eddings

IF PHARAOH WERE ALIVE TODAY

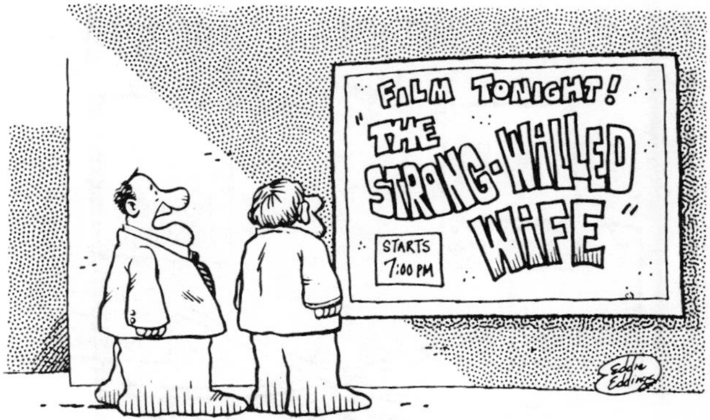
FILM TONIGHT!
"THE STRONG-WILLED WIFE"
STARTS 7:00 PM
Eddie Eddings

"SORRY, I WON'T BE HERE TONIGHT . . . MY WIFE SAID I COULDN'T SEE THIS FILM!"

CLEARANCE SALE
SALE!
CHS
ESCAPE TRICKS FOR PASTORS
THE ONE-MINUTE SERMON
SERMONS from HEZEKIAH ?
MY B.C. DAZE
BEN REDEEMED

"BOUND" TO SELL

MANUAL of CHURCH HISTORY
SYSTEMATIC THEOLOGY
GREEK LEXICON
EXHAUSTIVE CONCORDANCE

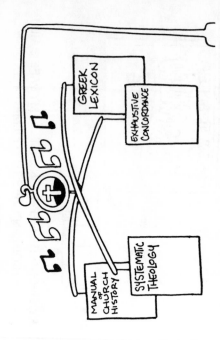

MUSICAL CRIB MOBILE FOR GROWING THEOLOGIAN

STUDY BIBLES
THE COMPLETE WORKS OF C.H. SPURGEON and JOHN OWEN
VARIOUS SETS OF THEOLOGICAL WORKS
Eddie Eddings

FOOT-PRINTS
PASTOR
Eddie Eddings

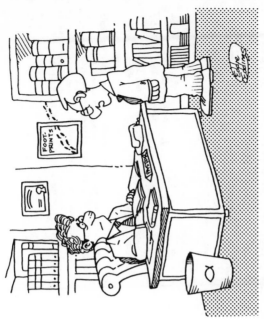

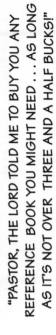

"PASTOR, THE LORD TOLD ME TO BUY YOU ANY REFERENCE BOOK YOU MIGHT NEED . . . AS LONG AS IT'S NOT OVER THREE AND A HALF BUCKS!"

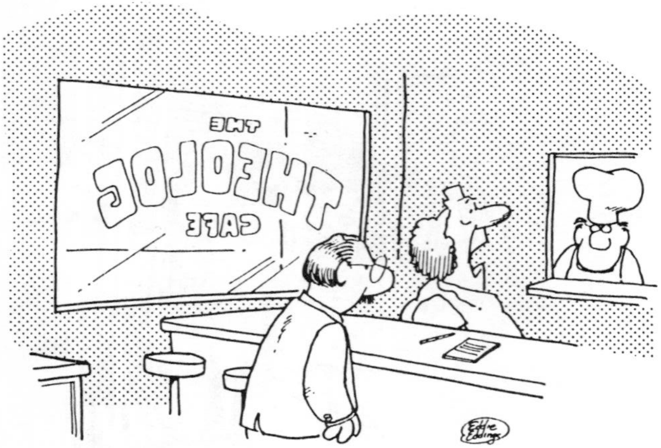
THE
THEOLOG
CAFE

"TWO LUTHERS AND SIDE OF EDWARDS TO GO! HOLD THE FINNEY!"

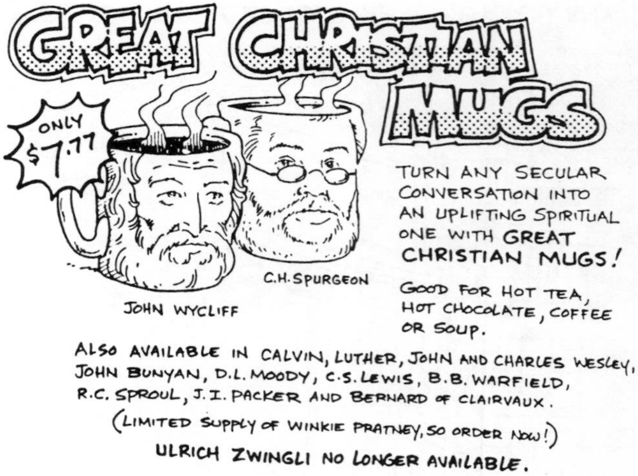
GREAT CHRISTIAN MUGS
ONLY $7.77
JOHN WYCLIFF
C.H. SPURGEON
TURN ANY SECULAR CONVERSATION INTO AN UPLIFTING SPIRITUAL ONE WITH GREAT CHRISTIAN MUGS!
GOOD FOR HOT TEA, HOT CHOCOLATE, COFFEE OR SOUP.
ALSO AVAILABLE IN CALVIN, LUTHER, JOHN AND CHARLES WESLEY, JOHN BUNYAN, D.L. MOODY, C.S. LEWIS, B.B. WARFIELD, R.C. SPROUL, J.I. PACKER AND BERNARD OF CLAIRVAUX.
(LIMITED SUPPLY OF WINKIE PRATNEY, SO ORDER NOW!)
ULRICH ZWINGLI NO LONGER AVAILABLE.

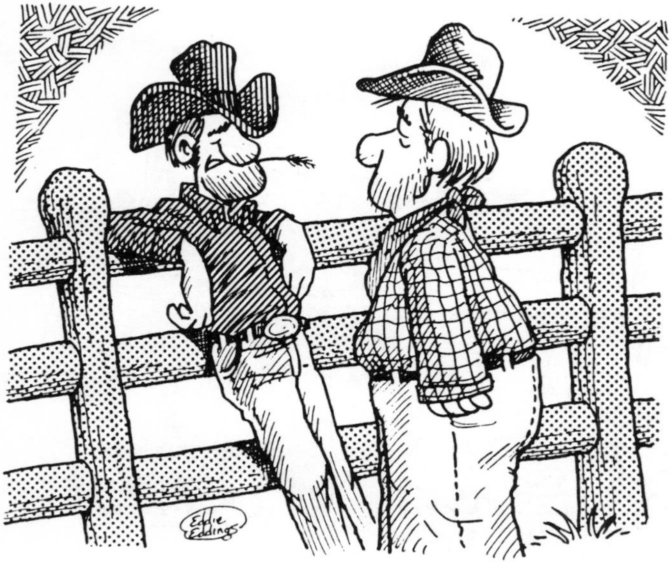
Eddie Eddings

"I DUNNO. . .I THINK **COW**VINISM HAS TO DO WITH CATTLE WORSHIP OF SOME KIND."

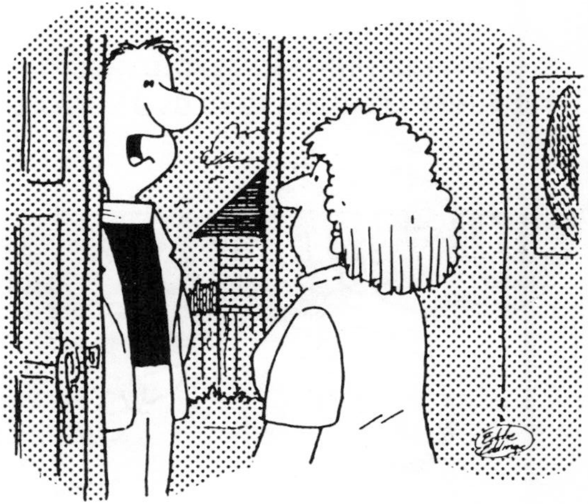

"CAN BOB COME OUT AND PRAY?"

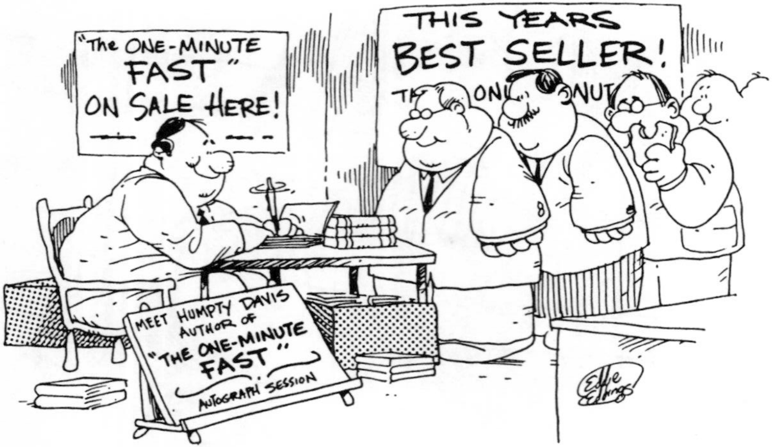
"The ONE-MINUTE
FAST"
ON SALE HERE!
THIS YEARS
BEST SELLER!
MEET HUMPTY DAVIS
AUTHOR OF
"THE ONE-MINUTE
FAST"
AUTOGRAPH SESSION
Eddie Eddings

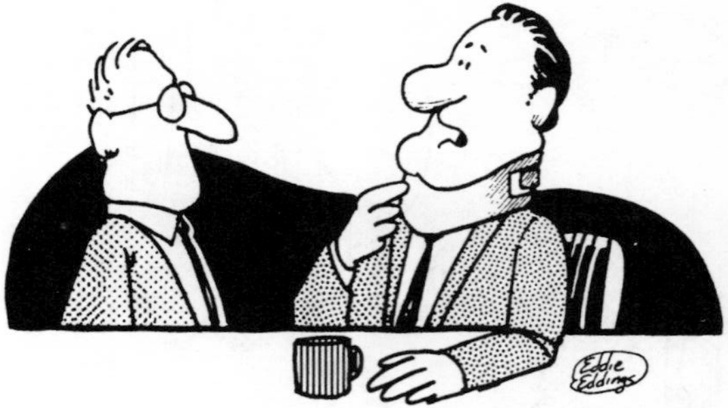
Eddie Eddings

"I GOT A BAD CASE OF 'QUIPLASH' FROM OUR PASTOR'S OPENING REMARKS."

BIBLE
Eddie Eddings

"NO, IT'S NOT AN ULTRA-THIN BIBLE . . . I PUT IT IN MY TRASH COMPACTOR BY MISTAKE!"

POWER DUDES
Eddie Eddings

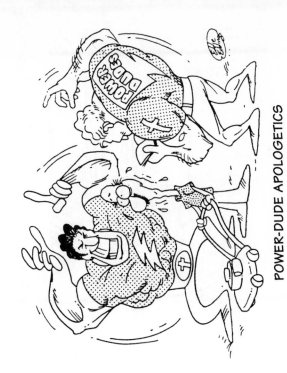

POWER-DUDE APOLOGETICS

HONK IF YOU HAVE SURVEYED THE HISTORICAL CONTEXT OF NAHUM OR JOB

NOT ONE OF THE BETTER-SELLING BUMPER STICKERS.

IF THE RAPTURE OCCURS TODAY PLEASE DELIVER THIS CAR TO MY BROTHER-IN-LAW!

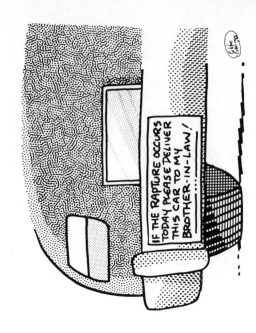

ONE OF THE BETTER-SELLING BUMPER STICKERS

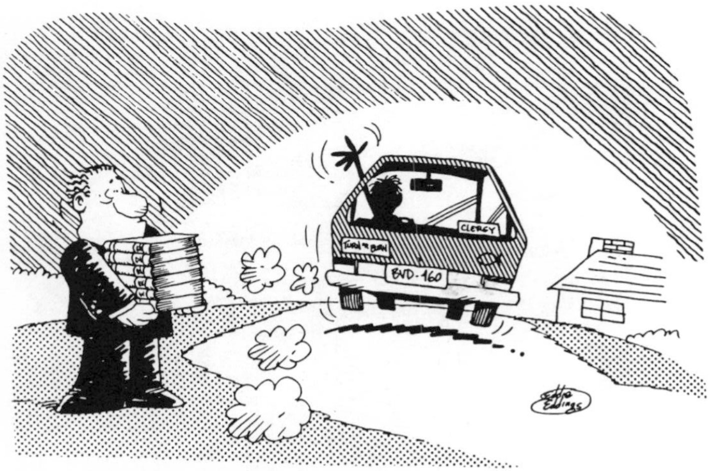
CLERGY
BVD-160

IN A MOMENT OF WEAKNESS, REV. J. HAROLD WEEMS TRADES HIS AUTOMOBILE FOR A SET OF SERMONS ON GODLY WISDOM.

THE CANNON OF SCRIPTURE

BIBLE
FIBER-PUFFS
BIBLE FIBER PUFFS
THE CEREAL FOR DISCIPLES
SHAPED LIKE TINY BIBLES
FREE INSIDE!
LARKIN'S DISPENSATIONAL CHARTS
PREACHER POPS
THE CEREAL SHAPED LIKE THE FATHERS of GREAT PASTORS OF THE PAST
WIN YOUR VERY OWN PEW
FREE GREEK DECODER RING
35¢ OFF
A NON-DENOMINATIONAL BREAKFAST CEREAL

SOUL-WINNING CEREALS

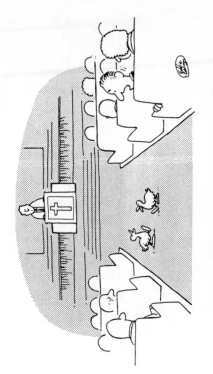

"OH . . . I THOUGHT HE WAS SAYING 'PARADOX'!"

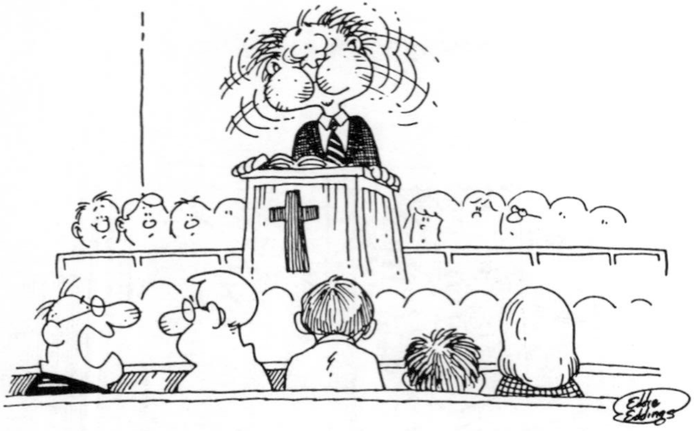
Eddie Eddings

"OUR PASTOR HAS AN UNCANNY ABILITY TO DEPICT THE DESTRUCTION OF JERICHO WITH FACIAL EXPRESSIONS ALONE."

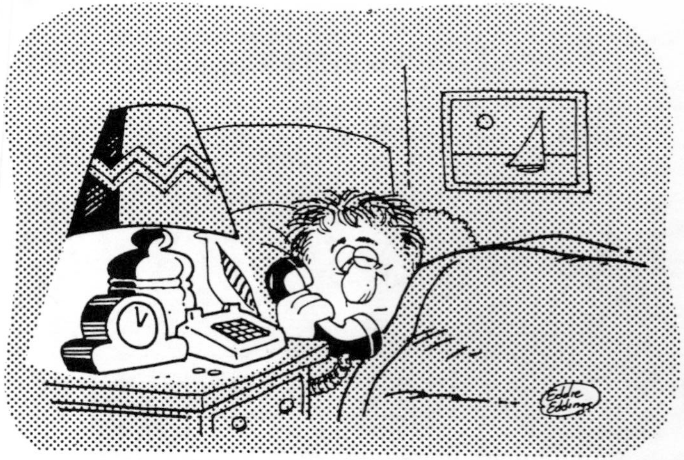
Eddie Eddings

"PASTOR . . . I'VE GOT A QUESTION CONCERNING YOUR THIRD POINT IN LAST NIGHT'S SERMON . . ."

Eddie Eddings

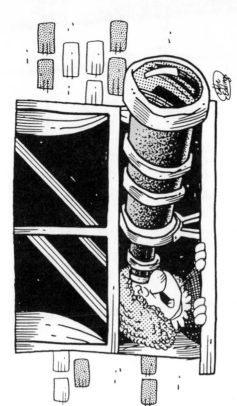

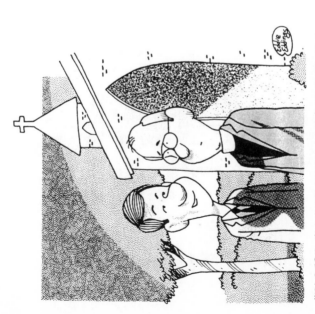

"PASTOR, I'M A REALTOR. I HAVE 'LOTS' TO BE THANKFUL FOR!"

Eddie Eddings

"WELL, LOOK AT THIS, ETHEL . . . OUR PASTOR IS WATCHING THAT SINFUL 'GILLIGAN'S ISLAND' AGAIN!"

HOPE I NEVER BECOME LEGALISTIC!
PASTOR

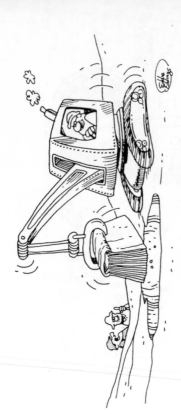

"HOW DO YOU LIKE THAT!
PASTOR BUNDY'S FIRST ARCHAEOLOGICAL DIG . . .
. . . AND HE DISCOVERS SOLOMON'S WEDDING ALBUM."

"YOU'VE MADE YOUR POINT HAROLD! I DON'T THINK YOU NEED TO ILLUSTRATE IT WITH A POEM FROM ONE OF YOUR SERMONS!"

PREACHED
SAME SERMON
4 TIMES
TO
CONGREGATION
Eddie Eddings

[redacted]

Eddie Eddings

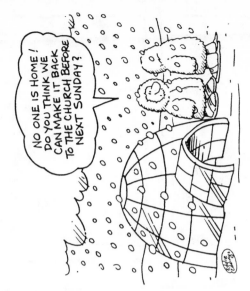

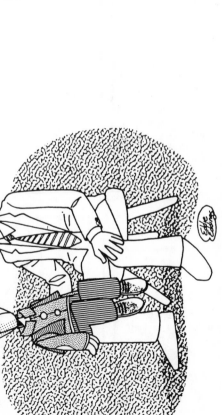

"WHY ARE YOU EXPLAINING THE GOSPEL TO ME? I'M A PIECE OF WOOD FOR CRYIN' OUT LOUD!"

NO ONE IS HOME! DO YOU THINK WE CAN MAKE IT BACK TO THE CHURCH BEFORE NEXT SUNDAY?
Eddie Eddings

THE UNIQUE TRIALS OF IGLOO TO IGLOO VISITATION

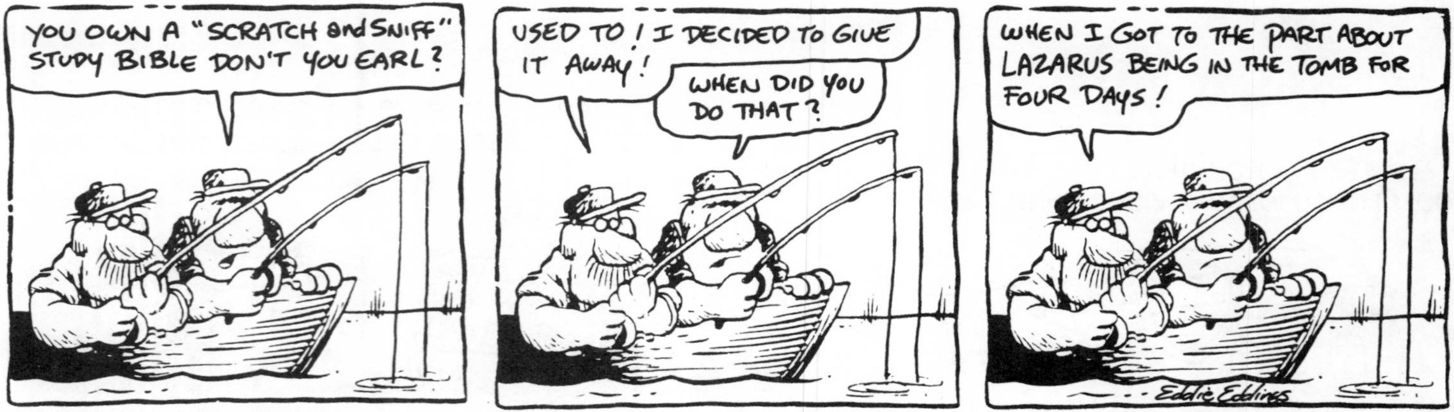
YOU OWN A "SCRATCH and SNIFF" STUDY BIBLE DON'T YOU EARL?
USED TO! I DECIDED TO GIVE IT AWAY!
WHEN DID YOU DO THAT?
WHEN I GOT TO THE PART ABOUT LAZARUS BEING IN THE TOMB FOR FOUR DAYS!
Eddie Eddings

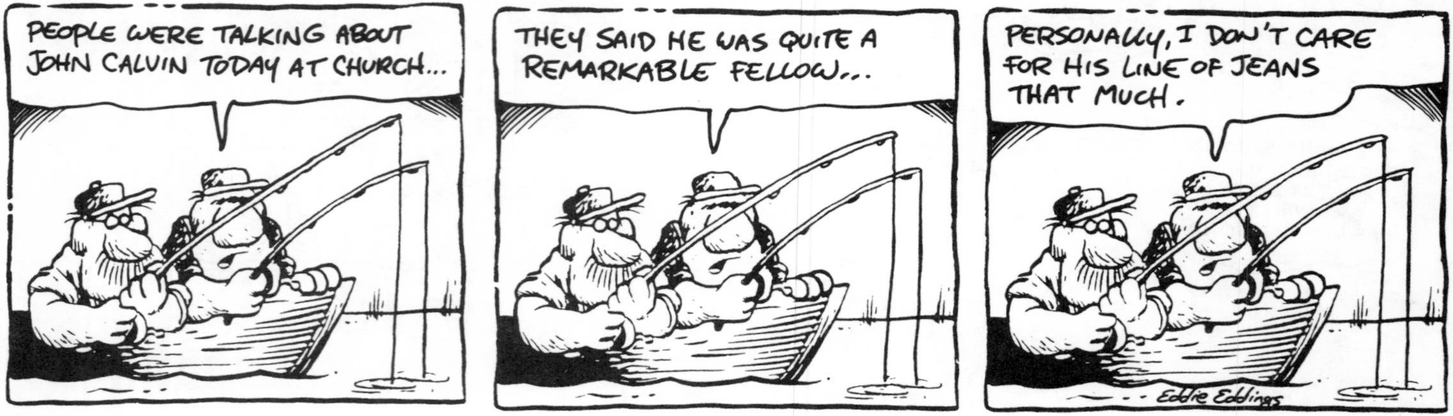
PEOPLE WERE TALKING ABOUT JOHN CALVIN TODAY AT CHURCH...
THEY SAID HE WAS QUITE A REMARKABLE FELLOW...
PERSONALLY, I DON'T CARE FOR HIS LINE OF JEANS THAT MUCH.
Eddie Eddings

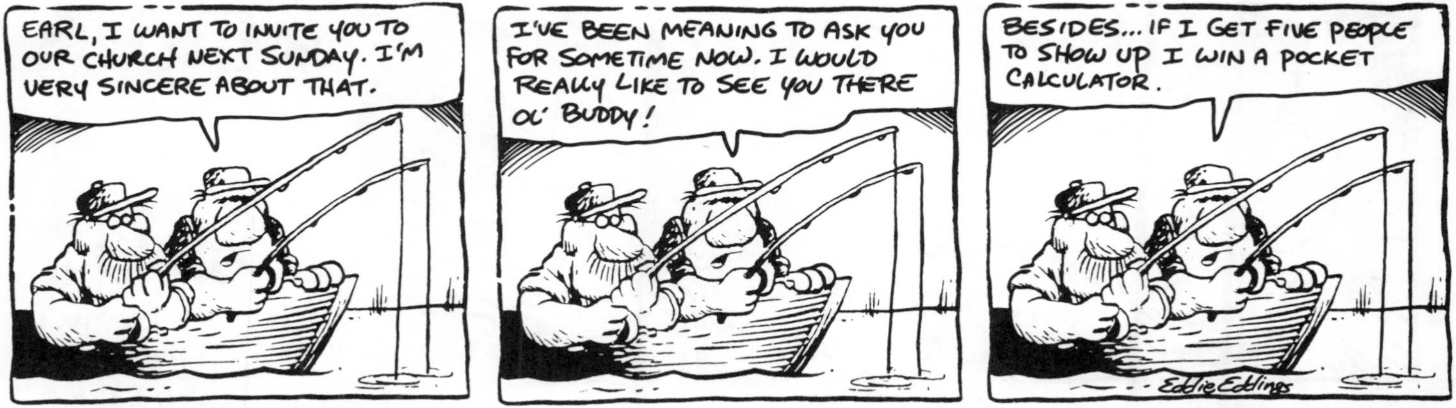
EARL, I WANT TO INVITE YOU TO OUR CHURCH NEXT SUNDAY. I'M VERY SINCERE ABOUT THAT.
I'VE BEEN MEANING TO ASK YOU FOR SOMETIME NOW. I WOULD REALLY LIKE TO SEE YOU THERE OL' BUDDY!
BESIDES... IF I GET FIVE PEOPLE TO SHOW UP I WIN A POCKET CALCULATOR.
Eddie Eddings

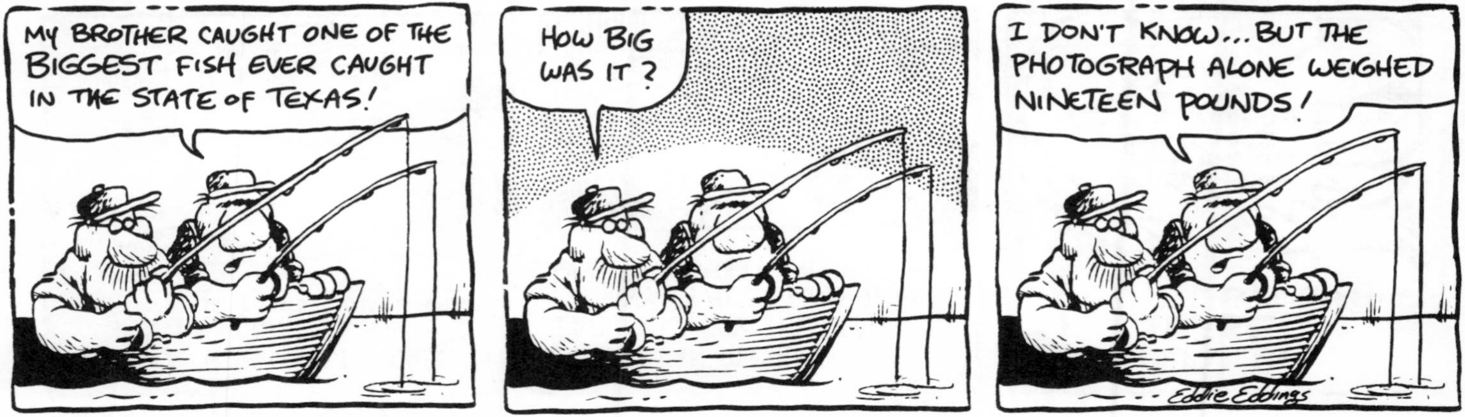
MY BROTHER CAUGHT ONE OF THE BIGGEST FISH EVER CAUGHT IN THE STATE OF TEXAS!
HOW BIG WAS IT?
I DON'T KNOW... BUT THE PHOTOGRAPH ALONE WEIGHED NINETEEN POUNDS!
Eddie Eddings

SWEET TATER McSPOON

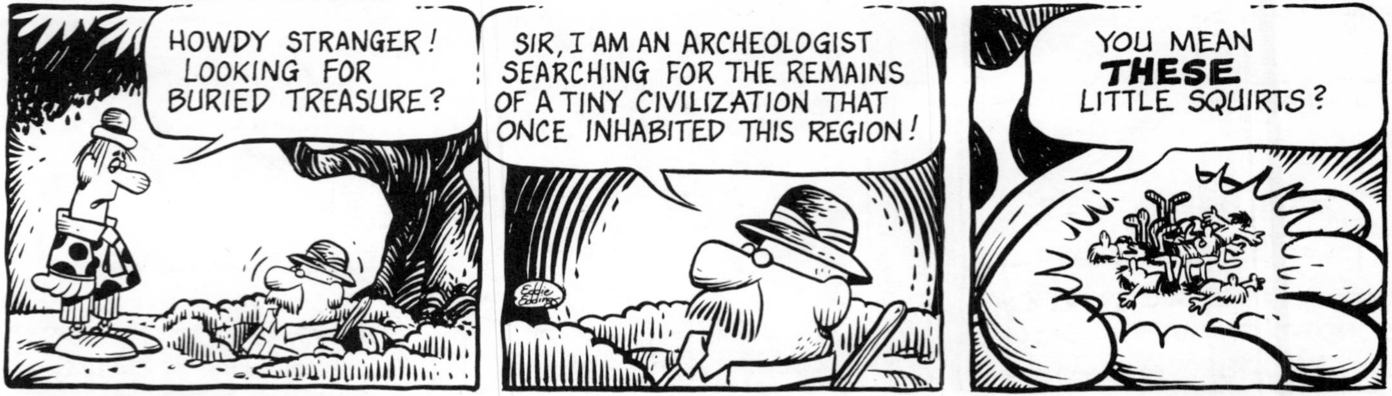
HOWDY STRANGER! LOOKING FOR BURIED TREASURE?
SIR, I AM AN ARCHEOLOGIST SEARCHING FOR THE REMAINS OF A TINY CIVILIZATION THAT ONCE INHABITED THIS REGION!
Eddie Eddings
YOU MEAN **THESE** LITTLE SQUIRTS?

SWEET TATER McSPOON

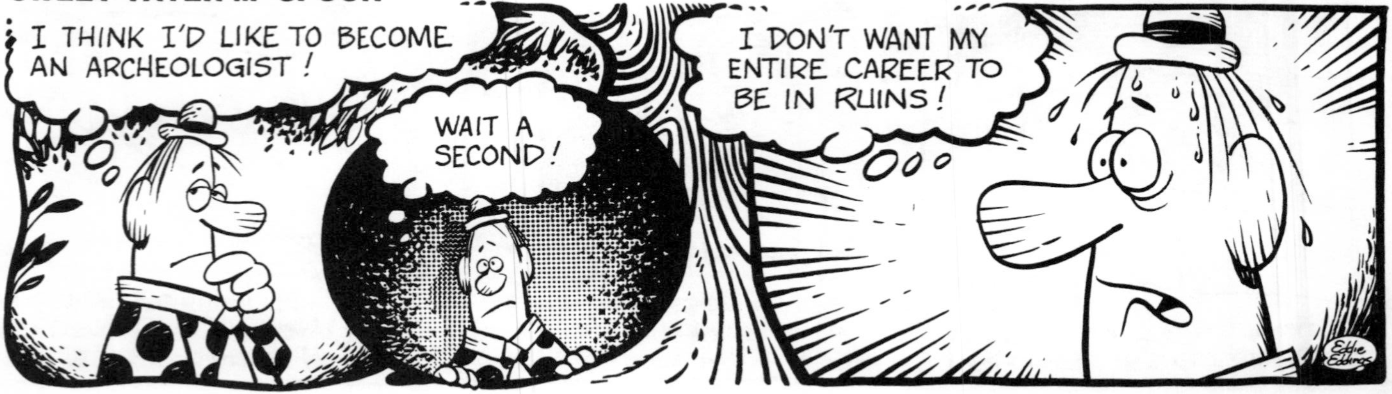
I THINK I'D LIKE TO BECOME AN ARCHEOLOGIST!
WAIT A SECOND!
I DON'T WANT MY ENTIRE CAREER TO BE IN RUINS!
Eddie Eddings

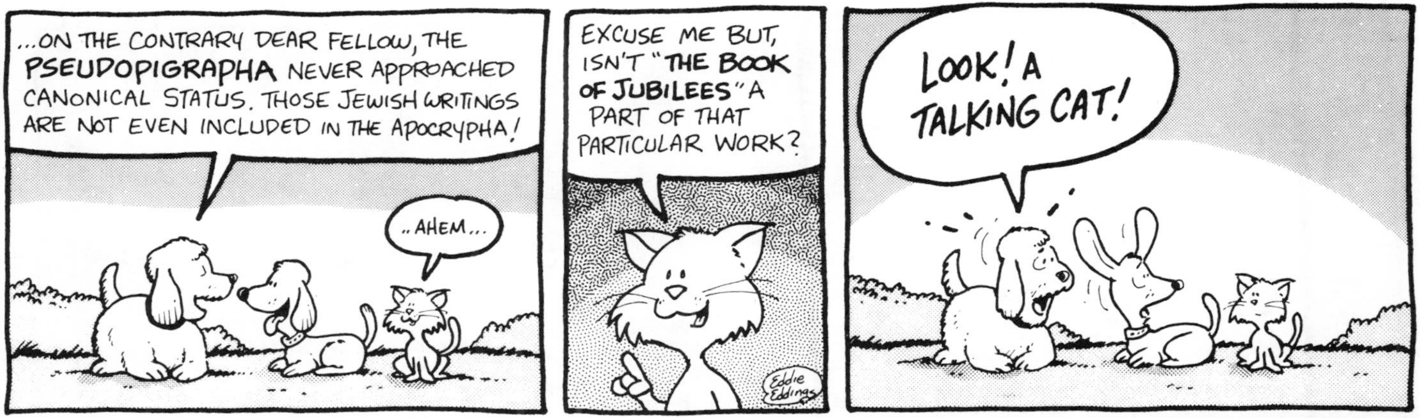
...ON THE CONTRARY DEAR FELLOW, THE PSEUDOPIGRAPHA NEVER APPROACHED CANONICAL STATUS. THOSE JEWISH WRITINGS ARE NOT EVEN INCLUDED IN THE APOCRYPHA!
..AHEM...
EXCUSE ME BUT, ISN'T "THE BOOK OF JUBILEES" A PART OF THAT PARTICULAR WORK?
Eddie Eddings
LOOK! A TALKING CAT!

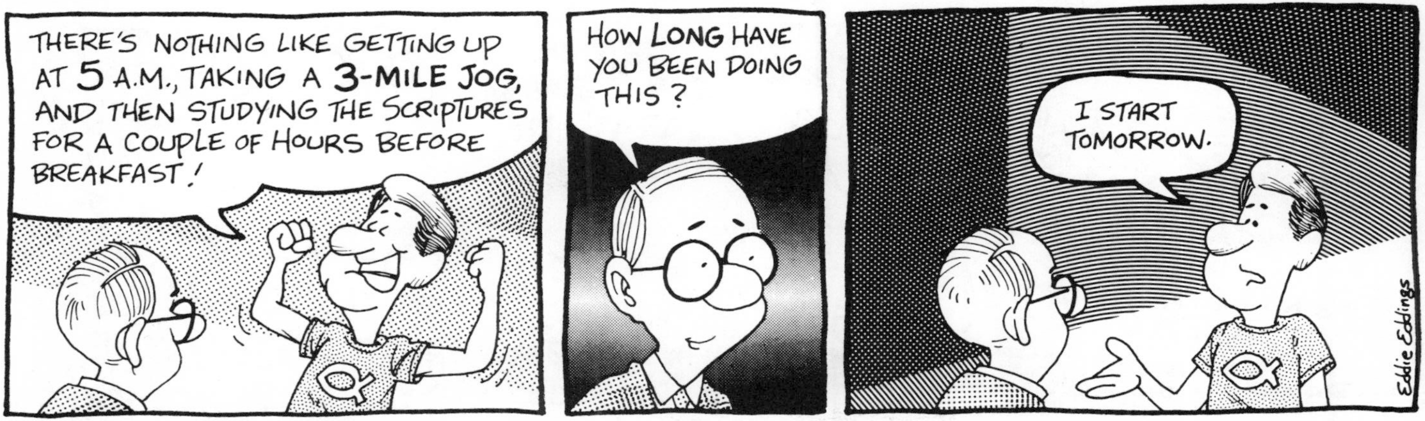
THERE'S NOTHING LIKE GETTING UP AT 5 A.M., TAKING A 3-MILE JOG, AND THEN STUDYING THE SCRIPTURES FOR A COUPLE OF HOURS BEFORE BREAKFAST!
HOW LONG HAVE YOU BEEN DOING THIS?
I START TOMORROW.
Eddie Eddings

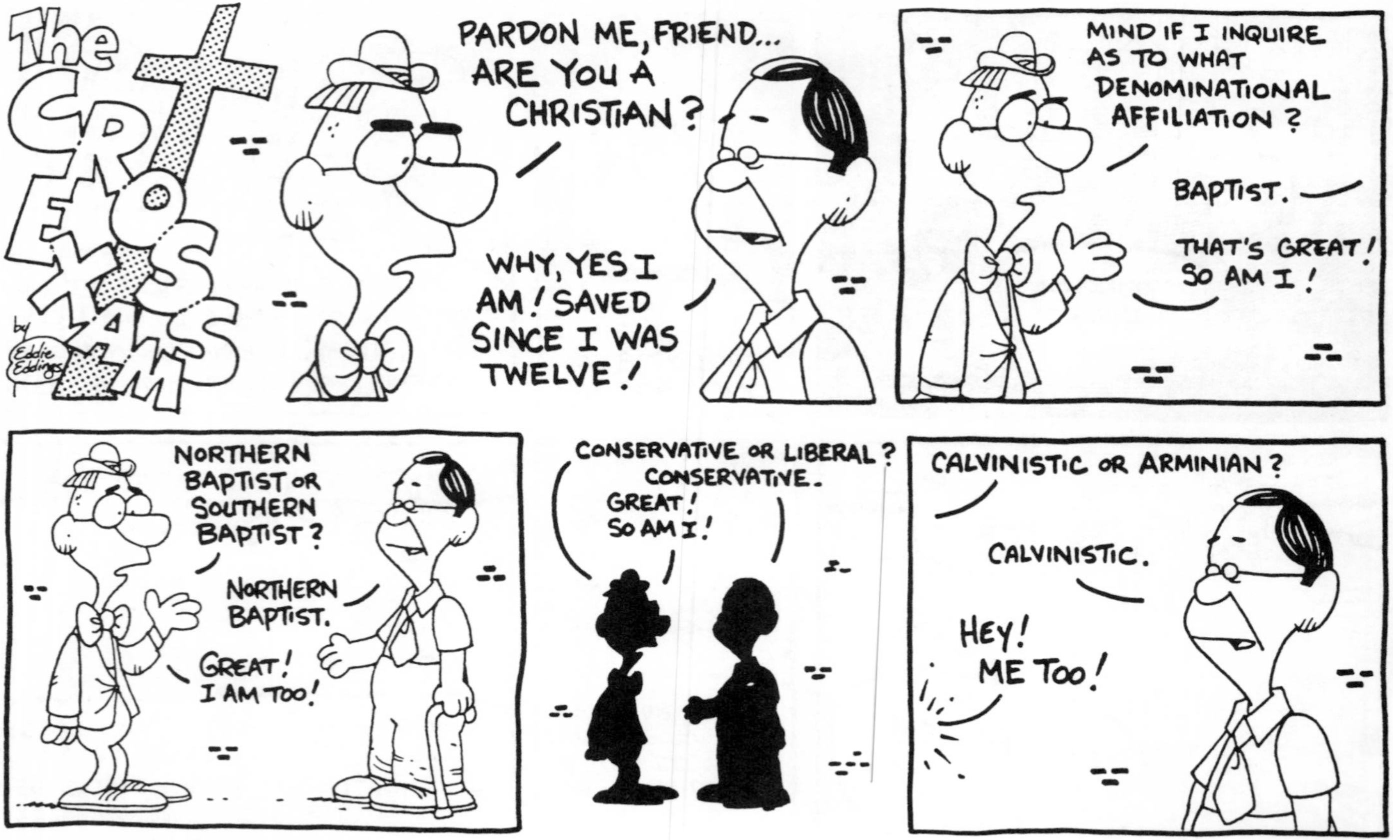
The CROSS EXAMS
by Eddie Eddings
PARDON ME, FRIEND... ARE YOU A CHRISTIAN?
WHY, YES I AM! SAVED SINCE I WAS TWELVE!
MIND IF I INQUIRE AS TO WHAT DENOMINATIONAL AFFILIATION?
BAPTIST.
THAT'S GREAT! SO AM I!
NORTHERN BAPTIST OR SOUTHERN BAPTIST?
NORTHERN BAPTIST.
GREAT! I AM TOO!
CONSERVATIVE OR LIBERAL?
CONSERVATIVE.
GREAT! SO AM I!
CALVINISTIC OR ARMINIAN?
CALVINISTIC.
HEY! ME TOO!

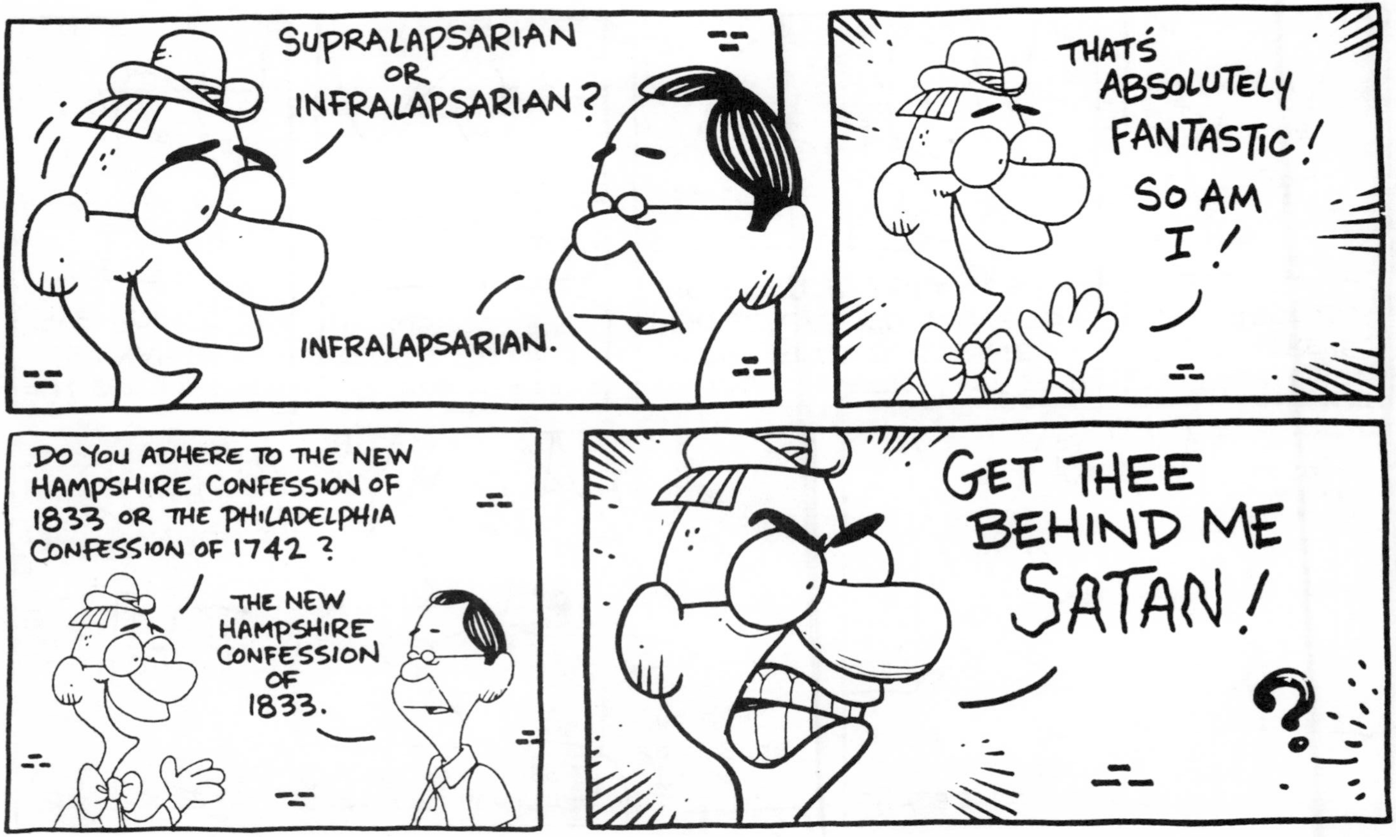
SUPRALAPSARIAN OR INFRALAPSARIAN?
INFRALAPSARIAN.
THAT'S ABSOLUTELY FANTASTIC!
SO AM I!
DO YOU ADHERE TO THE NEW HAMPSHIRE CONFESSION OF 1833 OR THE PHILADELPHIA CONFESSION OF 1742?
THE NEW HAMPSHIRE CONFESSION OF 1833.
GET THEE BEHIND ME SATAN!
?

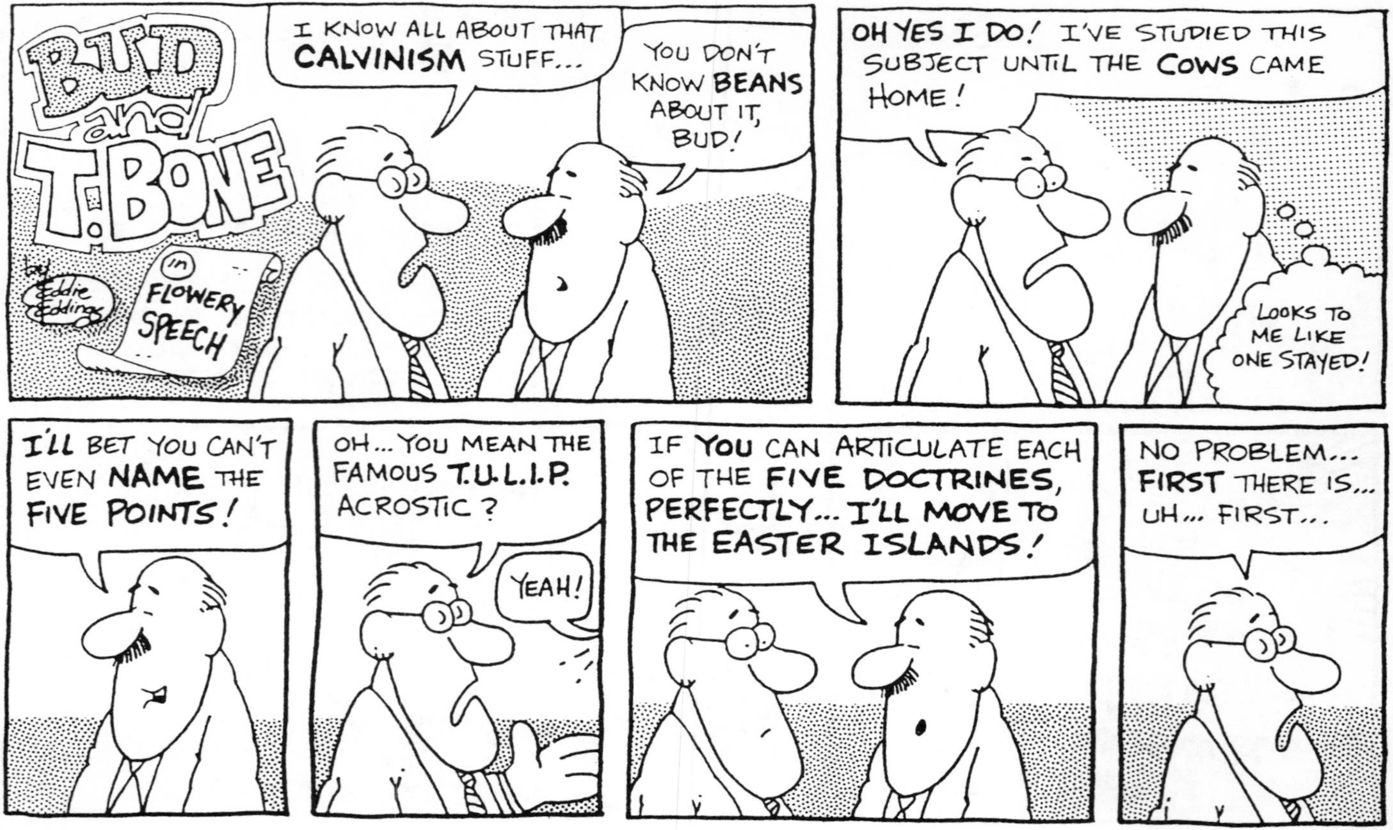
BUD and T.BONE
by Eddie Eddings
in FLOWERY SPEECH
I KNOW ALL ABOUT THAT CALVINISM STUFF...
YOU DON'T KNOW BEANS ABOUT IT, BUD!
OH YES I DO! I'VE STUDIED THIS SUBJECT UNTIL THE COWS CAME HOME!
LOOKS TO ME LIKE ONE STAYED!
I'LL BET YOU CAN'T EVEN NAME THE FIVE POINTS!
OH... YOU MEAN THE FAMOUS T.U.L.I.P. ACROSTIC?
YEAH!
IF YOU CAN ARTICULATE EACH OF THE FIVE DOCTRINES, PERFECTLY... I'LL MOVE TO THE EASTER ISLANDS!
NO PROBLEM... FIRST THERE IS... UH... FIRST...

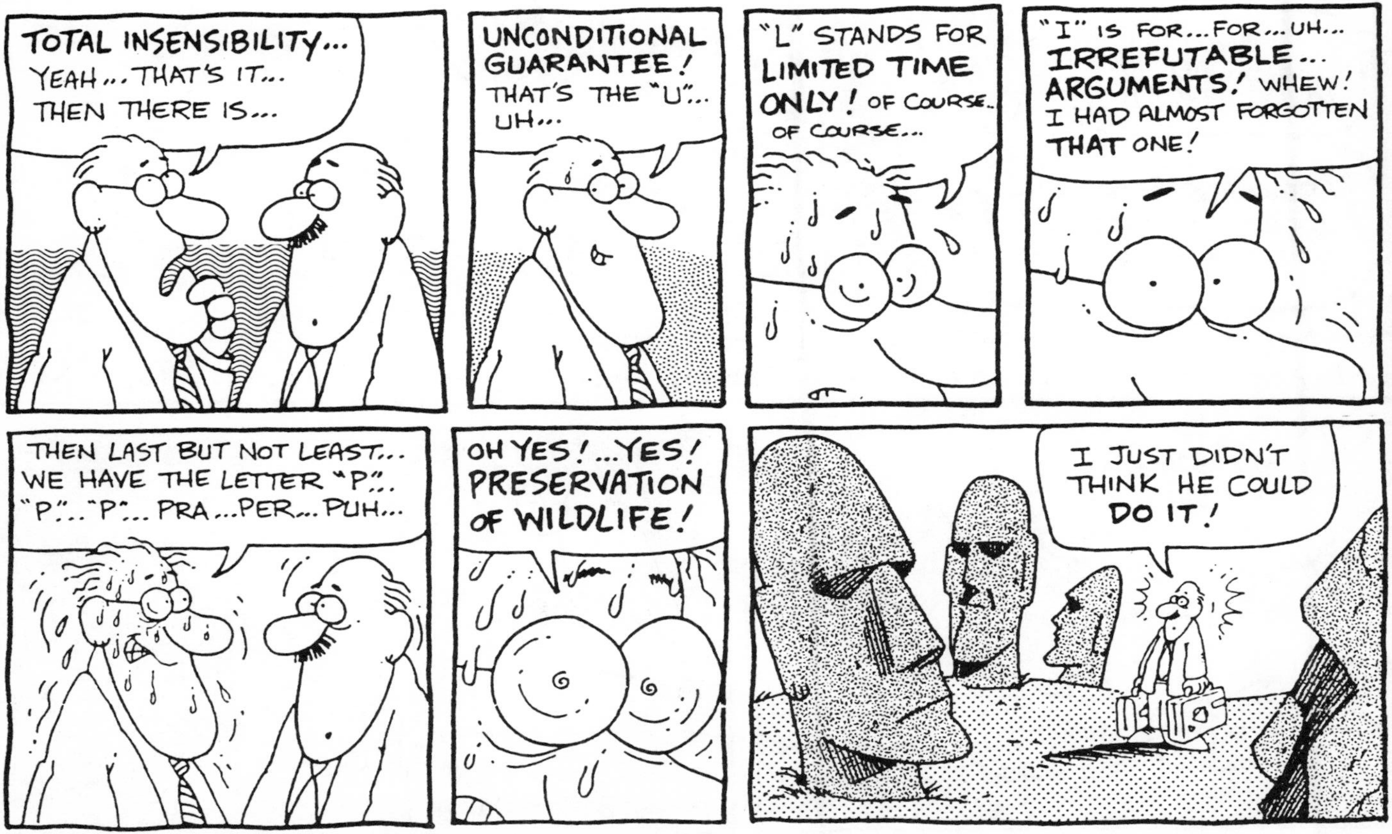
TOTAL INSENSIBILITY... YEAH... THAT'S IT... THEN THERE IS...
UNCONDITIONAL GUARANTEE! THAT'S THE "U"... UH...
"L" STANDS FOR LIMITED TIME ONLY! OF COURSE.. OF COURSE...
"I" IS FOR... FOR... UH... IRREFUTABLE... ARGUMENTS! WHEW! I HAD ALMOST FORGOTTEN THAT ONE!
THEN LAST BUT NOT LEAST... WE HAVE THE LETTER "P"... "P"... "P"... PRA... PER... PUH...
OH YES! ...YES! PRESERVATION OF WILDLIFE!
I JUST DIDN'T THINK HE COULD DO IT!

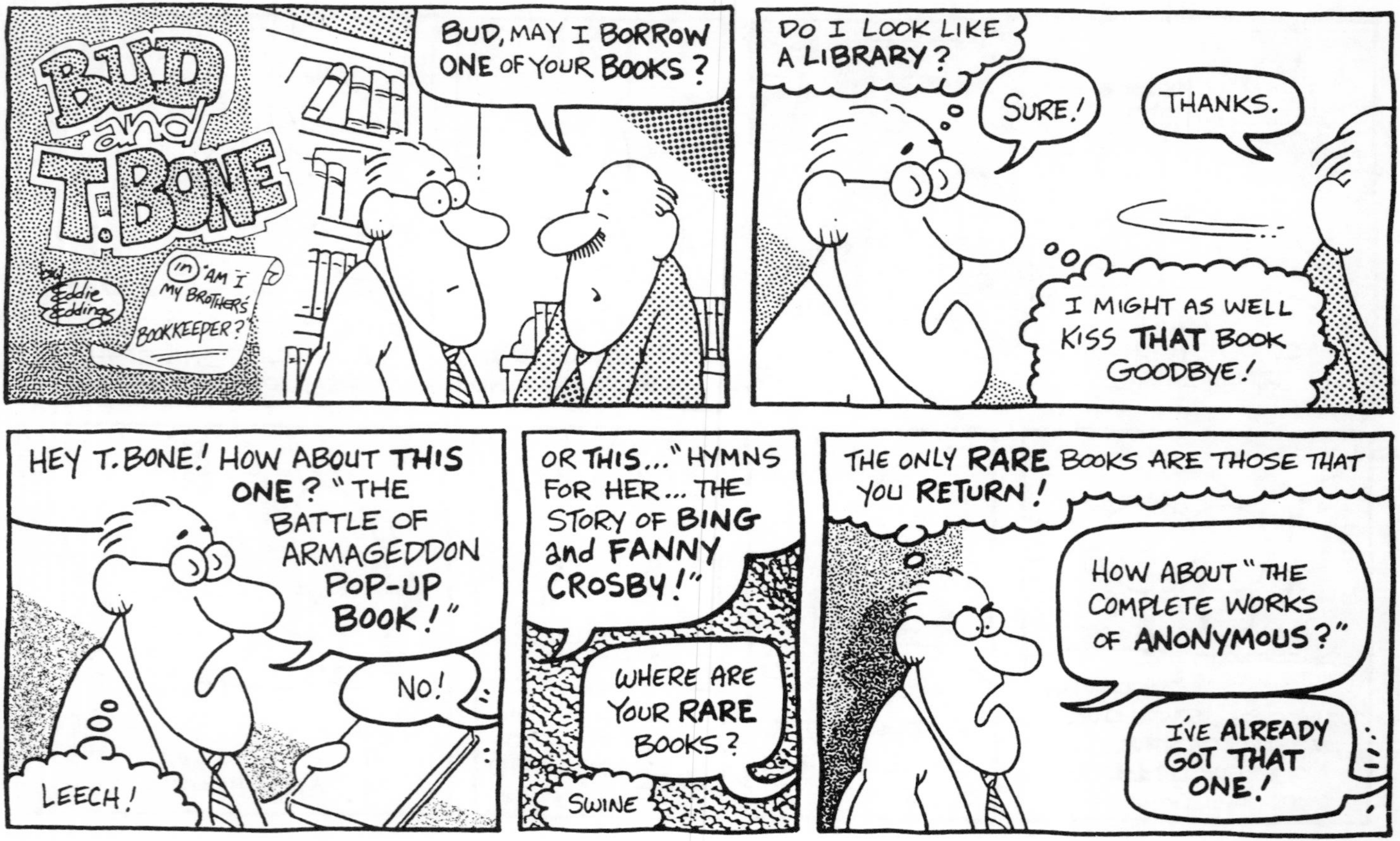
BUD and T. BONE
by Eddie Eddings
(in) "AM I MY BROTHER'S BOOKKEEPER?"
BUD, MAY I BORROW ONE OF YOUR BOOKS?
DO I LOOK LIKE A LIBRARY?
SURE!
THANKS.
I MIGHT AS WELL KISS THAT BOOK GOODBYE!
HEY T. BONE! HOW ABOUT THIS ONE? "THE BATTLE OF ARMAGEDDON POP-UP BOOK!"
NO!
LEECH!
OR THIS..."HYMNS FOR HER... THE STORY OF BING and FANNY CROSBY!"
WHERE ARE YOUR RARE BOOKS?
SWINE
THE ONLY RARE BOOKS ARE THOSE THAT YOU RETURN!
HOW ABOUT "THE COMPLETE WORKS OF ANONYMOUS?"
I'VE ALREADY GOT THAT ONE!

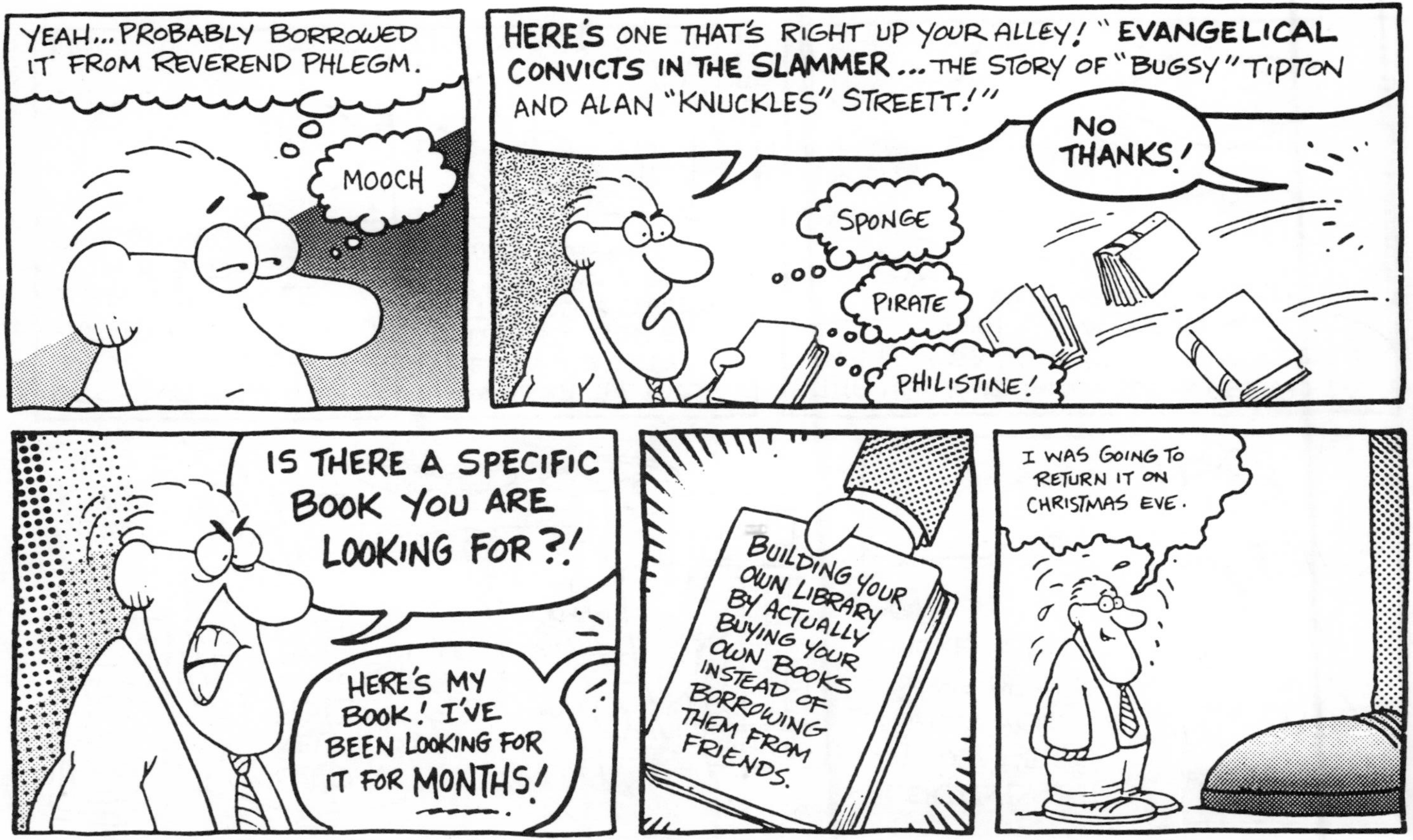
YEAH...PROBABLY BORROWED IT FROM REVEREND PHLEGM.
MOOCH
HERE'S ONE THAT'S RIGHT UP YOUR ALLEY! "EVANGELICAL CONVICTS IN THE SLAMMER ... THE STORY OF "BUGSY" TIPTON AND ALAN "KNUCKLES" STREETT!"
SPONGE
PIRATE
PHILISTINE!
NO THANKS!
IS THERE A SPECIFIC BOOK YOU ARE LOOKING FOR?!
HERE'S MY BOOK! I'VE BEEN LOOKING FOR IT FOR MONTHS!
BUILDING YOUR OWN LIBRARY BY ACTUALLY BUYING YOUR OWN BOOKS INSTEAD OF BORROWING THEM FROM FRIENDS.
I WAS GOING TO RETURN IT ON CHRISTMAS EVE.

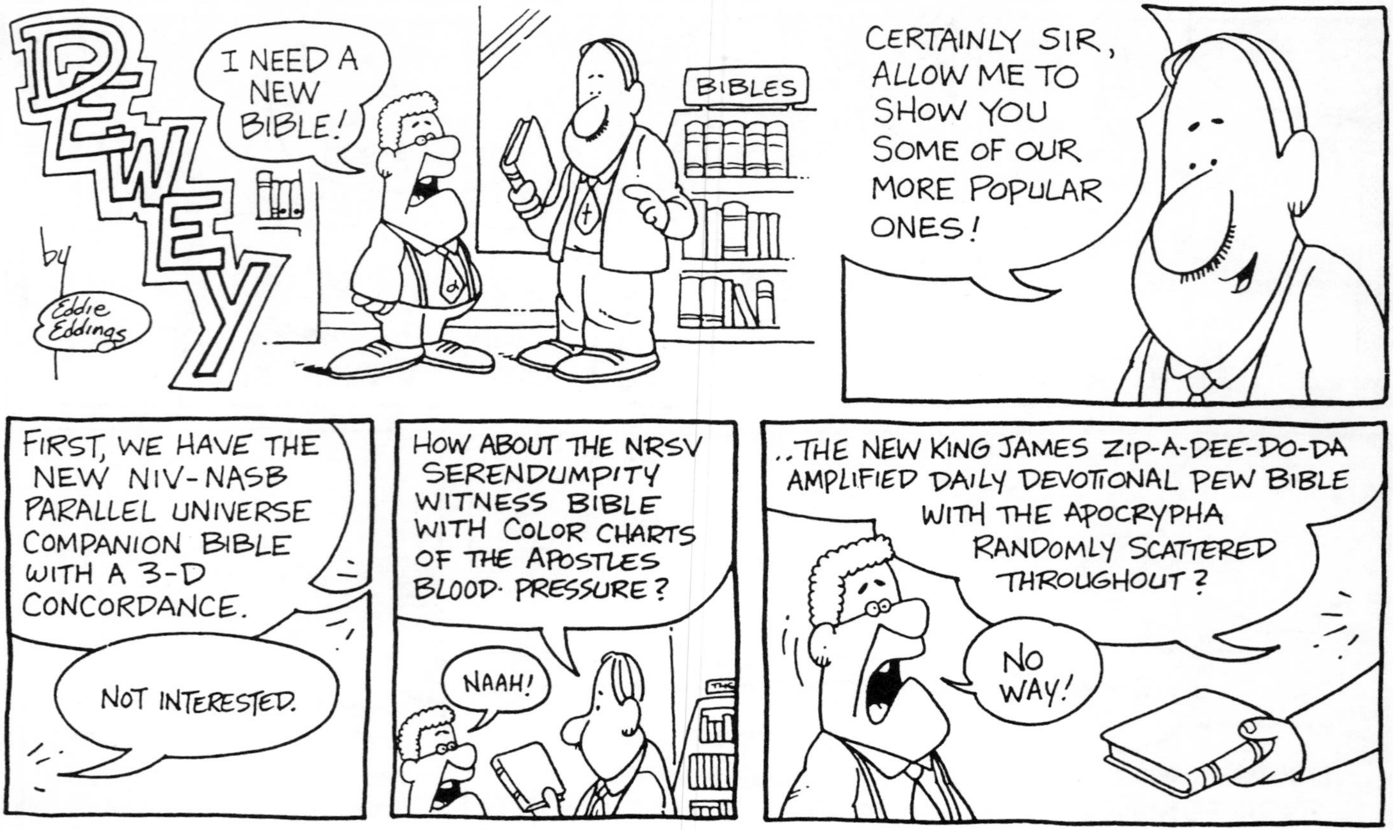
DEWEY
by Eddie Eddings
I NEED A NEW BIBLE!
BIBLES
CERTAINLY SIR, ALLOW ME TO SHOW YOU SOME OF OUR MORE POPULAR ONES!
FIRST, WE HAVE THE NEW NIV-NASB PARALLEL UNIVERSE COMPANION BIBLE WITH A 3-D CONCORDANCE.
NOT INTERESTED.
HOW ABOUT THE NRSV SERENDUMPITY WITNESS BIBLE WITH COLOR CHARTS OF THE APOSTLES BLOOD PRESSURE?
NAAH!
..THE NEW KING JAMES ZIP-A-DEE-DO-DA AMPLIFIED DAILY DEVOTIONAL PEW BIBLE WITH THE APOCRYPHA RANDOMLY SCATTERED THROUGHOUT?
NO WAY!

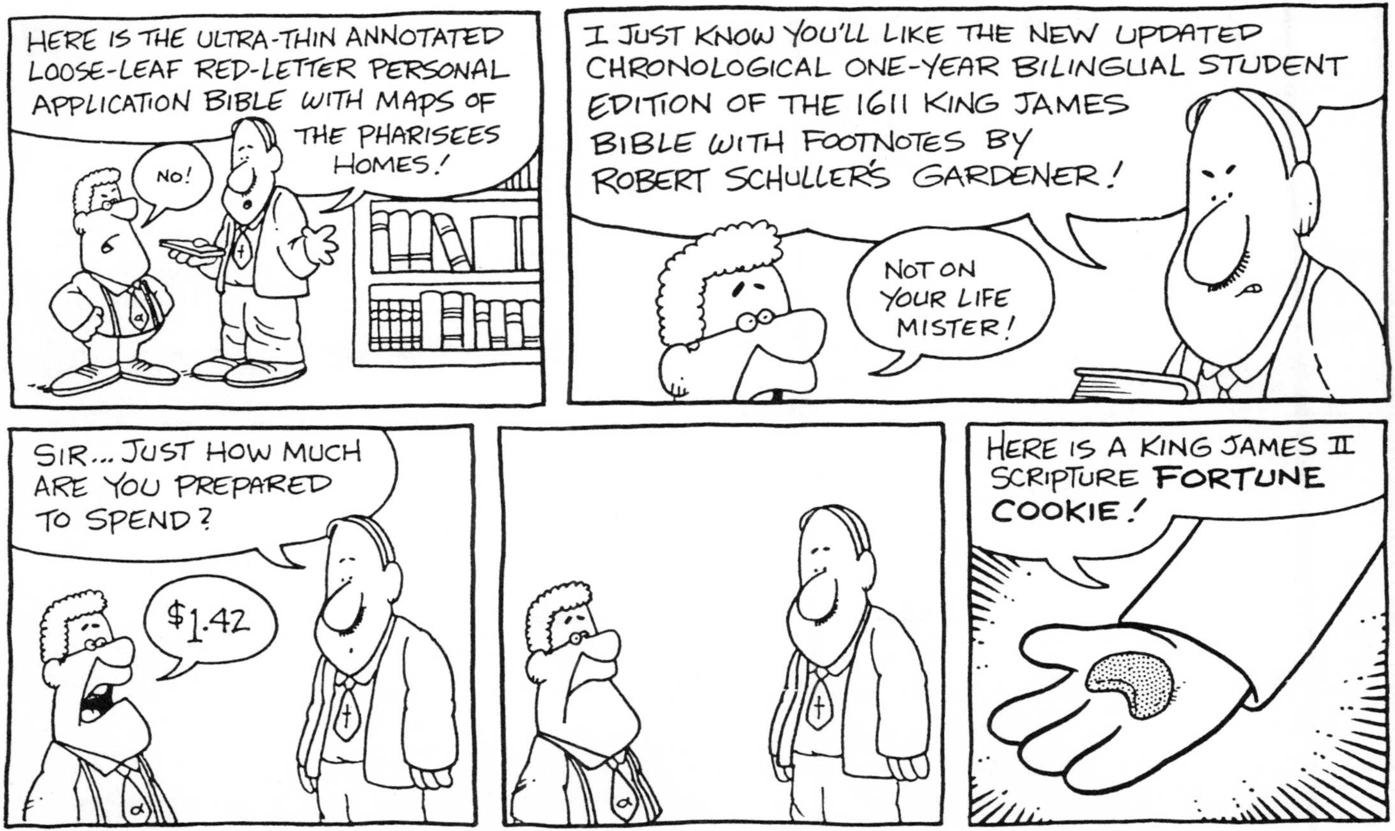
HERE IS THE ULTRA-THIN ANNOTATED LOOSE-LEAF RED-LETTER PERSONAL APPLICATION BIBLE WITH MAPS OF THE PHARISEES HOMES!
NO!
I JUST KNOW YOU'LL LIKE THE NEW UPDATED CHRONOLOGICAL ONE-YEAR BILINGUAL STUDENT EDITION OF THE 1611 KING JAMES BIBLE WITH FOOTNOTES BY ROBERT SCHULLER'S GARDENER!
NOT ON YOUR LIFE MISTER!
SIR... JUST HOW MUCH ARE YOU PREPARED TO SPEND?
$1.42
HERE IS A KING JAMES II SCRIPTURE FORTUNE COOKIE!

Did You Know? Features

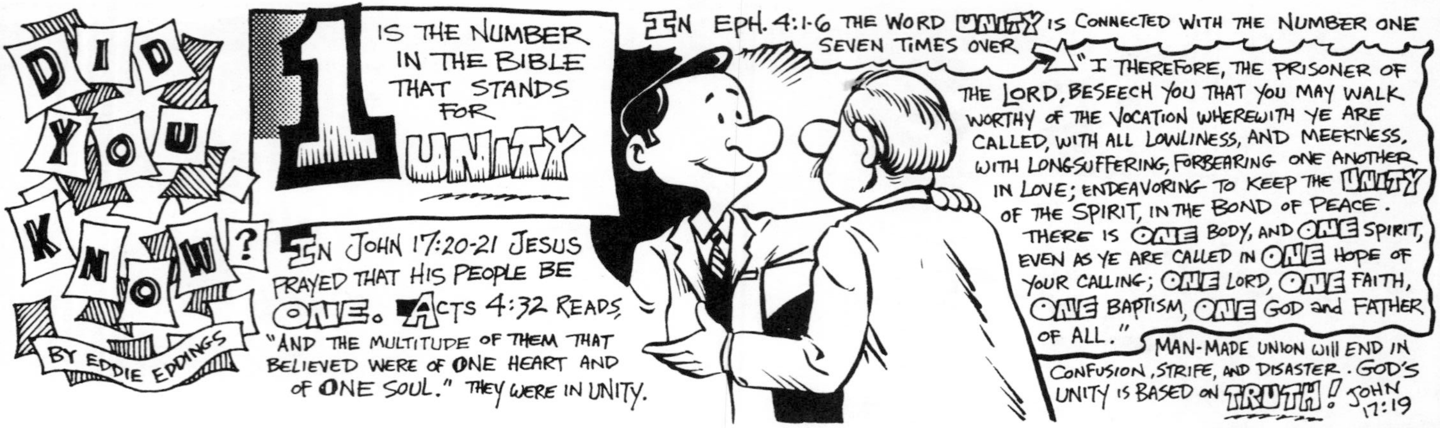
DID YOU KNOW?
BY EDDIE EDDINGS
1 IS THE NUMBER IN THE BIBLE THAT STANDS FOR UNITY
IN JOHN 17:20-21 JESUS PRAYED THAT HIS PEOPLE BE ONE. ACTS 4:32 READS, "AND THE MULTITUDE OF THEM THAT BELIEVED WERE OF ONE HEART AND OF ONE SOUL." THEY WERE IN UNITY.
IN EPH. 4:1-6 THE WORD UNITY IS CONNECTED WITH THE NUMBER ONE SEVEN TIMES OVER
"I THEREFORE, THE PRISONER OF THE LORD, BESEECH YOU THAT YOU MAY WALK WORTHY OF THE VOCATION WHEREWITH YE ARE CALLED, WITH ALL LOWLINESS, AND MEEKNESS, WITH LONGSUFFERING, FORBEARING ONE ANOTHER IN LOVE; ENDEAVORING TO KEEP THE UNITY OF THE SPIRIT, IN THE BOND OF PEACE. THERE IS ONE BODY, AND ONE SPIRIT, EVEN AS YE ARE CALLED IN ONE HOPE OF YOUR CALLING; ONE LORD, ONE FAITH, ONE BAPTISM, ONE GOD and FATHER OF ALL."
MAN-MADE UNION WILL END IN CONFUSION, STRIFE, AND DISASTER. GOD'S UNITY IS BASED ON TRUTH! JOHN 17:19

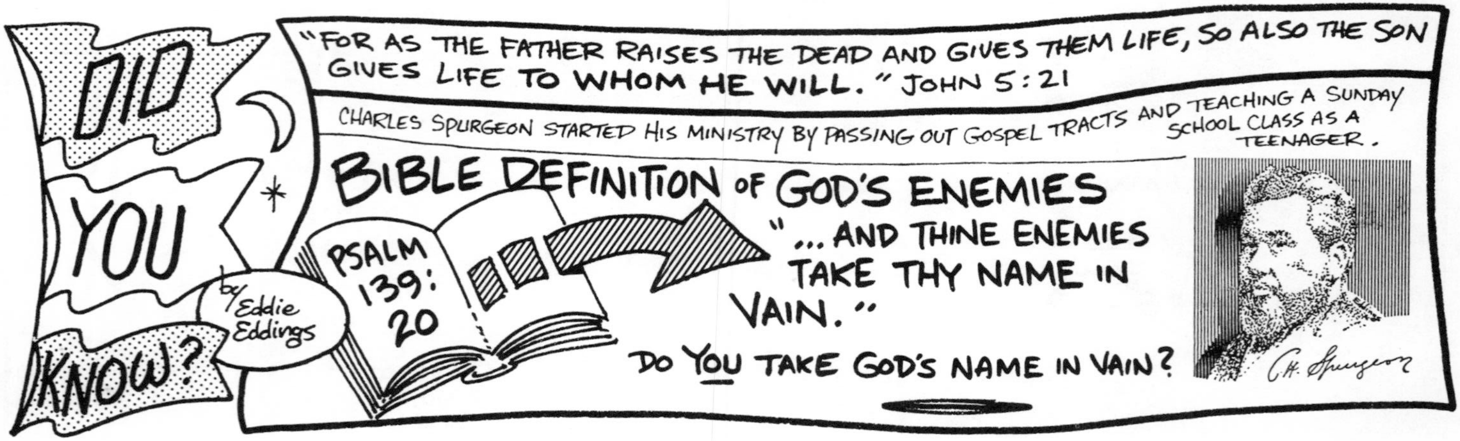
DID YOU KNOW?
by Eddie Eddings
"FOR AS THE FATHER RAISES THE DEAD AND GIVES THEM LIFE, SO ALSO THE SON GIVES LIFE TO WHOM HE WILL." JOHN 5:21
CHARLES SPURGEON STARTED HIS MINISTRY BY PASSING OUT GOSPEL TRACTS AND TEACHING A SUNDAY SCHOOL CLASS AS A TEENAGER.
C.H. Spurgeon
BIBLE DEFINITION OF GOD'S ENEMIES
PSALM 139:20
"... AND THINE ENEMIES TAKE THY NAME IN VAIN."
DO YOU TAKE GOD'S NAME IN VAIN?

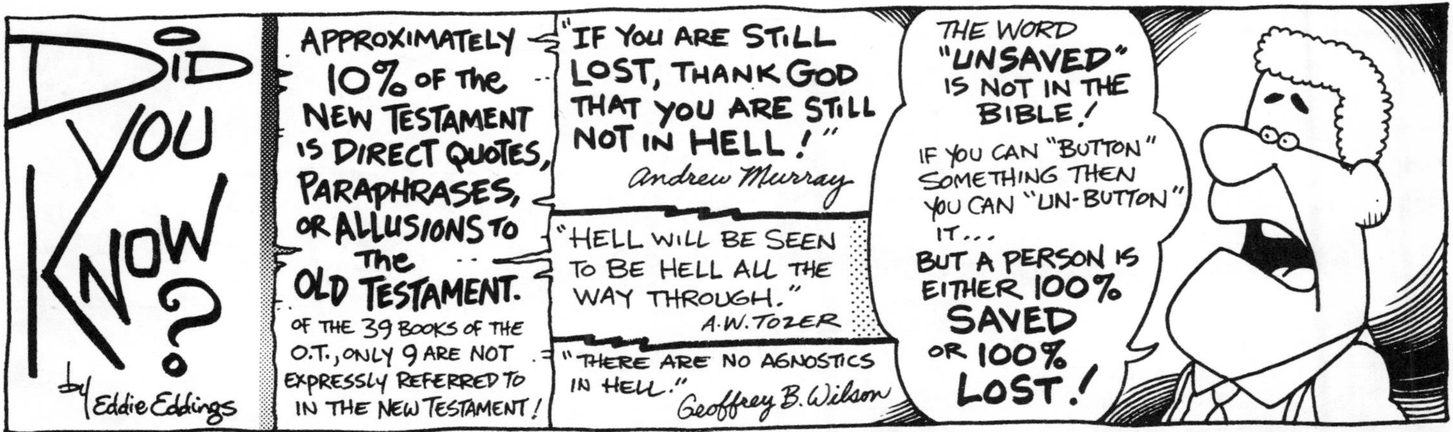
DID YOU KNOW?
by Eddie Eddings
APPROXIMATELY 10% OF THE NEW TESTAMENT IS DIRECT QUOTES, PARAPHRASES, OR ALLUSIONS TO THE OLD TESTAMENT.
OF THE 39 BOOKS OF THE O.T., ONLY 9 ARE NOT EXPRESSLY REFERRED TO IN THE NEW TESTAMENT!
"IF YOU ARE STILL LOST, THANK GOD THAT YOU ARE STILL NOT IN HELL!" Andrew Murray
"HELL WILL BE SEEN TO BE HELL ALL THE WAY THROUGH." A.W. TOZER
"THERE ARE NO AGNOSTICS IN HELL." Geoffrey B. Wilson
THE WORD "UNSAVED" IS NOT IN THE BIBLE!
IF YOU CAN "BUTTON" SOMETHING THEN YOU CAN "UN-BUTTON" IT...
BUT A PERSON IS EITHER 100% SAVED OR 100% LOST!

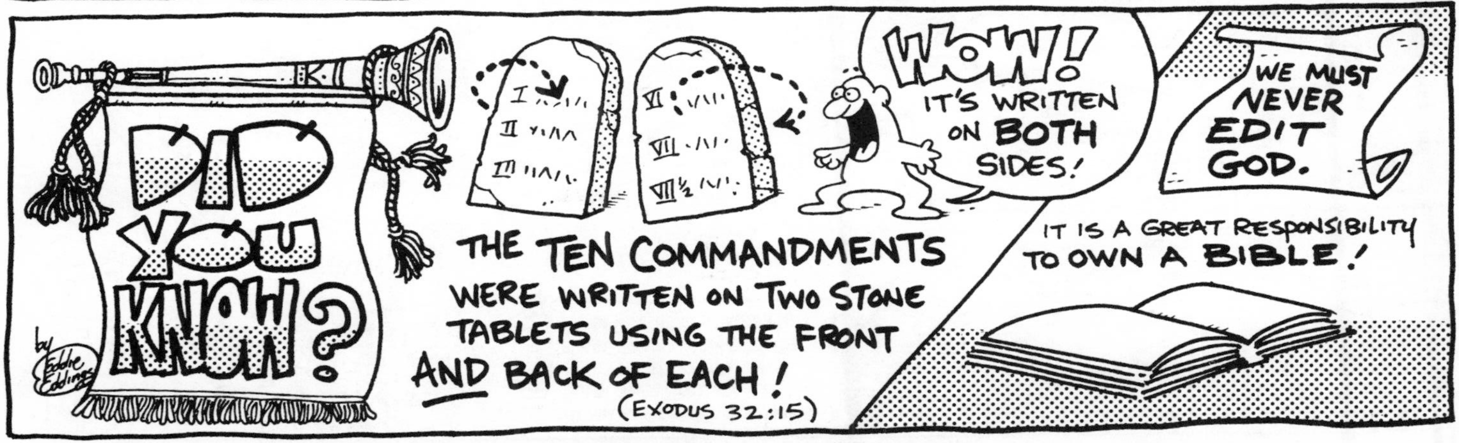
DID YOU KNOW?
by Eddie Eddings
THE TEN COMMANDMENTS WERE WRITTEN ON TWO STONE TABLETS USING THE FRONT AND BACK OF EACH!
(EXODUS 32:15)
WOW! IT'S WRITTEN ON BOTH SIDES!
WE MUST NEVER EDIT GOD.
IT IS A GREAT RESPONSIBILITY TO OWN A BIBLE!

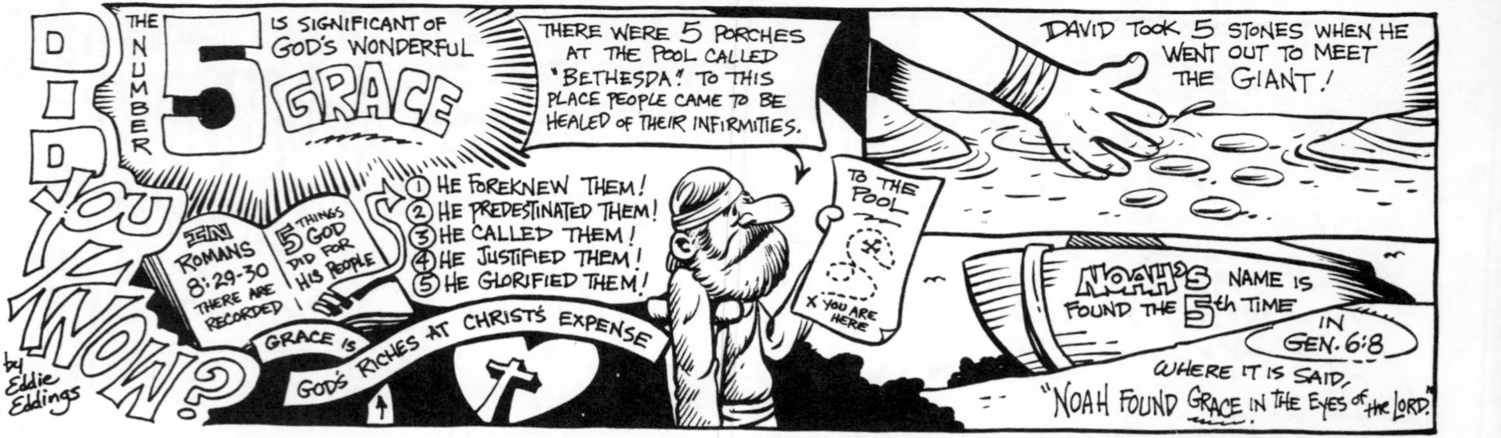
DID YOU KNOW?
THE NUMBER 5 IS SIGNIFICANT OF GOD'S WONDERFUL GRACE
by Eddie Eddings
IN ROMANS 8:29-30 THERE ARE RECORDED 5 THINGS GOD DID FOR HIS PEOPLE
① HE FOREKNEW THEM!
② HE PREDESTINATED THEM!
③ HE CALLED THEM!
④ HE JUSTIFIED THEM!
⑤ HE GLORIFIED THEM!
GRACE IS GOD'S RICHES AT CHRIST'S EXPENSE
THERE WERE 5 PORCHES AT THE POOL CALLED "BETHESDA." TO THIS PLACE PEOPLE CAME TO BE HEALED OF THEIR INFIRMITIES.
TO THE POOL
X YOU ARE HERE
DAVID TOOK 5 STONES WHEN HE WENT OUT TO MEET THE GIANT!
NOAH'S NAME IS FOUND THE 5th TIME IN GEN. 6:8
WHERE IT IS SAID, "NOAH FOUND GRACE IN THE EYES of the LORD."

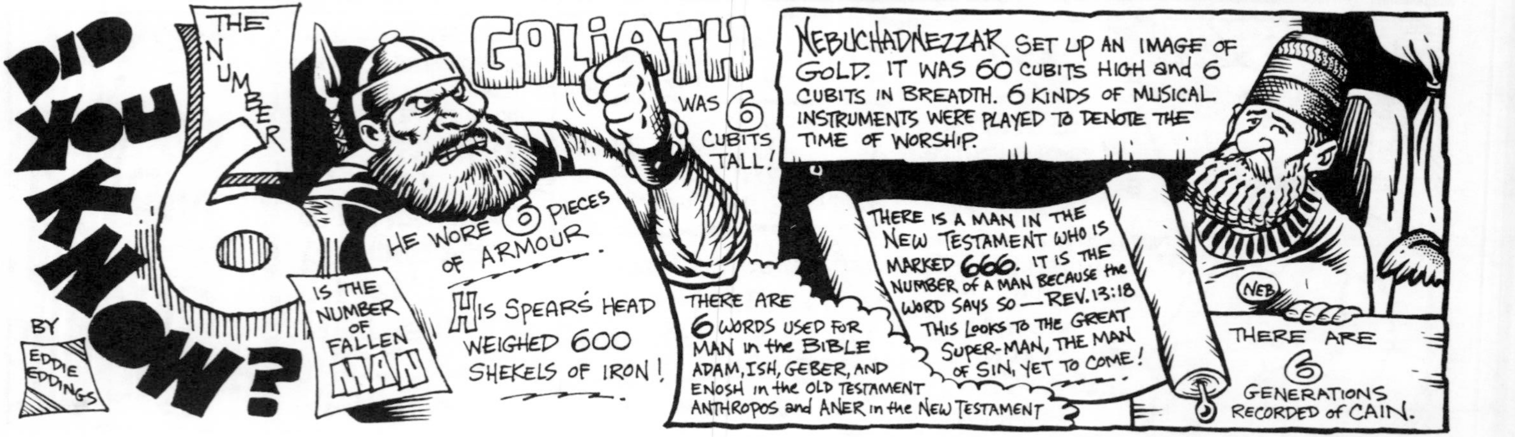
DID YOU KNOW?
BY EDDIE EDDINGS
THE NUMBER 6 IS THE NUMBER OF FALLEN MAN
GOLIATH WAS 6 CUBITS TALL!
HE WORE 6 PIECES OF ARMOUR.
HIS SPEAR'S HEAD WEIGHED 600 SHEKELS OF IRON!
THERE ARE 6 WORDS USED FOR MAN in the BIBLE ADAM, ISH, GEBER, AND ENOSH in the OLD TESTAMENT ANTHROPOS and ANER in the NEW TESTAMENT
NEBUCHADNEZZAR SET UP AN IMAGE OF GOLD. IT WAS 60 CUBITS HIGH and 6 CUBITS IN BREADTH. 6 KINDS OF MUSICAL INSTRUMENTS WERE PLAYED TO DENOTE THE TIME OF WORSHIP.
THERE IS A MAN IN THE NEW TESTAMENT WHO IS MARKED 666. IT IS THE NUMBER OF A MAN BECAUSE the WORD SAYS SO — REV. 13:18
THIS LOOKS TO THE GREAT SUPER-MAN, THE MAN OF SIN, YET TO COME!
NEB
THERE ARE 6 GENERATIONS RECORDED of CAIN.

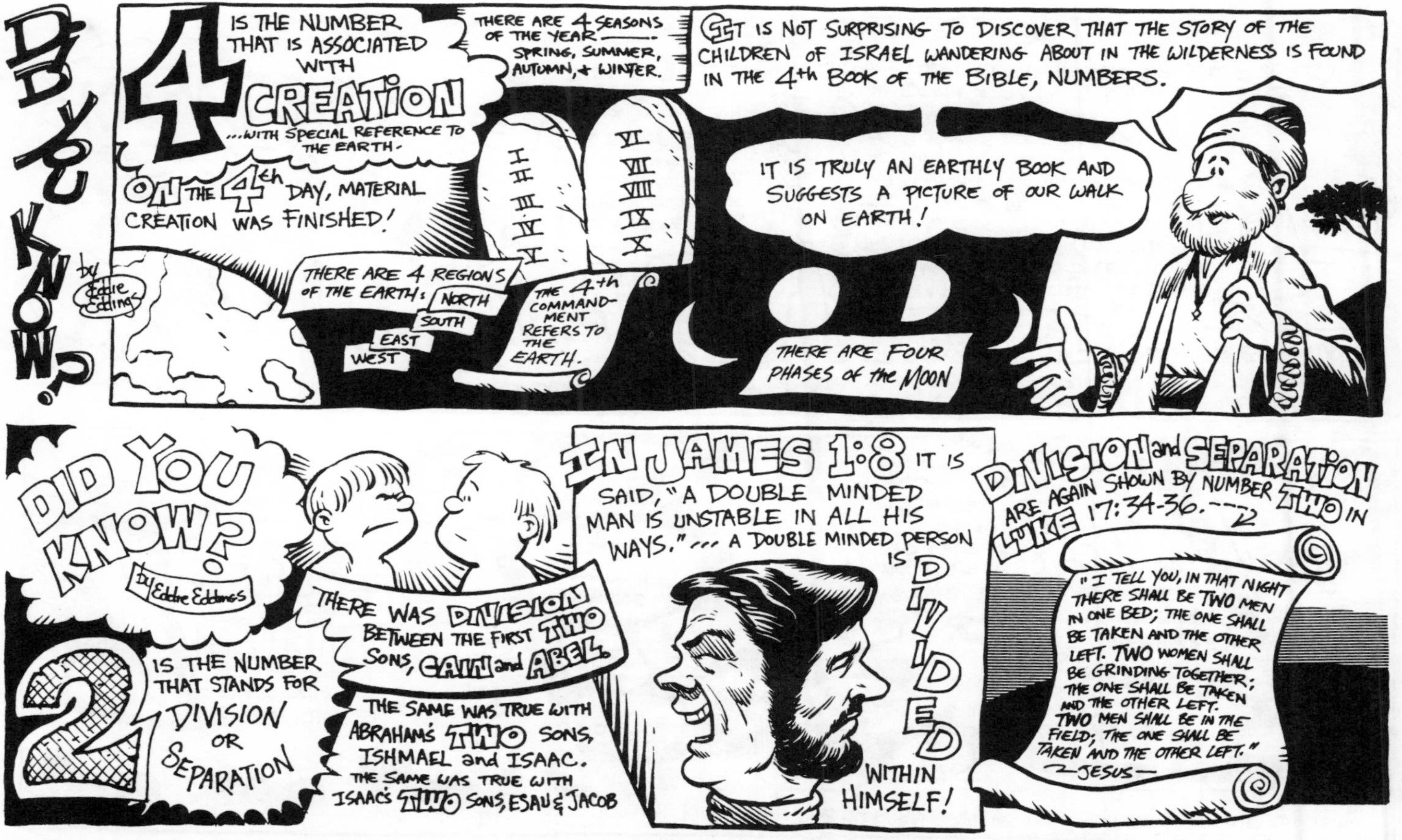
DID YOU KNOW?
by Eddie Eddings
4 IS THE NUMBER THAT IS ASSOCIATED WITH CREATION ...WITH SPECIAL REFERENCE TO THE EARTH.
ON THE 4th DAY, MATERIAL CREATION WAS FINISHED!
THERE ARE 4 SEASONS OF THE YEAR — SPRING, SUMMER, AUTUMN, & WINTER.
I II III IV V
VI VII VIII IX X
THERE ARE 4 REGIONS OF THE EARTH: NORTH SOUTH EAST WEST
THE 4th COMMANDMENT REFERS TO THE EARTH.
IT IS NOT SURPRISING TO DISCOVER THAT THE STORY OF THE CHILDREN OF ISRAEL WANDERING ABOUT IN THE WILDERNESS IS FOUND IN THE 4th BOOK OF THE BIBLE, NUMBERS.
IT IS TRULY AN EARTHLY BOOK AND SUGGESTS A PICTURE OF OUR WALK ON EARTH!
THERE ARE FOUR PHASES OF THE MOON
DID YOU KNOW?
by Eddie Eddings
2 IS THE NUMBER THAT STANDS FOR DIVISION OR SEPARATION
THERE WAS DIVISION BETWEEN THE FIRST TWO SONS, CAIN and ABEL.
THE SAME WAS TRUE WITH ABRAHAM'S TWO SONS, ISHMAEL and ISAAC.
THE SAME WAS TRUE WITH ISAAC'S TWO SONS, ESAU & JACOB
IN JAMES 1:8 IT IS SAID, "A DOUBLE MINDED MAN IS UNSTABLE IN ALL HIS WAYS." ... A DOUBLE MINDED PERSON IS DIVIDED WITHIN HIMSELF!
DIVISION and SEPARATION ARE AGAIN SHOWN BY NUMBER TWO IN LUKE 17:34-36.
"I TELL YOU, IN THAT NIGHT THERE SHALL BE TWO MEN IN ONE BED; THE ONE SHALL BE TAKEN AND THE OTHER LEFT. TWO WOMEN SHALL BE GRINDING TOGETHER; THE ONE SHALL BE TAKEN AND THE OTHER LEFT. TWO MEN SHALL BE IN THE FIELD; THE ONE SHALL BE TAKEN AND THE OTHER LEFT."
— JESUS —

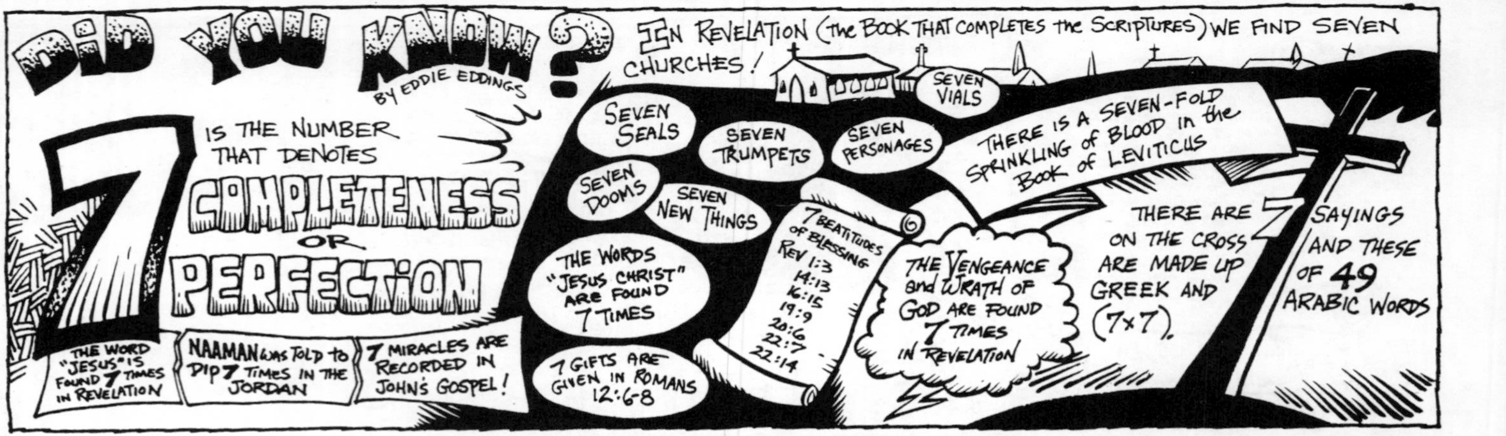
DID YOU KNOW?
BY EDDIE EDDINGS
IN REVELATION (the BOOK THAT COMPLETES the SCRIPTURES) WE FIND SEVEN CHURCHES!
7 IS THE NUMBER THAT DENOTES COMPLETENESS OR PERFECTION
THE WORD "JESUS" IS FOUND 7 TIMES IN REVELATION
NAAMAN WAS TOLD TO DIP 7 TIMES IN THE JORDAN
7 MIRACLES ARE RECORDED IN JOHN'S GOSPEL!
SEVEN SEALS
SEVEN DOOMS
SEVEN TRUMPETS
SEVEN NEW THINGS
SEVEN PERSONAGES
SEVEN VIALS
THE WORDS "JESUS CHRIST" ARE FOUND 7 TIMES
7 GIFTS ARE GIVEN IN ROMANS 12:6-8
7 BEATITUDES OF BLESSING REV 1:3 14:13 16:15 19:9 20:6 22:7 22:14
THERE IS A SEVEN-FOLD SPRINKLING of BLOOD in the BOOK of LEVITICUS
THE VENGEANCE and WRATH OF GOD ARE FOUND 7 TIMES IN REVELATION
THERE ARE 7 SAYINGS ON THE CROSS AND THESE ARE MADE UP OF 49 GREEK AND ARABIC WORDS (7×7).

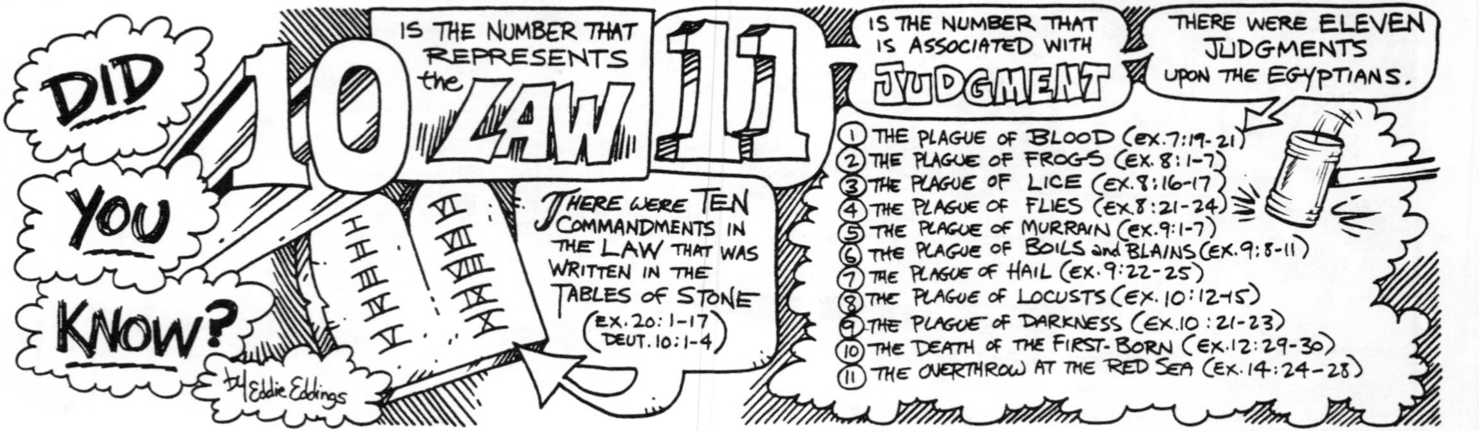
DID YOU KNOW?
by Eddie Eddings
10 IS THE NUMBER THAT REPRESENTS the LAW
I II III IV V VI VII VIII IX X
THERE WERE TEN COMMANDMENTS IN THE LAW THAT WAS WRITTEN IN THE TABLES OF STONE (EX. 20:1-17 DEUT. 10:1-4)
11 IS THE NUMBER THAT IS ASSOCIATED WITH JUDGMENT
THERE WERE ELEVEN JUDGMENTS UPON THE EGYPTIANS.
1 THE PLAGUE OF BLOOD (EX. 7:19-21)
2 THE PLAGUE OF FROGS (EX. 8:1-7)
3 THE PLAGUE OF LICE (EX. 8:16-17)
4 THE PLAGUE OF FLIES (EX. 8:21-24)
5 THE PLAGUE OF MURRAIN (EX. 9:1-7)
6 THE PLAGUE OF BOILS and BLAINS (EX. 9:8-11)
7 THE PLAGUE OF HAIL (EX. 9:22-25)
8 THE PLAGUE OF LOCUSTS (EX. 10:12-15)
9 THE PLAGUE OF DARKNESS (EX. 10:21-23)
10 THE DEATH OF THE FIRST-BORN (EX. 12:29-30)
11 THE OVERTHROW AT THE RED SEA (EX. 14:24-28)

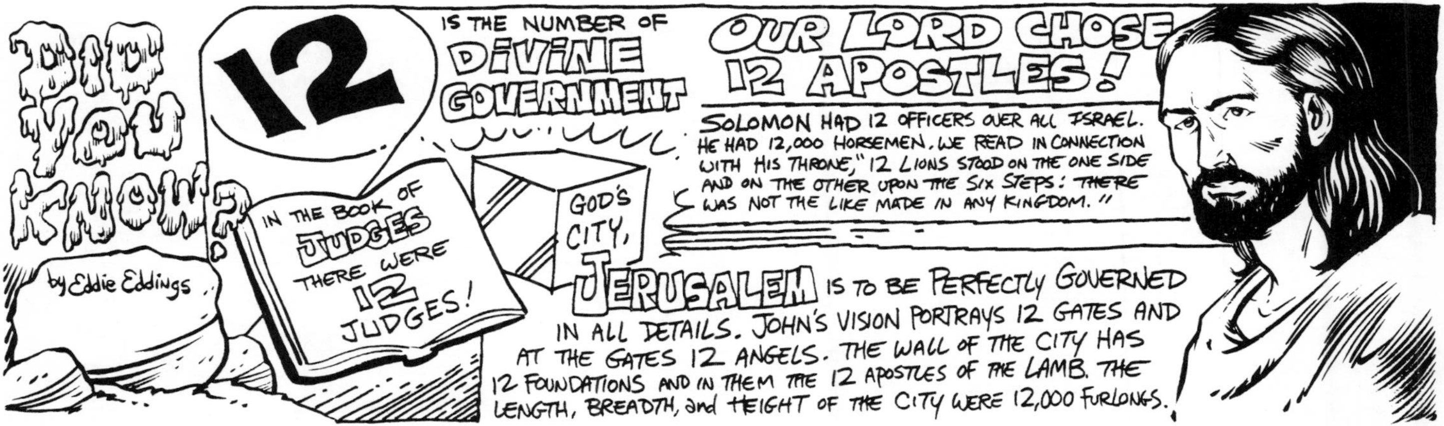
DID YOU KNOW?
by Eddie Eddings
12
IS THE NUMBER OF DIVINE GOVERNMENT
IN THE BOOK OF JUDGES THERE WERE 12 JUDGES!
OUR LORD CHOSE 12 APOSTLES!
SOLOMON HAD 12 OFFICERS OVER ALL ISRAEL. HE HAD 12,000 HORSEMEN. WE READ IN CONNECTION WITH HIS THRONE, "12 LIONS STOOD ON THE ONE SIDE AND ON THE OTHER UPON THE SIX STEPS: THERE WAS NOT THE LIKE MADE IN ANY KINGDOM."
GOD'S CITY, JERUSALEM IS TO BE PERFECTLY GOVERNED IN ALL DETAILS. JOHN'S VISION PORTRAYS 12 GATES AND AT THE GATES 12 ANGELS. THE WALL OF THE CITY HAS 12 FOUNDATIONS AND IN THEM THE 12 APOSTLES OF THE LAMB. THE LENGTH, BREADTH, and HEIGHT OF THE CITY WERE 12,000 FURLONGS.

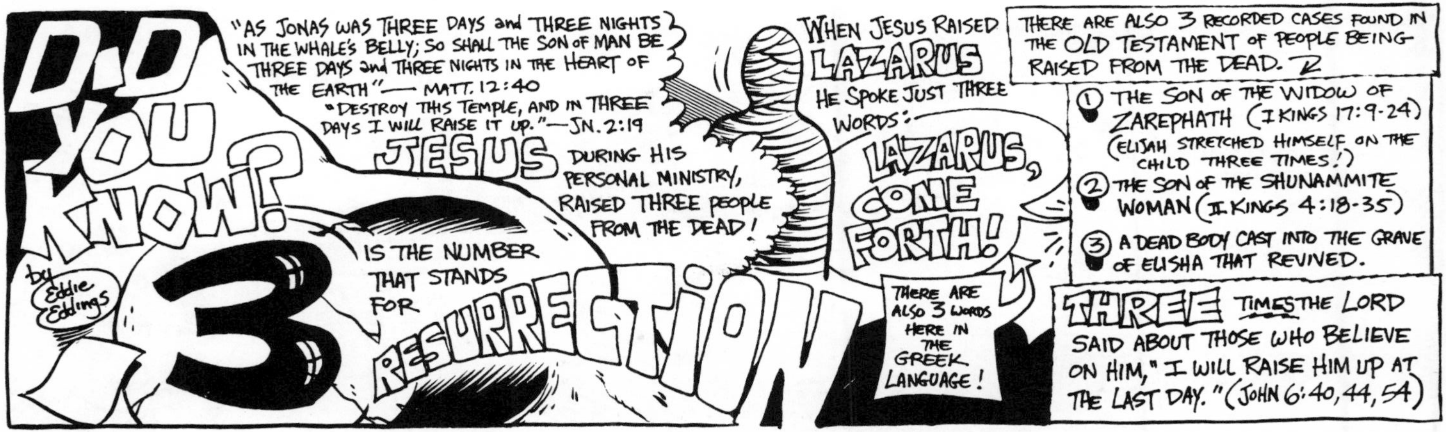
DID YOU KNOW?
by Eddie Eddings
"AS JONAS WAS THREE DAYS and THREE NIGHTS IN THE WHALE'S BELLY; SO SHALL THE SON OF MAN BE THREE DAYS and THREE NIGHTS IN THE HEART OF THE EARTH" — MATT. 12:40
"DESTROY THIS TEMPLE, AND IN THREE DAYS I WILL RAISE IT UP." — JN. 2:19
JESUS DURING HIS PERSONAL MINISTRY, RAISED THREE PEOPLE FROM THE DEAD!
3 IS THE NUMBER THAT STANDS FOR RESURRECTION!
WHEN JESUS RAISED LAZARUS HE SPOKE JUST THREE WORDS:
LAZARUS, COME FORTH!
THERE ARE ALSO 3 WORDS HERE IN THE GREEK LANGUAGE!
THERE ARE ALSO 3 RECORDED CASES FOUND IN THE OLD TESTAMENT OF PEOPLE BEING RAISED FROM THE DEAD.
1 THE SON OF THE WIDOW OF ZAREPHATH (I KINGS 17:9-24) (ELIJAH STRETCHED HIMSELF ON THE CHILD THREE TIMES!)
2 THE SON OF THE SHUNAMMITE WOMAN (II KINGS 4:18-35)
3 A DEAD BODY CAST INTO THE GRAVE OF ELISHA THAT REVIVED.
THREE TIMES THE LORD SAID ABOUT THOSE WHO BELIEVE ON HIM, "I WILL RAISE HIM UP AT THE LAST DAY." (JOHN 6:40, 44, 54)

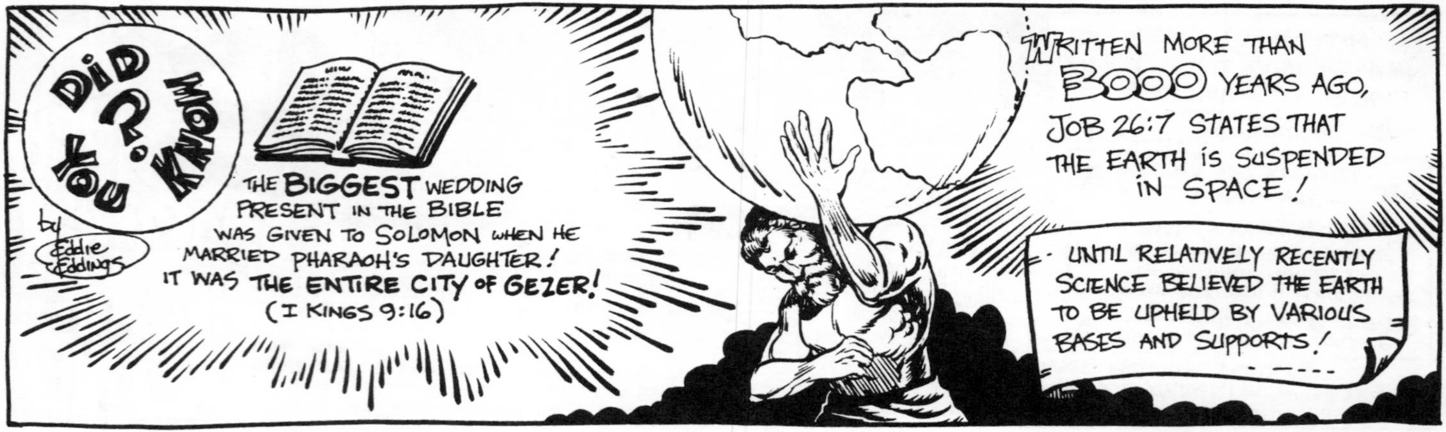
DID YOU KNOW?
by Eddie Eddings
THE BIGGEST WEDDING PRESENT IN THE BIBLE WAS GIVEN TO SOLOMON WHEN HE MARRIED PHARAOH'S DAUGHTER! IT WAS THE ENTIRE CITY OF GEZER! (I KINGS 9:16)
WRITTEN MORE THAN 3000 YEARS AGO, JOB 26:7 STATES THAT THE EARTH IS SUSPENDED IN SPACE!
UNTIL RELATIVELY RECENTLY SCIENCE BELIEVED THE EARTH TO BE UPHELD BY VARIOUS BASES AND SUPPORTS!

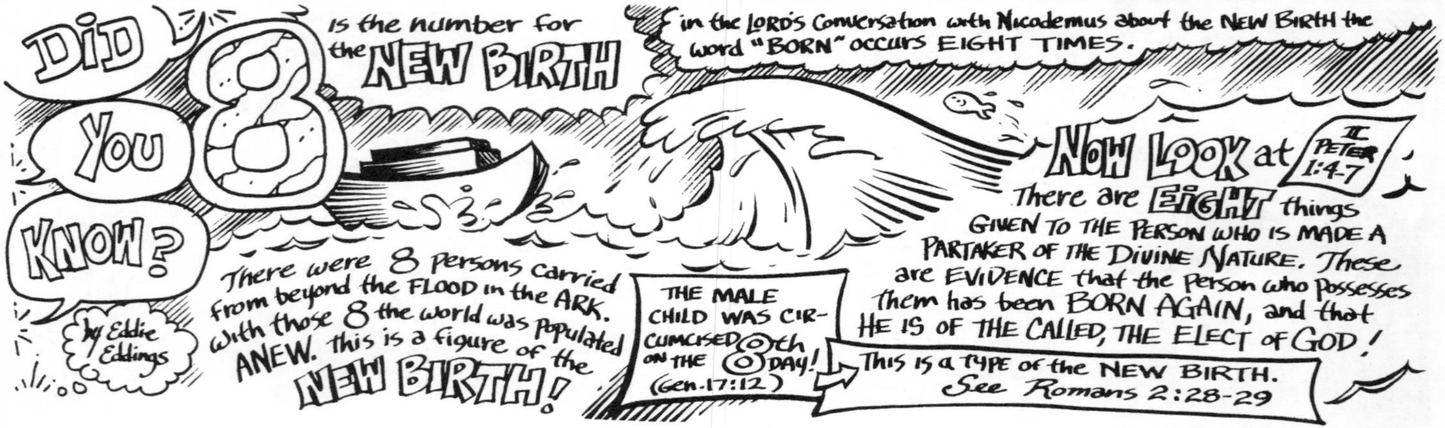
DID YOU KNOW?
by Eddie Eddings
8 is the number for the NEW BIRTH
in the LORD'S Conversation with Nicodemus about the NEW BIRTH the word "BORN" occurs EIGHT TIMES.
There were 8 persons carried from beyond the FLOOD in the ARK. With those 8 the world was populated ANEW. this is a figure of the NEW BIRTH!
THE MALE CHILD WAS CIRCUMCISED ON THE 8th DAY! (Gen. 17:12)
NOW LOOK at II PETER 1:4-7
There are EIGHT things GIVEN TO THE PERSON WHO IS MADE A PARTAKER OF THE DIVINE NATURE. These are EVIDENCE that the person who possesses them has been BORN AGAIN, and that HE IS OF THE CALLED, THE ELECT of GOD!
This is a TYPE of the NEW BIRTH. See Romans 2:28-29

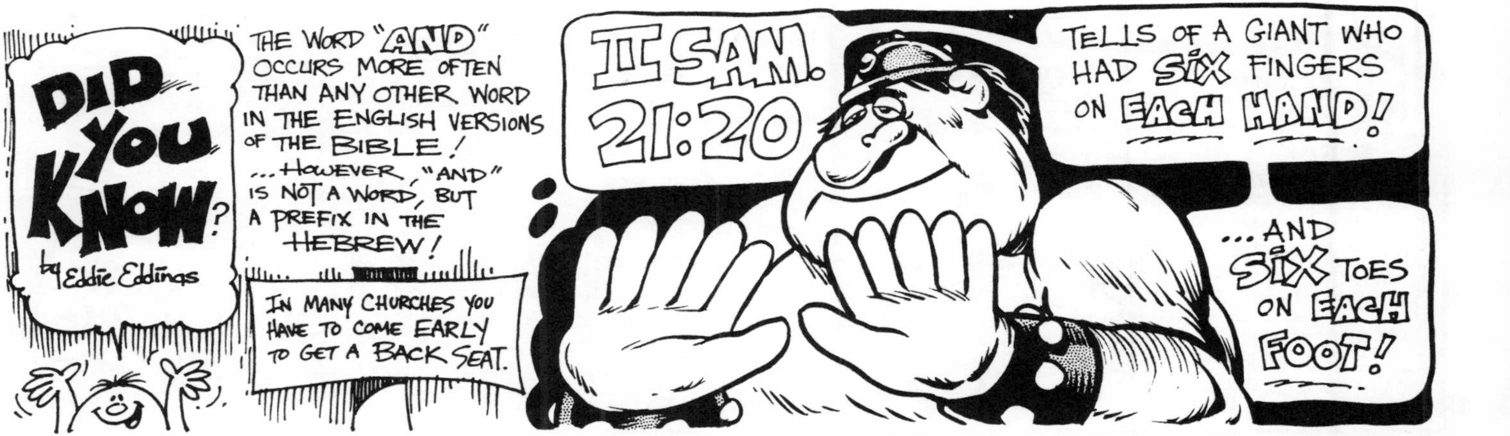
DID YOU KNOW?
by Eddie Eddings
THE WORD "AND" OCCURS MORE OFTEN THAN ANY OTHER WORD IN THE ENGLISH VERSIONS OF THE BIBLE! ...HOWEVER, "AND" IS NOT A WORD, BUT A PREFIX IN THE HEBREW!
IN MANY CHURCHES YOU HAVE TO COME EARLY TO GET A BACK SEAT.
II SAM. 21:20
TELLS OF A GIANT WHO HAD SIX FINGERS ON EACH HAND!
...AND SIX TOES ON EACH FOOT!

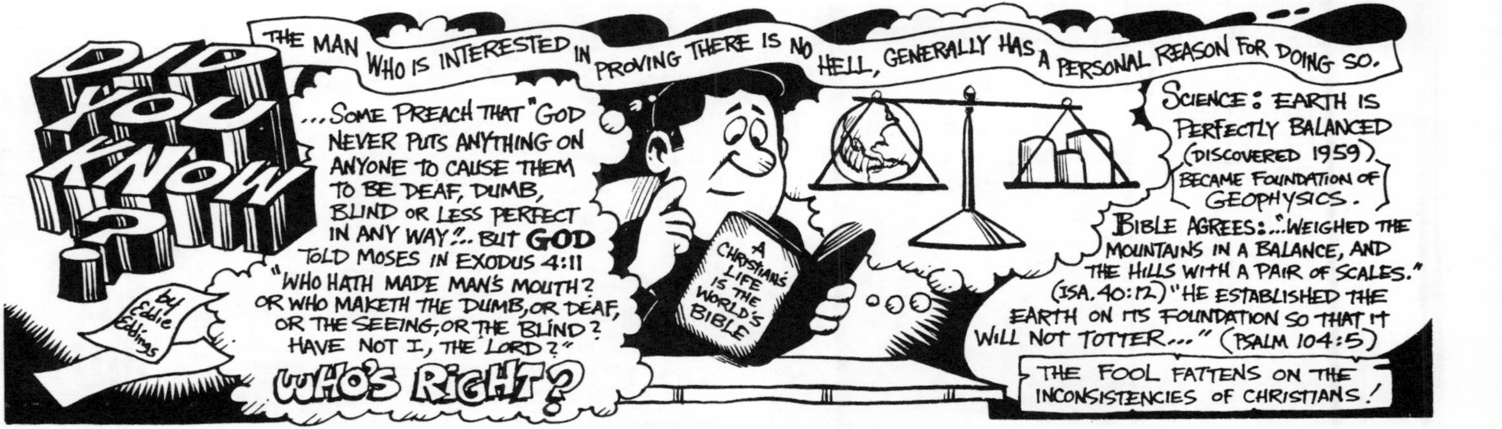
DID YOU KNOW?
by Eddie Eddings
THE MAN WHO IS INTERESTED IN PROVING THERE IS NO HELL, GENERALLY HAS A PERSONAL REASON FOR DOING SO.
...SOME PREACH THAT "GOD NEVER PUTS ANYTHING ON ANYONE TO CAUSE THEM TO BE DEAF, DUMB, BLIND OR LESS PERFECT IN ANY WAY"... BUT GOD TOLD MOSES IN EXODUS 4:11 "WHO HATH MADE MAN'S MOUTH? OR WHO MAKETH THE DUMB, OR DEAF, OR THE SEEING, OR THE BLIND? HAVE NOT I, THE LORD?"
WHO'S RIGHT?
A CHRISTIAN'S LIFE IS THE WORLD'S BIBLE
SCIENCE: EARTH IS PERFECTLY BALANCED (DISCOVERED 1959) BECAME FOUNDATION OF GEOPHYSICS.
BIBLE AGREES: "WEIGHED THE MOUNTAINS IN A BALANCE, AND THE HILLS WITH A PAIR OF SCALES." (ISA. 40:12) "HE ESTABLISHED THE EARTH ON ITS FOUNDATION SO THAT IT WILL NOT TOTTER..." (PSALM 104:5)
THE FOOL FATTENS ON THE INCONSISTENCIES OF CHRISTIANS!

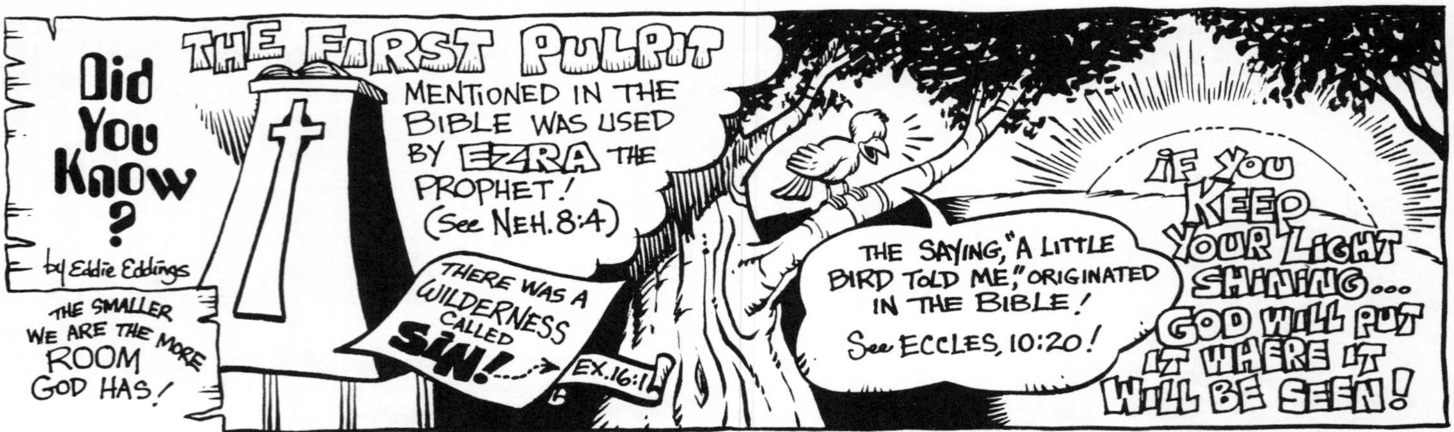
Did You Know?
by Eddie Eddings
THE FIRST PULPIT
MENTIONED IN THE BIBLE WAS USED BY EZRA THE PROPHET! (See NEH. 8:4)
THERE WAS A WILDERNESS CALLED SIN! EX. 16:1
THE SMALLER WE ARE THE MORE ROOM GOD HAS!
THE SAYING, "A LITTLE BIRD TOLD ME," ORIGINATED IN THE BIBLE! See ECCLES, 10:20!
IF YOU KEEP YOUR LIGHT SHINING... GOD WILL PUT IT WHERE IT WILL BE SEEN!

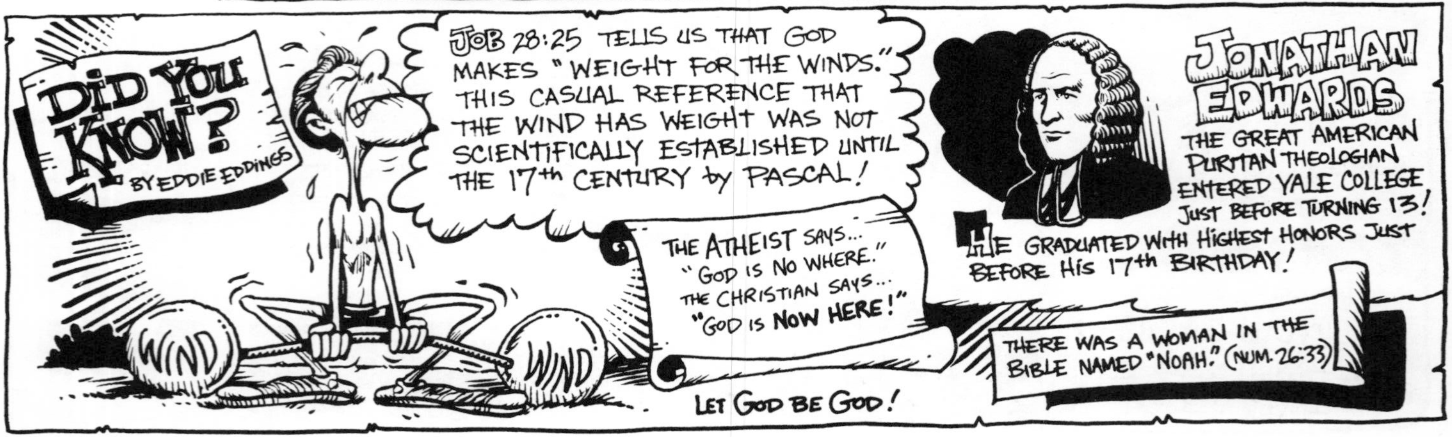
DID YOU KNOW?
BY EDDIE EDDINGS
JOB 28:25 TELLS US THAT GOD MAKES "WEIGHT FOR THE WINDS." THIS CASUAL REFERENCE THAT THE WIND HAS WEIGHT WAS NOT SCIENTIFICALLY ESTABLISHED UNTIL THE 17th CENTURY by PASCAL!
WIND
WIND
THE ATHEIST SAYS... "GOD IS NO WHERE." THE CHRISTIAN SAYS... "GOD IS NOW HERE!"
LET GOD BE GOD!
JONATHAN EDWARDS
THE GREAT AMERICAN PURITAN THEOLOGIAN ENTERED YALE COLLEGE JUST BEFORE TURNING 13!
HE GRADUATED WITH HIGHEST HONORS JUST BEFORE HIS 17th BIRTHDAY!
THERE WAS A WOMAN IN THE BIBLE NAMED "NOAH." (NUM. 26:33)

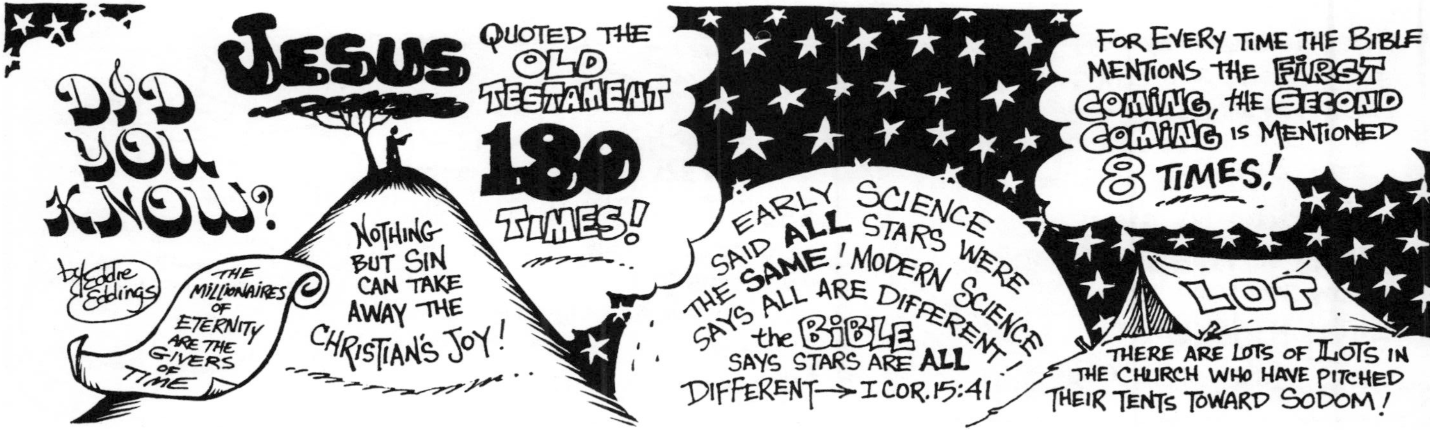
DID YOU KNOW?
by Eddie Eddings
THE MILLIONAIRES OF ETERNITY ARE THE GIVERS OF TIME
JESUS QUOTED THE OLD TESTAMENT 180 TIMES!
NOTHING BUT SIN CAN TAKE AWAY THE CHRISTIAN'S JOY!
EARLY SCIENCE SAID ALL STARS WERE THE SAME! MODERN SCIENCE SAYS ALL ARE DIFFERENT! the BIBLE SAYS STARS ARE ALL DIFFERENT → I COR. 15:41
FOR EVERY TIME THE BIBLE MENTIONS THE FIRST COMING, THE SECOND COMING IS MENTIONED 8 TIMES!
LOT
THERE ARE LOTS OF LOTS IN THE CHURCH WHO HAVE PITCHED THEIR TENTS TOWARD SODOM!

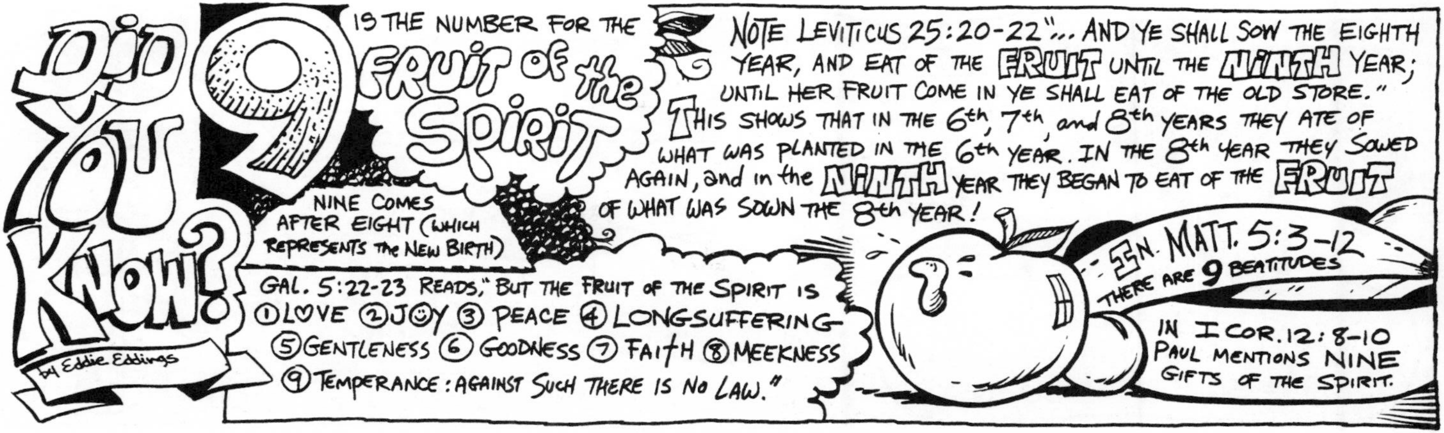
DID YOU KNOW?
by Eddie Eddings
9 IS THE NUMBER FOR THE FRUIT OF the SPIRIT
NINE COMES AFTER EIGHT (WHICH REPRESENTS the NEW BIRTH)
NOTE LEVITICUS 25:20-22 "... AND YE SHALL SOW THE EIGHTH YEAR, AND EAT OF THE FRUIT UNTIL THE NINTH YEAR; UNTIL HER FRUIT COME IN YE SHALL EAT OF THE OLD STORE."
THIS SHOWS THAT IN THE 6th, 7th, and 8th YEARS THEY ATE OF WHAT WAS PLANTED IN THE 6th YEAR. IN THE 8th YEAR THEY SOWED AGAIN, and in the NINTH YEAR THEY BEGAN TO EAT OF THE FRUIT OF WHAT WAS SOWN THE 8th YEAR!
GAL. 5:22-23 READS, "BUT THE FRUIT OF THE SPIRIT IS ① LOVE ② JOY ③ PEACE ④ LONGSUFFERING ⑤ GENTLENESS ⑥ GOODNESS ⑦ FAITH ⑧ MEEKNESS ⑨ TEMPERANCE: AGAINST SUCH THERE IS NO LAW."
IN MATT. 5:3-12 THERE ARE 9 BEATITUDES
IN I COR. 12:8-10 PAUL MENTIONS NINE GIFTS OF THE SPIRIT.

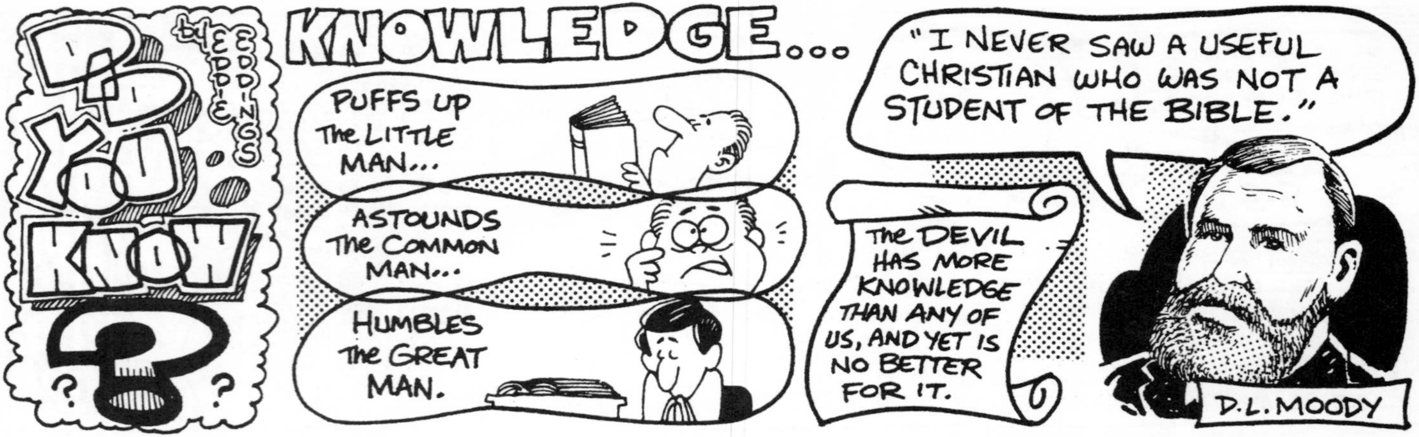
DID YOU KNOW ??
by EDDIE EDDINGS
KNOWLEDGE...
PUFFS UP The LITTLE MAN...
ASTOUNDS The COMMON MAN...
HUMBLES The GREAT MAN.
The DEVIL HAS MORE KNOWLEDGE THAN ANY OF US, AND YET IS NO BETTER FOR IT.
"I NEVER SAW A USEFUL CHRISTIAN WHO WAS NOT A STUDENT OF THE BIBLE."
D.L. MOODY

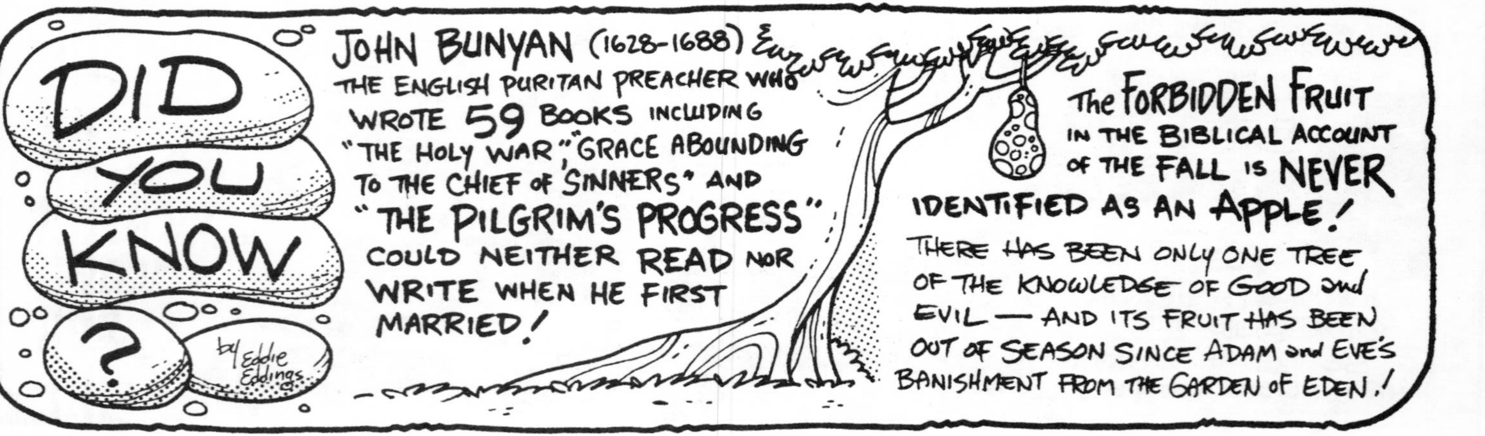
DID YOU KNOW ?
by Eddie Eddings
JOHN BUNYAN (1628-1688) THE ENGLISH PURITAN PREACHER WHO WROTE 59 BOOKS INCLUDING "THE HOLY WAR", "GRACE ABOUNDING TO THE CHIEF OF SINNERS" AND "THE PILGRIM'S PROGRESS" COULD NEITHER READ NOR WRITE WHEN HE FIRST MARRIED!
The FORBIDDEN FRUIT IN THE BIBLICAL ACCOUNT OF THE FALL IS NEVER IDENTIFIED AS AN APPLE!
THERE HAS BEEN ONLY ONE TREE OF THE KNOWLEDGE OF GOOD and EVIL — AND ITS FRUIT HAS BEEN OUT OF SEASON SINCE ADAM and EVE'S BANISHMENT FROM THE GARDEN OF EDEN!

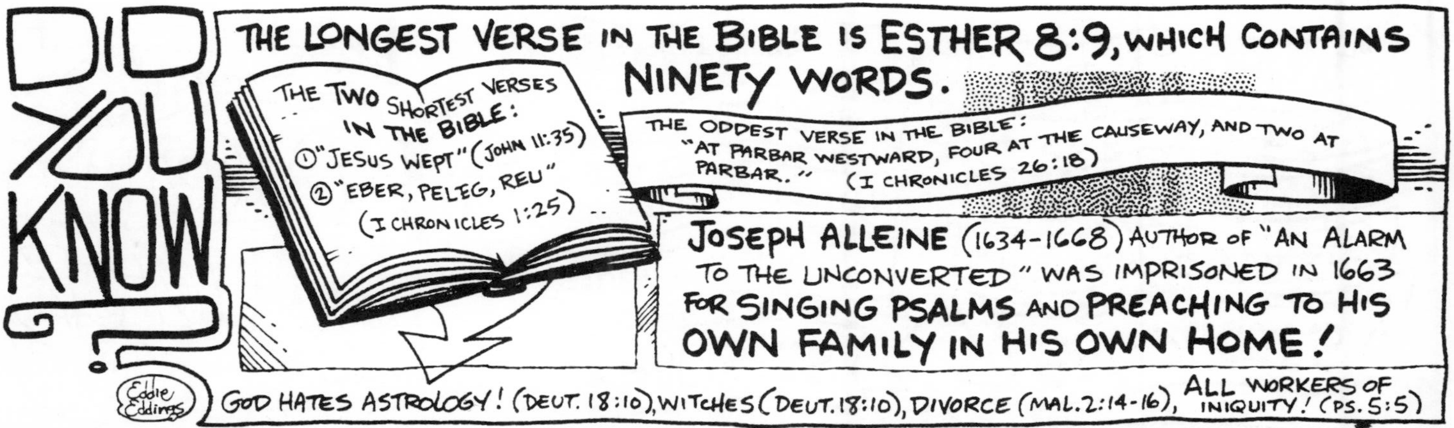
DID YOU KNOW?
THE LONGEST VERSE IN THE BIBLE IS ESTHER 8:9, WHICH CONTAINS NINETY WORDS.
THE TWO SHORTEST VERSES IN THE BIBLE:
① "JESUS WEPT" (JOHN 11:35)
② "EBER, PELEG, REU" (I CHRONICLES 1:25)
THE ODDEST VERSE IN THE BIBLE:
"AT PARBAR WESTWARD, FOUR AT THE CAUSEWAY, AND TWO AT PARBAR." (I CHRONICLES 26:18)
JOSEPH ALLEINE (1634-1668) AUTHOR OF "AN ALARM TO THE UNCONVERTED" WAS IMPRISONED IN 1663 FOR SINGING PSALMS AND PREACHING TO HIS OWN FAMILY IN HIS OWN HOME!
Eddie Eddings
GOD HATES ASTROLOGY! (DEUT. 18:10), WITCHES (DEUT. 18:10), DIVORCE (MAL. 2:14-16), ALL WORKERS OF INIQUITY! (PS. 5:5)

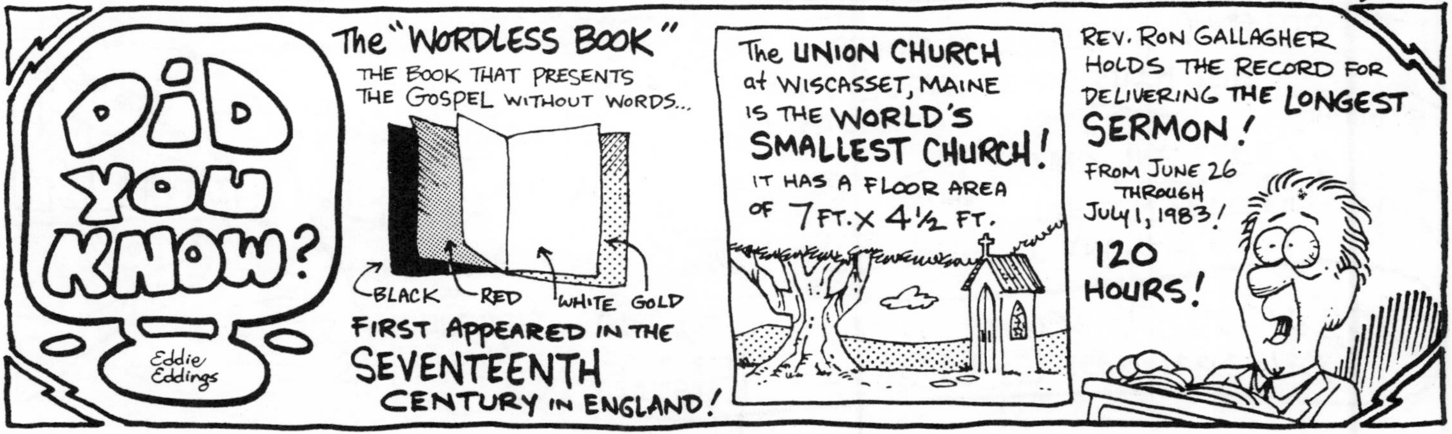
DID YOU KNOW?
Eddie Eddings
The "WORDLESS BOOK"
THE BOOK THAT PRESENTS THE GOSPEL WITHOUT WORDS...
BLACK
RED
WHITE
GOLD
FIRST APPEARED IN THE SEVENTEENTH CENTURY IN ENGLAND!
The UNION CHURCH at WISCASSET, MAINE IS THE WORLD'S SMALLEST CHURCH!
IT HAS A FLOOR AREA OF 7 FT. X 4½ FT.
REV. RON GALLAGHER HOLDS THE RECORD FOR DELIVERING THE LONGEST SERMON!
FROM JUNE 26 THROUGH JULY 1, 1983!
120 HOURS!

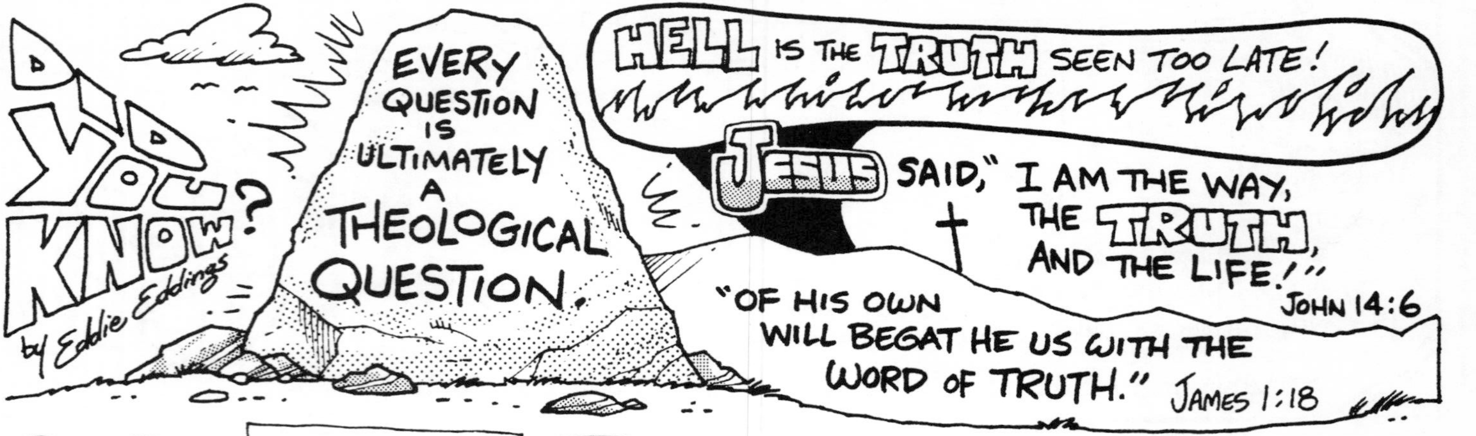
DID YOU KNOW?
by Eddie Eddings
EVERY QUESTION IS ULTIMATELY A THEOLOGICAL QUESTION.
HELL IS THE TRUTH SEEN TOO LATE!
JESUS SAID, "I AM THE WAY, THE TRUTH, AND THE LIFE!"
JOHN 14:6
"OF HIS OWN WILL BEGAT HE US WITH THE WORD OF TRUTH." JAMES 1:18

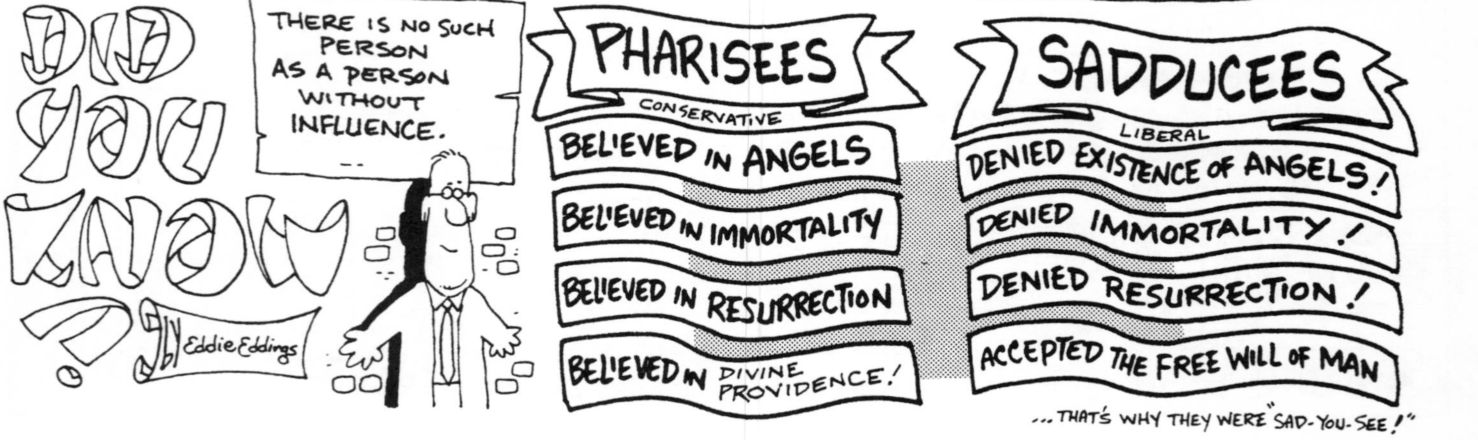
DID YOU KNOW?
by Eddie Eddings
THERE IS NO SUCH PERSON AS A PERSON WITHOUT INFLUENCE.
PHARISEES
CONSERVATIVE
BELIEVED IN ANGELS
BELIEVED IN IMMORTALITY
BELIEVED IN RESURRECTION
BELIEVED IN DIVINE PROVIDENCE!
SADDUCEES
LIBERAL
DENIED EXISTENCE OF ANGELS!
DENIED IMMORTALITY!
DENIED RESURRECTION!
ACCEPTED THE FREE WILL OF MAN
...THAT'S WHY THEY WERE "SAD-YOU-SEE!"

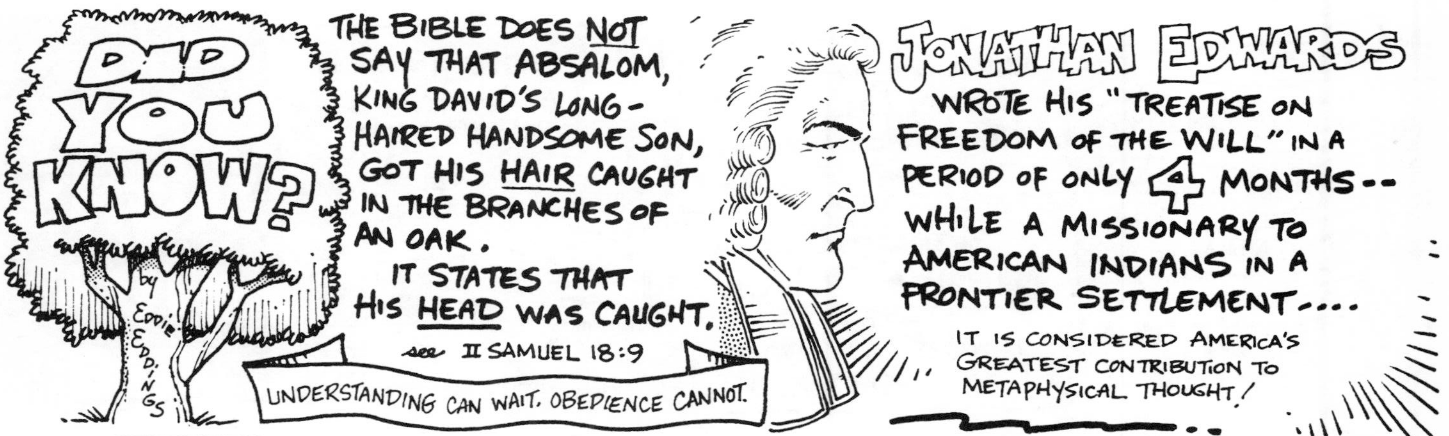
DID YOU KNOW?
by Eddie Eddings
THE BIBLE DOES NOT SAY THAT ABSALOM, KING DAVID'S LONG-HAIRED HANDSOME SON, GOT HIS HAIR CAUGHT IN THE BRANCHES OF AN OAK.
IT STATES THAT HIS HEAD WAS CAUGHT.
see II SAMUEL 18:9
UNDERSTANDING CAN WAIT. OBEDIENCE CANNOT.
JONATHAN EDWARDS
WROTE HIS "TREATISE ON FREEDOM OF THE WILL" IN A PERIOD OF ONLY 4 MONTHS-- WHILE A MISSIONARY TO AMERICAN INDIANS IN A FRONTIER SETTLEMENT....
IT IS CONSIDERED AMERICA'S GREATEST CONTRIBUTION TO METAPHYSICAL THOUGHT!

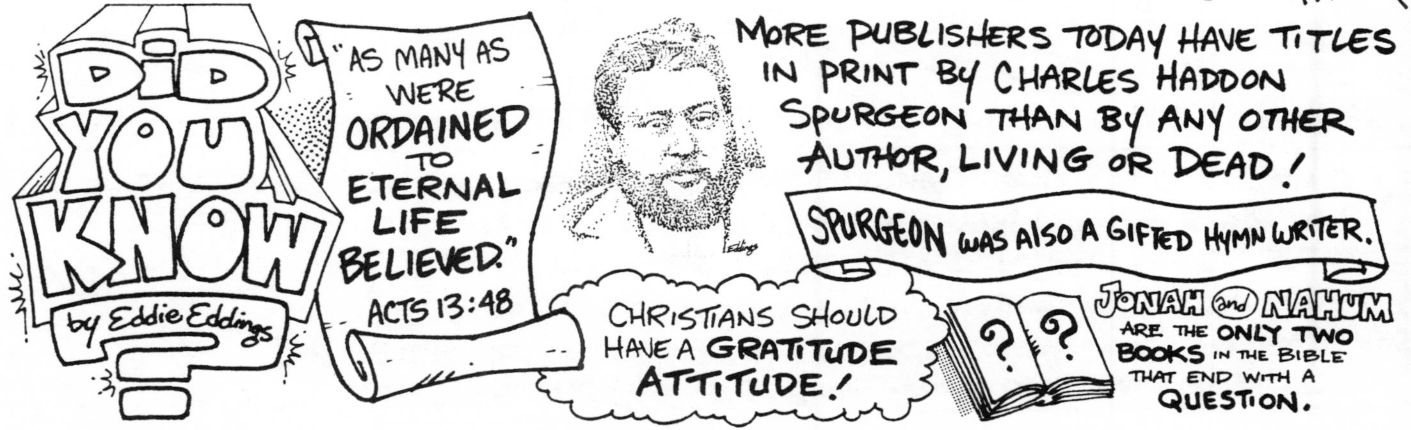
DID YOU KNOW
by Eddie Eddings
"AS MANY AS WERE ORDAINED TO ETERNAL LIFE BELIEVED."
ACTS 13:48
Eddings
MORE PUBLISHERS TODAY HAVE TITLES IN PRINT BY CHARLES HADDON SPURGEON THAN BY ANY OTHER AUTHOR, LIVING OR DEAD!
SPURGEON WAS ALSO A GIFTED HYMN WRITER.
CHRISTIANS SHOULD HAVE A GRATITUDE ATTITUDE!
JONAH and NAHUM ARE THE ONLY TWO BOOKS IN THE BIBLE THAT END WITH A QUESTION.

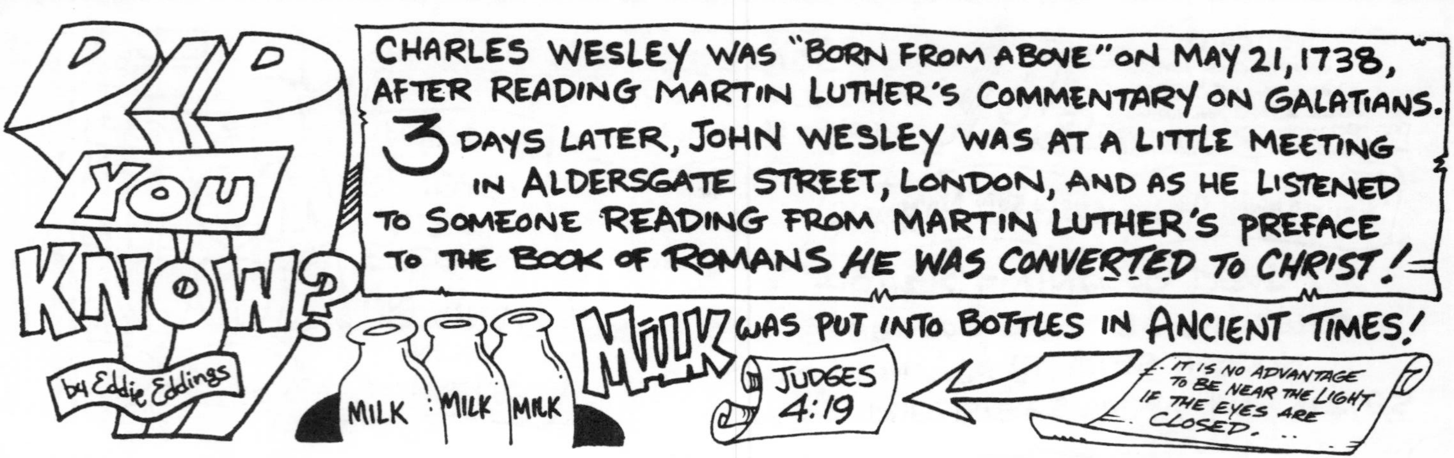
DID YOU KNOW?
by Eddie Eddings
CHARLES WESLEY WAS "BORN FROM ABOVE" ON MAY 21, 1738, AFTER READING MARTIN LUTHER'S COMMENTARY ON GALATIANS.
3 DAYS LATER, JOHN WESLEY WAS AT A LITTLE MEETING IN ALDERSGATE STREET, LONDON, AND AS HE LISTENED TO SOMEONE READING FROM MARTIN LUTHER'S PREFACE TO THE BOOK OF ROMANS HE WAS CONVERTED TO CHRIST!
MILK MILK MILK
MILK WAS PUT INTO BOTTLES IN ANCIENT TIMES!
JUDGES 4:19
IT IS NO ADVANTAGE TO BE NEAR THE LIGHT IF THE EYES ARE CLOSED.

DID YOU KNOW ?

By Eddie Eddings

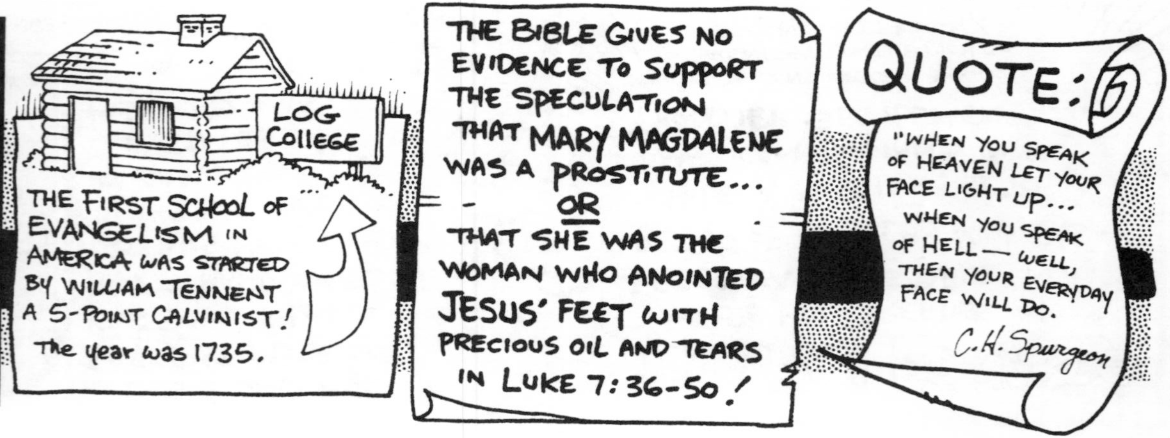
LOG COLLEGE
THE FIRST SCHOOL OF EVANGELISM IN AMERICA WAS STARTED BY WILLIAM TENNENT A 5-POINT CALVINIST!
The year was 1735.
THE BIBLE GIVES NO EVIDENCE TO SUPPORT THE SPECULATION THAT MARY MAGDALENE WAS A PROSTITUTE... OR THAT SHE WAS THE WOMAN WHO ANOINTED JESUS' FEET WITH PRECIOUS OIL AND TEARS IN LUKE 7:36-50!
QUOTE:
"WHEN YOU SPEAK OF HEAVEN LET YOUR FACE LIGHT UP... WHEN YOU SPEAK OF HELL — WELL, THEN YOUR EVERYDAY FACE WILL DO.
C.H. Spurgeon

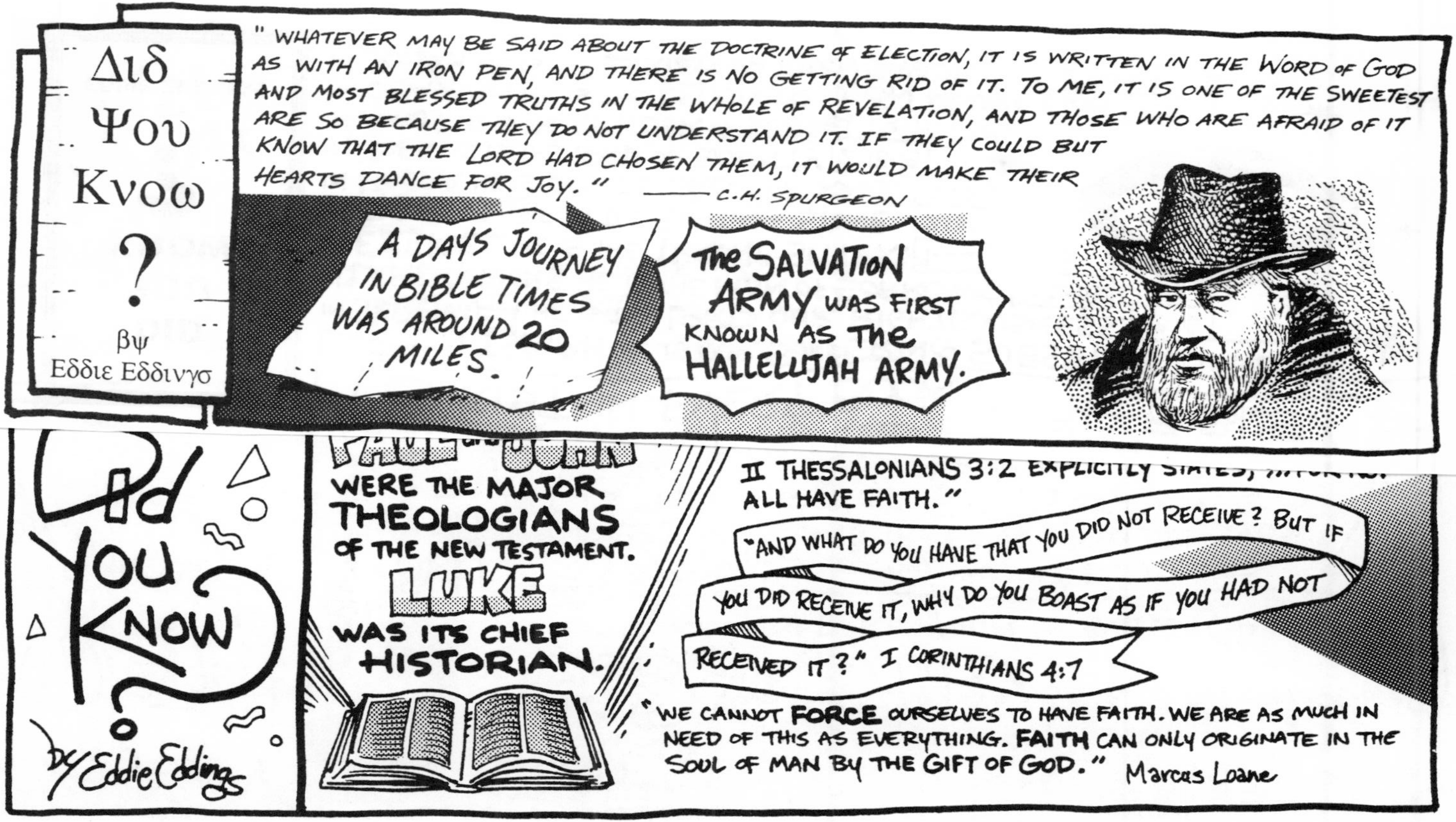
Διδ Ψου Κνοω ?
βψ Εδδιε Εδδινγσ
" WHATEVER MAY BE SAID ABOUT THE DOCTRINE OF ELECTION, IT IS WRITTEN IN THE WORD OF GOD AS WITH AN IRON PEN, AND THERE IS NO GETTING RID OF IT. TO ME, IT IS ONE OF THE SWEETEST AND MOST BLESSED TRUTHS IN THE WHOLE OF REVELATION, AND THOSE WHO ARE AFRAID OF IT ARE SO BECAUSE THEY DO NOT UNDERSTAND IT. IF THEY COULD BUT KNOW THAT THE LORD HAD CHOSEN THEM, IT WOULD MAKE THEIR HEARTS DANCE FOR JOY. " —— C.H. SPURGEON
A DAYS JOURNEY IN BIBLE TIMES WAS AROUND 20 MILES.
The SALVATION ARMY WAS FIRST KNOWN AS The HALLELUJAH ARMY.
Did You Know?
by Eddie Eddings
WERE THE MAJOR THEOLOGIANS OF THE NEW TESTAMENT.
LUKE WAS ITS CHIEF HISTORIAN.
II THESSALONIANS 3:2 EXPLICITLY STATES,
ALL HAVE FAITH."
"AND WHAT DO YOU HAVE THAT YOU DID NOT RECEIVE? BUT IF YOU DID RECEIVE IT, WHY DO YOU BOAST AS IF YOU HAD NOT RECEIVED IT?" I CORINTHIANS 4:7
"WE CANNOT FORCE OURSELVES TO HAVE FAITH. WE ARE AS MUCH IN NEED OF THIS AS EVERYTHING. FAITH CAN ONLY ORIGINATE IN THE SOUL OF MAN BY THE GIFT OF GOD." Marcus Loane

DID YOU KNOW?

by Eddie Eddings

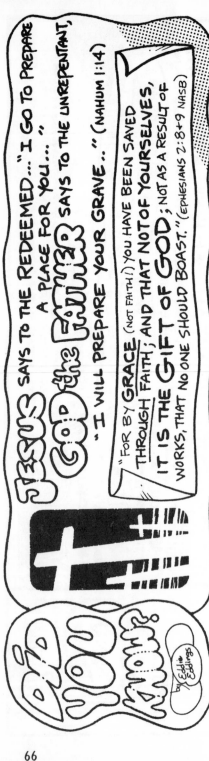

JESUS SAYS TO THE REDEEMED..."I GO TO PREPARE A PLACE FOR YOU..."

GOD the FATHER SAYS TO THE UNREPENTANT, "I WILL PREPARE YOUR GRAVE.." (NAHUM 1:14)

"FOR BY GRACE (NOT FAITH!) YOU HAVE BEEN SAVED THROUGH FAITH; AND THAT NOT OF YOURSELVES, IT IS THE GIFT OF GOD; NOT AS A RESULT OF WORKS, THAT NO ONE SHOULD BOAST." (EPHESIANS 2:8+9 NASB)

DID YOU KNOW ?

by Eddie Eddings

ISAIAH IS A MINIATURE BIBLE!

THIS BOOK HAS THE SAME NUMBER OF CHAPTERS THAT THE BIBLE HAS BOOKS—66. THERE ARE TWO GREAT DIVISIONS, JUST AS THERE ARE IN THE BIBLE, WITH 39 CHAPTERS IN THE FIRST (LIKE THE O.T.) AND 27 CHAPTERS IN THE SECOND (LIKE THE N.T.). ISAIAH BEGINS WHERE THE FIRST BOOK OF THE BIBLE BEGINS—WITH THE HEAVENS AND THE EARTH (ISA. 1:2 WITH GEN. 1:1). THE 39th CHAPTER OF ISAIAH AND THE 39th BOOK OF THE O.T. (MALACHI) ENDS WITH A PREDICTION OF JUDGMENT (39:6 WITH MALACHI 4:1). THE "N.T." SECTION OF ISAIAH (CHPTS. 40-66) BEGINS WHERE THE 40th BOOK OF THE BIBLE (MATTHEW) BEGINS—WITH "THE VOICE OF ONE CRYING IN THE WILDERNESS" (JOHN THE BAPTIST). THE LAST CHAPTER OF ISAIAH ENDS JUST WHERE THE LAST BOOK OF THE BIBLE ENDS—WITH A NEW HEAVEN AND A NEW EARTH (66:22 WITH REVELATION 21:1).

"SIN AND HELL ARE MARRIED UNLESS REPENTANCE PROCLAIMS THE DIVORCE."
C.H. SPURGEON

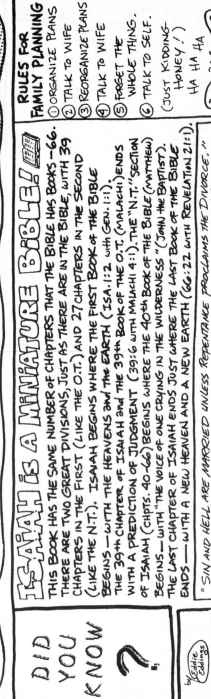

RULES FOR FAMILY PLANNING

1. ORGANIZE PLANS
2. TALK TO WIFE
3. REORGANIZE PLANS
4. TALK TO WIFE
5. FORGET THE WHOLE THING.
6. TALK TO SELF.

(JUST KIDDING HONEY!)
HA HA HA

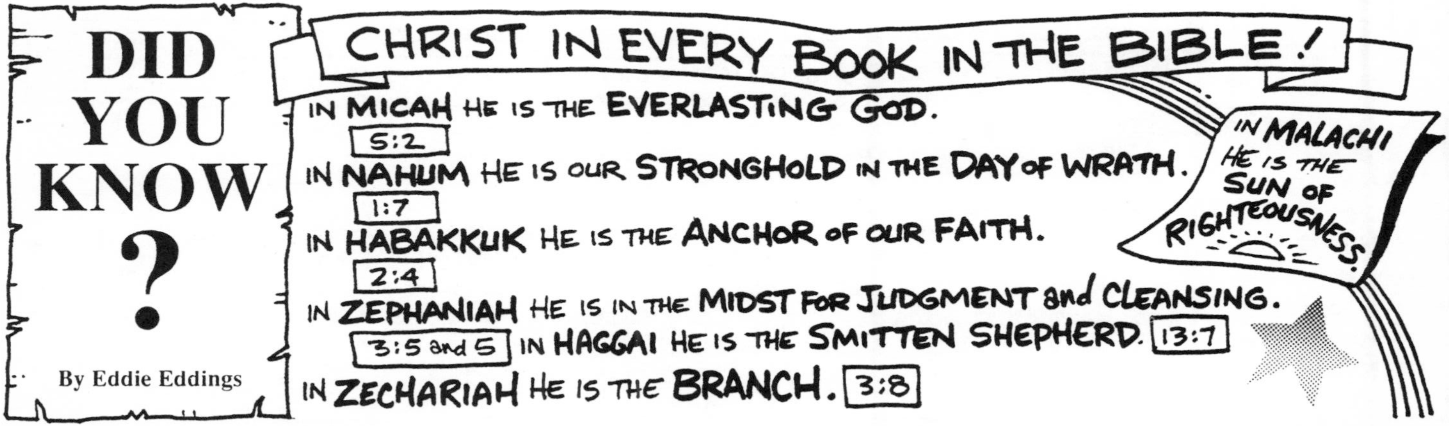
DID YOU KNOW ?
By Eddie Eddings
CHRIST IN EVERY BOOK IN THE BIBLE!
IN MICAH HE IS THE EVERLASTING GOD. 5:2
IN NAHUM HE IS OUR STRONGHOLD IN THE DAY OF WRATH. 1:7
IN HABAKKUK HE IS THE ANCHOR OF OUR FAITH. 2:4
IN ZEPHANIAH HE IS IN THE MIDST FOR JUDGMENT and CLEANSING. 3:5 and 5
IN HAGGAI HE IS THE SMITTEN SHEPHERD. 13:7
IN ZECHARIAH HE IS THE BRANCH. 3:8
IN MALACHI HE IS THE SUN OF RIGHTEOUSNESS.

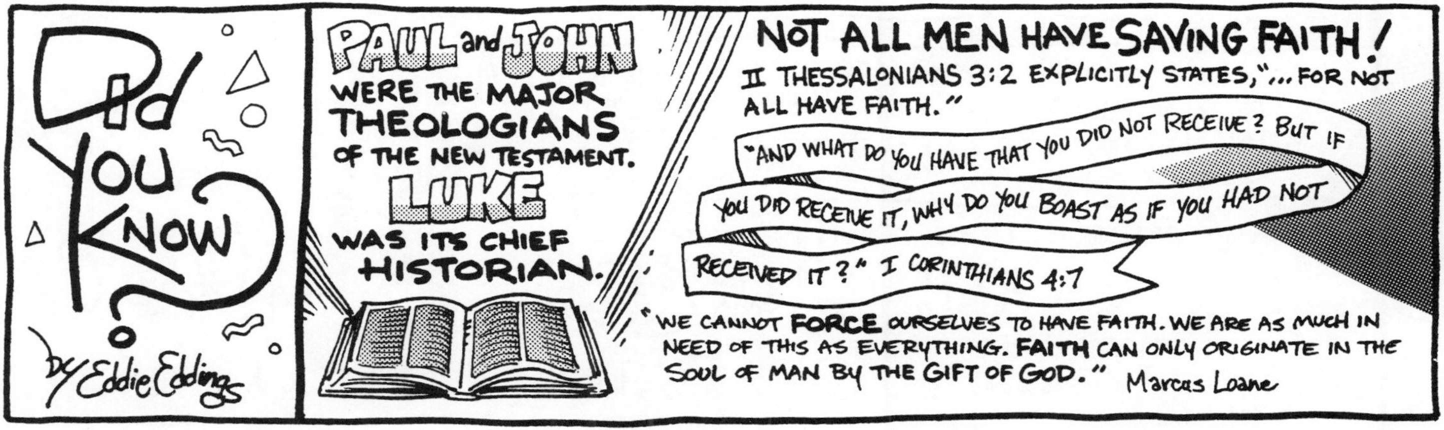
Did You Know?
by Eddie Eddings
PAUL and JOHN WERE THE MAJOR THEOLOGIANS OF THE NEW TESTAMENT.
LUKE WAS ITS CHIEF HISTORIAN.
NOT ALL MEN HAVE SAVING FAITH!
II THESSALONIANS 3:2 EXPLICITLY STATES, "... FOR NOT ALL HAVE FAITH."
"AND WHAT DO YOU HAVE THAT YOU DID NOT RECEIVE? BUT IF
YOU DID RECEIVE IT, WHY DO YOU BOAST AS IF YOU HAD NOT
RECEIVED IT?" I CORINTHIANS 4:7
"WE CANNOT FORCE OURSELVES TO HAVE FAITH. WE ARE AS MUCH IN NEED OF THIS AS EVERYTHING. FAITH CAN ONLY ORIGINATE IN THE SOUL OF MAN BY THE GIFT OF GOD." Marcus Loane

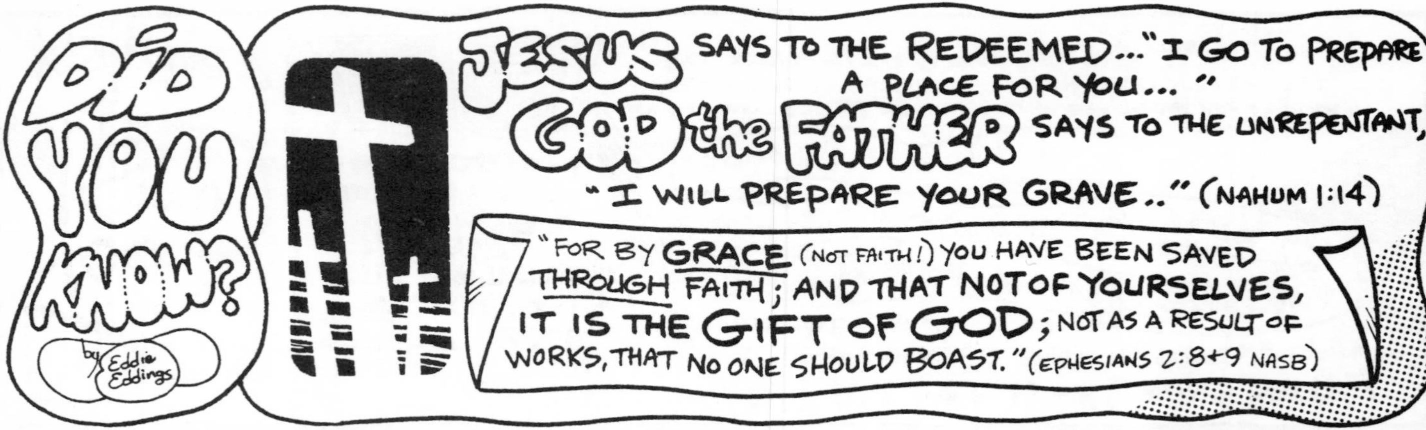
DID YOU KNOW?
by Eddie Eddings
JESUS SAYS TO THE REDEEMED..."I GO TO PREPARE A PLACE FOR YOU..."
GOD the FATHER SAYS TO THE UNREPENTANT, "I WILL PREPARE YOUR GRAVE.." (NAHUM 1:14)
"FOR BY GRACE (NOT FAITH!) YOU HAVE BEEN SAVED THROUGH FAITH; AND THAT NOT OF YOURSELVES, IT IS THE GIFT OF GOD; NOT AS A RESULT OF WORKS, THAT NO ONE SHOULD BOAST." (EPHESIANS 2:8+9 NASB)

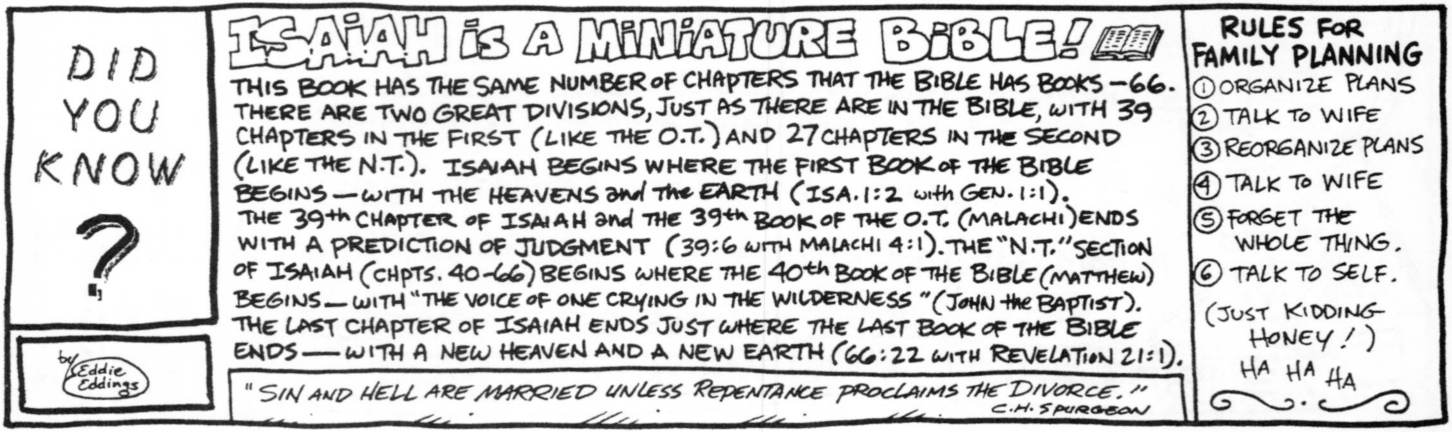
DID YOU KNOW ?
by Eddie Eddings
ISAIAH is A MINIATURE BIBLE!
THIS BOOK HAS THE SAME NUMBER OF CHAPTERS THAT THE BIBLE HAS BOOKS—66. THERE ARE TWO GREAT DIVISIONS, JUST AS THERE ARE IN THE BIBLE, WITH 39 CHAPTERS IN THE FIRST (LIKE THE O.T.) AND 27 CHAPTERS IN THE SECOND (LIKE THE N.T.). ISAIAH BEGINS WHERE THE FIRST BOOK OF THE BIBLE BEGINS—WITH THE HEAVENS and the EARTH (ISA. 1:2 with GEN. 1:1).
THE 39th CHAPTER OF ISAIAH and THE 39th BOOK OF THE O.T. (MALACHI) ENDS WITH A PREDICTION OF JUDGMENT (39:6 WITH MALACHI 4:1). THE "N.T." SECTION OF ISAIAH (CHPTS. 40-66) BEGINS WHERE THE 40th BOOK OF THE BIBLE (MATTHEW) BEGINS—WITH "THE VOICE OF ONE CRYING IN THE WILDERNESS" (JOHN the BAPTIST).
THE LAST CHAPTER OF ISAIAH ENDS JUST WHERE THE LAST BOOK OF THE BIBLE ENDS—WITH A NEW HEAVEN AND A NEW EARTH (66:22 WITH REVELATION 21:1).
"SIN AND HELL ARE MARRIED UNLESS REPENTANCE PROCLAIMS THE DIVORCE." C.H. SPURGEON
RULES FOR FAMILY PLANNING
① ORGANIZE PLANS
② TALK TO WIFE
③ REORGANIZE PLANS
④ TALK TO WIFE
⑤ FORGET THE WHOLE THING.
⑥ TALK TO SELF.
(JUST KIDDING HONEY!)
HA HA HA

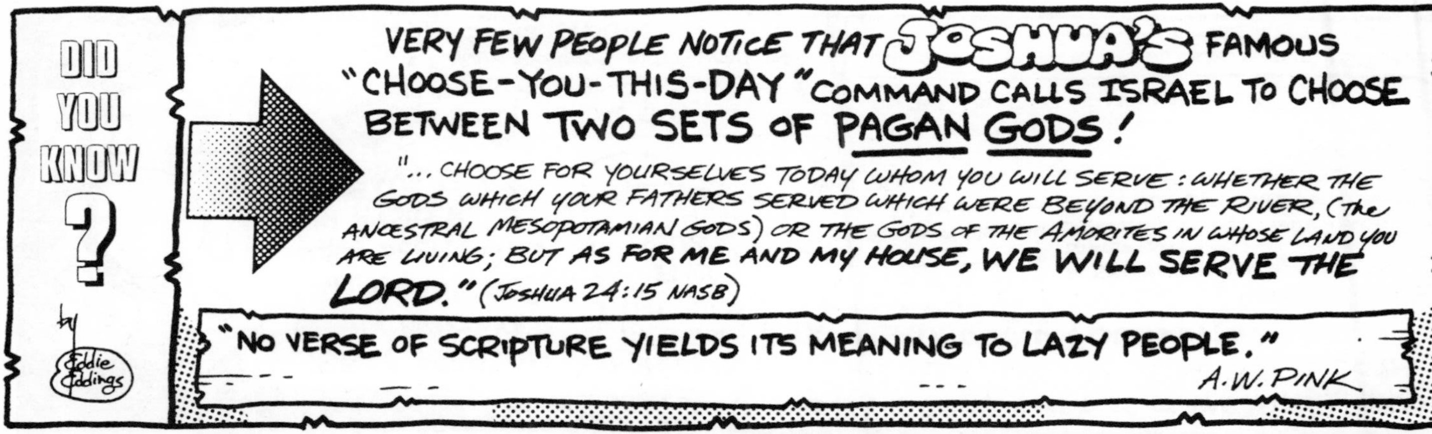
DID YOU KNOW ?
by Eddie Eddings
VERY FEW PEOPLE NOTICE THAT JOSHUA'S FAMOUS "CHOOSE-YOU-THIS-DAY" COMMAND CALLS ISRAEL TO CHOOSE BETWEEN TWO SETS OF PAGAN GODS!
"... CHOOSE FOR YOURSELVES TODAY WHOM YOU WILL SERVE: WHETHER THE GODS WHICH YOUR FATHERS SERVED WHICH WERE BEYOND THE RIVER, (the ANCESTRAL MESOPOTAMIAN GODS) OR THE GODS OF THE AMORITES IN WHOSE LAND YOU ARE LIVING; BUT AS FOR ME AND MY HOUSE, WE WILL SERVE THE LORD." (JOSHUA 24:15 NASB)
"NO VERSE OF SCRIPTURE YIELDS ITS MEANING TO LAZY PEOPLE."
A.W. PINK

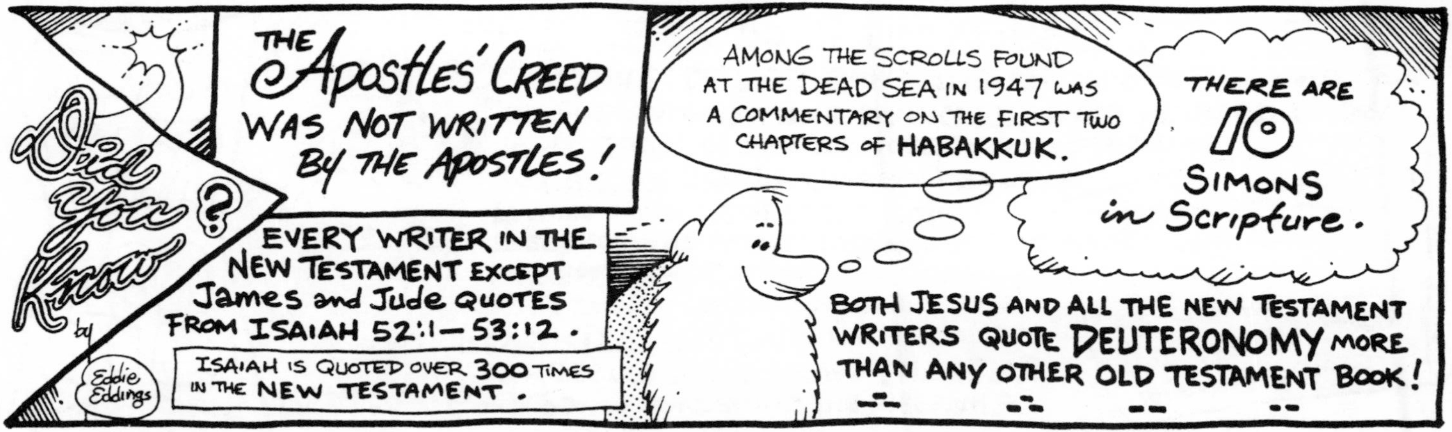
Did You Know ?
by Eddie Eddings
THE Apostles' CREED WAS NOT WRITTEN BY THE APOSTLES!
EVERY WRITER IN THE NEW TESTAMENT EXCEPT James and Jude QUOTES FROM ISAIAH 52:1—53:12.
ISAIAH IS QUOTED OVER 300 TIMES IN THE NEW TESTAMENT.
AMONG THE SCROLLS FOUND AT THE DEAD SEA IN 1947 WAS A COMMENTARY ON THE FIRST TWO CHAPTERS OF HABAKKUK.
THERE ARE 10 SIMONS in Scripture.
BOTH JESUS AND ALL THE NEW TESTAMENT WRITERS QUOTE DEUTERONOMY MORE THAN ANY OTHER OLD TESTAMENT BOOK!

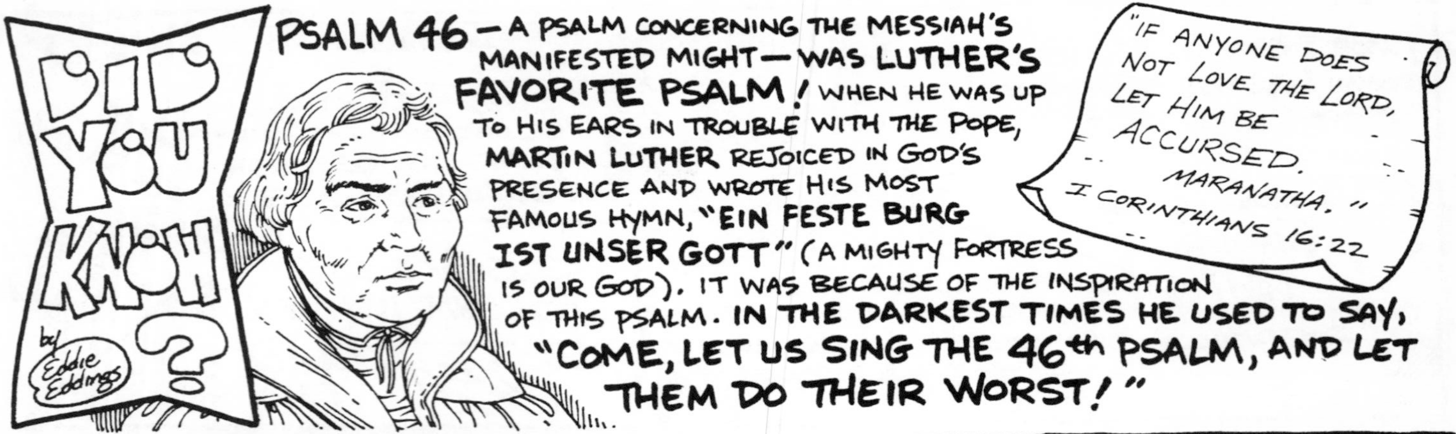
DID YOU KNOW?
by Eddie Eddings
PSALM 46 — A PSALM CONCERNING THE MESSIAH'S MANIFESTED MIGHT — WAS LUTHER'S FAVORITE PSALM! WHEN HE WAS UP TO HIS EARS IN TROUBLE WITH THE POPE, MARTIN LUTHER REJOICED IN GOD'S PRESENCE AND WROTE HIS MOST FAMOUS HYMN, "EIN FESTE BURG IST UNSER GOTT" (A MIGHTY FORTRESS IS OUR GOD). IT WAS BECAUSE OF THE INSPIRATION OF THIS PSALM. IN THE DARKEST TIMES HE USED TO SAY, "COME, LET US SING THE 46th PSALM, AND LET THEM DO THEIR WORST!"
"IF ANYONE DOES NOT LOVE THE LORD, LET HIM BE ACCURSED. MARANATHA." I CORINTHIANS 16:22

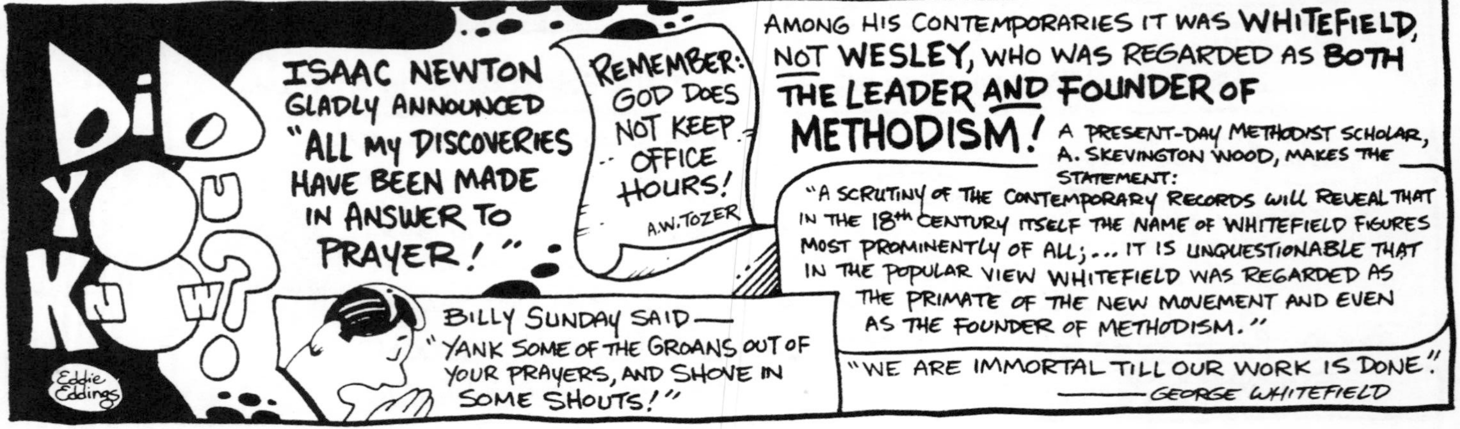
DID YOU KNOW?
Eddie Eddings
ISAAC NEWTON GLADLY ANNOUNCED "ALL MY DISCOVERIES HAVE BEEN MADE IN ANSWER TO PRAYER!"
REMEMBER: GOD DOES NOT KEEP OFFICE HOURS! A.W. TOZER
BILLY SUNDAY SAID — "YANK SOME OF THE GROANS OUT OF YOUR PRAYERS, AND SHOVE IN SOME SHOUTS!"
AMONG HIS CONTEMPORARIES IT WAS WHITEFIELD, NOT WESLEY, WHO WAS REGARDED AS BOTH THE LEADER AND FOUNDER OF METHODISM! A PRESENT-DAY METHODIST SCHOLAR, A. SKEVINGTON WOOD, MAKES THE STATEMENT:
"A SCRUTINY OF THE CONTEMPORARY RECORDS WILL REVEAL THAT IN THE 18th CENTURY ITSELF THE NAME OF WHITEFIELD FIGURES MOST PROMINENTLY OF ALL; ... IT IS UNQUESTIONABLE THAT IN THE POPULAR VIEW WHITEFIELD WAS REGARDED AS THE PRIMATE OF THE NEW MOVEMENT AND EVEN AS THE FOUNDER OF METHODISM."
"WE ARE IMMORTAL TILL OUR WORK IS DONE." — GEORGE WHITEFIELD

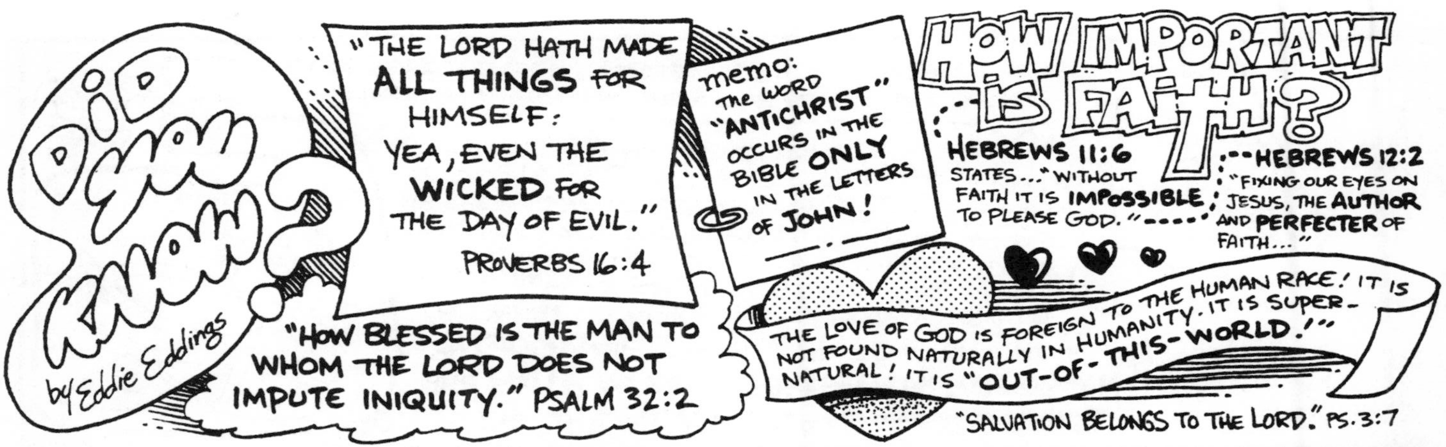
DID YOU KNOW?
by Eddie Eddings
"THE LORD HATH MADE ALL THINGS FOR HIMSELF: YEA, EVEN THE WICKED FOR THE DAY OF EVIL." PROVERBS 16:4
"HOW BLESSED IS THE MAN TO WHOM THE LORD DOES NOT IMPUTE INIQUITY." PSALM 32:2
memo: The word "ANTICHRIST" occurs in the BIBLE ONLY IN THE LETTERS OF JOHN!
HOW IMPORTANT IS FAITH?
HEBREWS 11:6 STATES..."WITHOUT FAITH IT IS IMPOSSIBLE TO PLEASE GOD."
HEBREWS 12:2 "FIXING OUR EYES ON JESUS, THE AUTHOR AND PERFECTER OF FAITH..."
THE LOVE OF GOD IS FOREIGN TO THE HUMAN RACE! IT IS NOT FOUND NATURALLY IN HUMANITY. IT IS SUPER-NATURAL! IT IS "OUT-OF-THIS-WORLD!"
"SALVATION BELONGS TO THE LORD." PS. 3:7

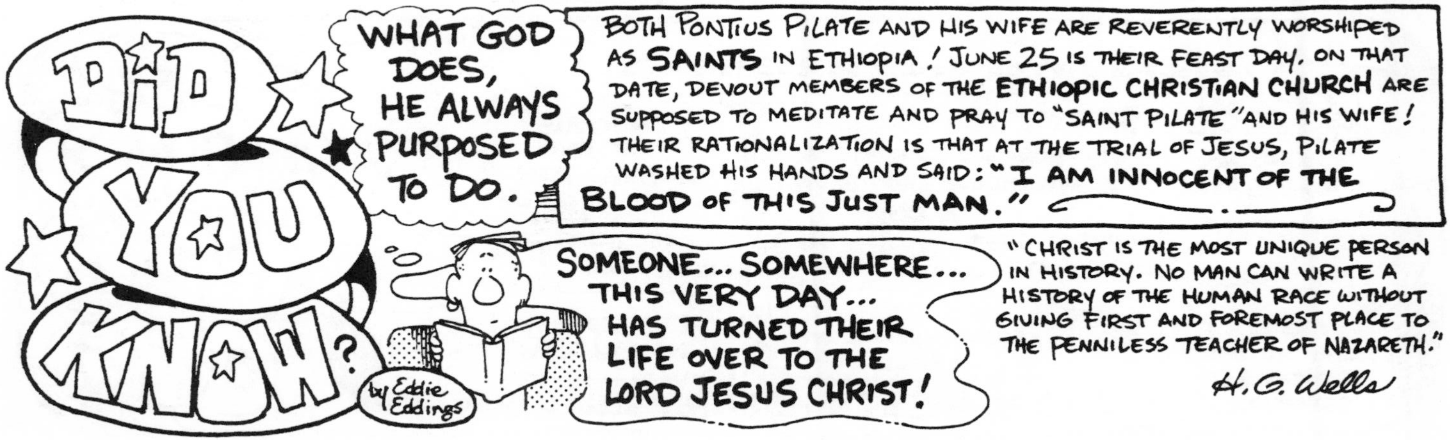
DID YOU KNOW?
WHAT GOD DOES, HE ALWAYS PURPOSED TO DO.
BOTH PONTIUS PILATE AND HIS WIFE ARE REVERENTLY WORSHIPED AS SAINTS IN ETHIOPIA! JUNE 25 IS THEIR FEAST DAY. ON THAT DATE, DEVOUT MEMBERS OF THE ETHIOPIC CHRISTIAN CHURCH ARE SUPPOSED TO MEDITATE AND PRAY TO "SAINT PILATE" AND HIS WIFE! THEIR RATIONALIZATION IS THAT AT THE TRIAL OF JESUS, PILATE WASHED HIS HANDS AND SAID: "I AM INNOCENT OF THE BLOOD OF THIS JUST MAN."
SOMEONE... SOMEWHERE... THIS VERY DAY... HAS TURNED THEIR LIFE OVER TO THE LORD JESUS CHRIST!
"CHRIST IS THE MOST UNIQUE PERSON IN HISTORY. NO MAN CAN WRITE A HISTORY OF THE HUMAN RACE WITHOUT GIVING FIRST AND FOREMOST PLACE TO THE PENNILESS TEACHER OF NAZARETH."
H. G. Wells
by Eddie Eddings

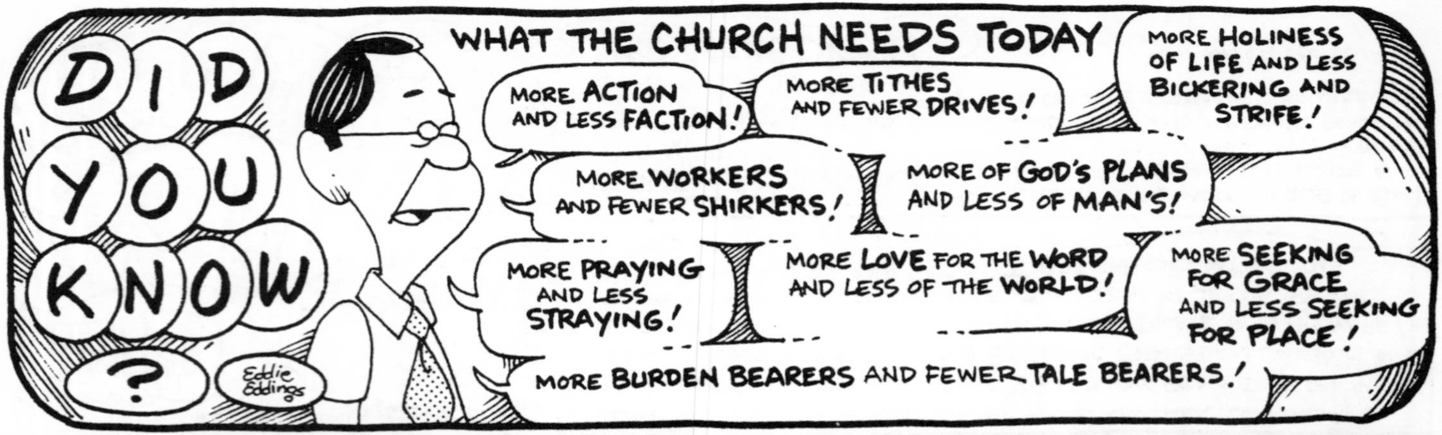
DID YOU KNOW ?
Eddie Eddings
WHAT THE CHURCH NEEDS TODAY
MORE ACTION AND LESS FACTION!
MORE TITHES AND FEWER DRIVES!
MORE HOLINESS OF LIFE AND LESS BICKERING AND STRIFE!
MORE WORKERS AND FEWER SHIRKERS!
MORE OF GOD'S PLANS AND LESS OF MAN'S!
MORE PRAYING AND LESS STRAYING!
MORE LOVE FOR THE WORD AND LESS OF THE WORLD!
MORE SEEKING FOR GRACE AND LESS SEEKING FOR PLACE!
MORE BURDEN BEARERS AND FEWER TALE BEARERS!

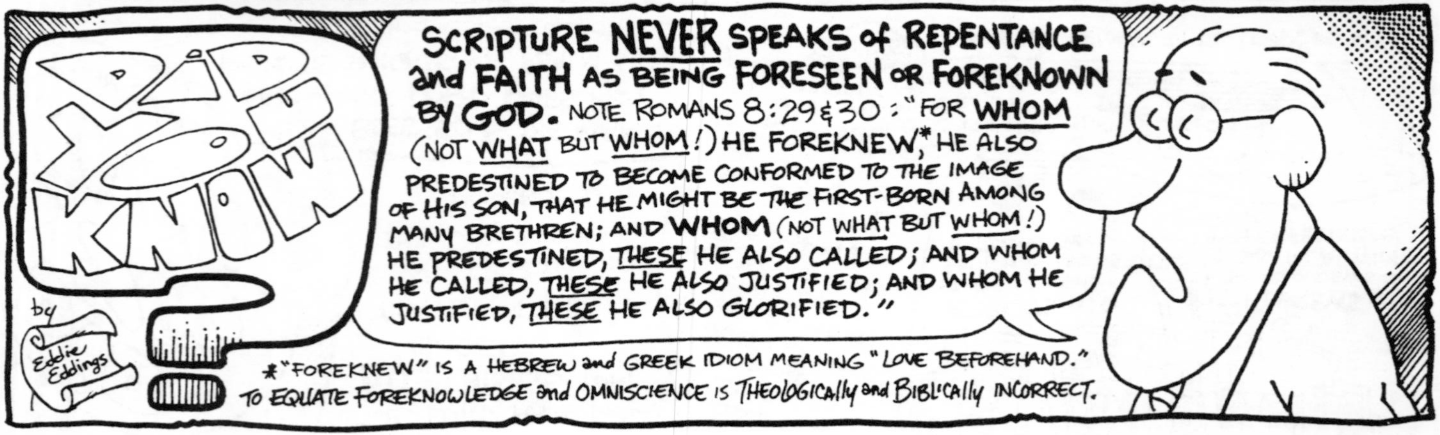
DID YOU KNOW ?
by Eddie Eddings
SCRIPTURE NEVER SPEAKS of REPENTANCE and FAITH AS BEING FORESEEN OR FOREKNOWN BY GOD. NOTE ROMANS 8:29 & 30: "FOR WHOM (NOT WHAT BUT WHOM!) HE FOREKNEW,* HE ALSO PREDESTINED TO BECOME CONFORMED TO THE IMAGE OF HIS SON, THAT HE MIGHT BE THE FIRST-BORN AMONG MANY BRETHREN; AND WHOM (NOT WHAT BUT WHOM!) HE PREDESTINED, THESE HE ALSO CALLED; AND WHOM HE CALLED, THESE HE ALSO JUSTIFIED; AND WHOM HE JUSTIFIED, THESE HE ALSO GLORIFIED."
* "FOREKNEW" IS A HEBREW and GREEK IDIOM MEANING "LOVE BEFOREHAND." TO EQUATE FOREKNOWLEDGE and OMNISCIENCE IS THEOLOGICALLY and BIBLICALLY INCORRECT.

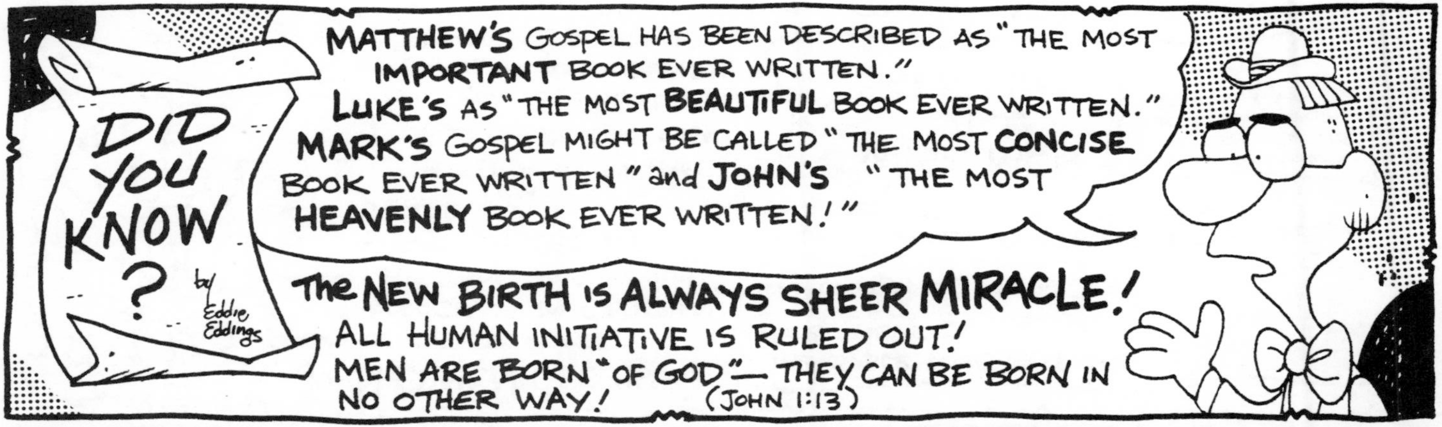
DID YOU KNOW ?
by Eddie Eddings
MATTHEW'S GOSPEL HAS BEEN DESCRIBED AS "THE MOST IMPORTANT BOOK EVER WRITTEN."
LUKE'S AS "THE MOST BEAUTIFUL BOOK EVER WRITTEN."
MARK'S GOSPEL MIGHT BE CALLED "THE MOST CONCISE BOOK EVER WRITTEN" and JOHN'S "THE MOST HEAVENLY BOOK EVER WRITTEN!"
The NEW BIRTH IS ALWAYS SHEER MIRACLE!
ALL HUMAN INITIATIVE IS RULED OUT!
MEN ARE BORN "OF GOD"— THEY CAN BE BORN IN NO OTHER WAY! (JOHN 1:13)

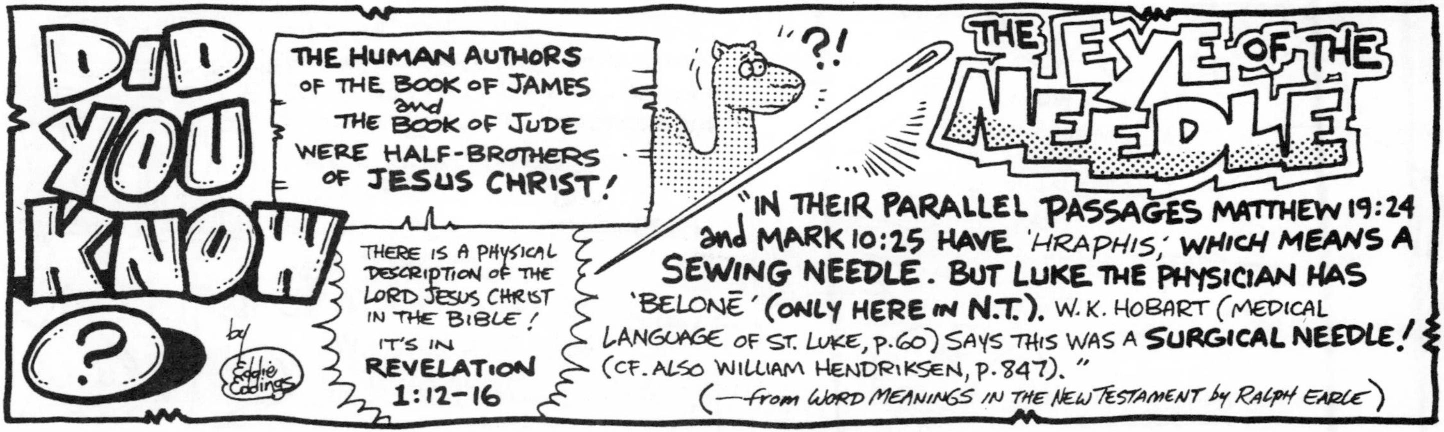
DID YOU KNOW ?
by Eddie Eddings
THE HUMAN AUTHORS OF THE BOOK OF JAMES and THE BOOK OF JUDE WERE HALF-BROTHERS OF JESUS CHRIST!
THERE IS A PHYSICAL DESCRIPTION OF THE LORD JESUS CHRIST IN THE BIBLE! IT'S IN REVELATION 1:12-16
"?!
THE EYE OF THE NEEDLE
"IN THEIR PARALLEL PASSAGES MATTHEW 19:24 and MARK 10:25 HAVE 'HRAPHIS,' WHICH MEANS A SEWING NEEDLE. BUT LUKE THE PHYSICIAN HAS 'BELONĒ' (ONLY HERE IN N.T.). W.K. HOBART (MEDICAL LANGUAGE OF ST. LUKE, P.60) SAYS THIS WAS A SURGICAL NEEDLE! (CF. ALSO WILLIAM HENDRIKSEN, P.847)."
(—from WORD MEANINGS IN THE NEW TESTAMENT by RALPH EARLE)

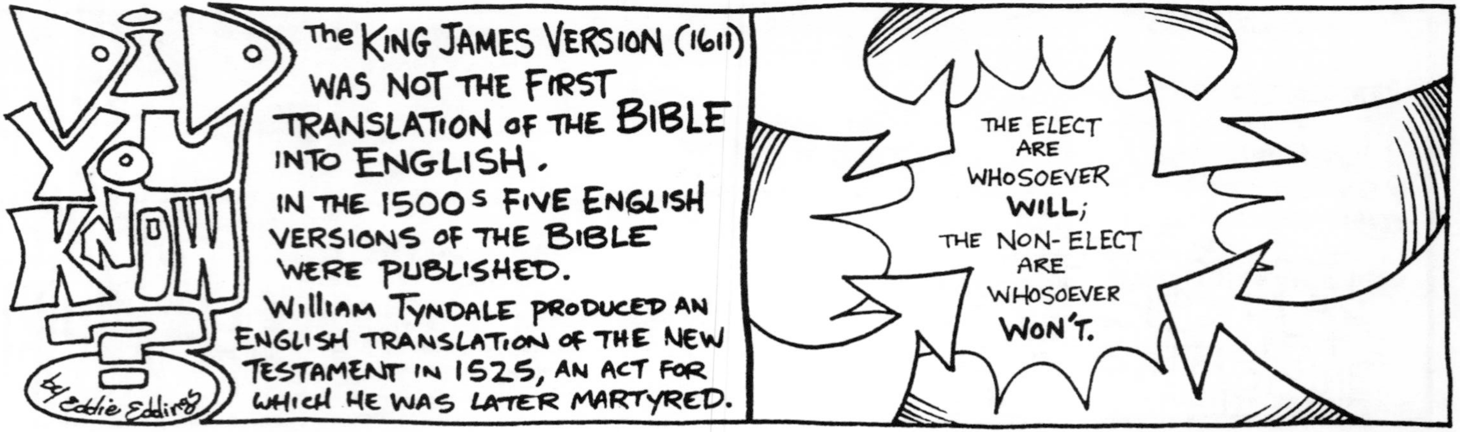
DID YOU KNOW?
by Eddie Eddings
The KING JAMES VERSION (1611) WAS NOT THE FIRST TRANSLATION OF THE BIBLE INTO ENGLISH.
IN THE 1500s FIVE ENGLISH VERSIONS OF THE BIBLE WERE PUBLISHED.
WILLIAM TYNDALE PRODUCED AN ENGLISH TRANSLATION OF THE NEW TESTAMENT IN 1525, AN ACT FOR WHICH HE WAS LATER MARTYRED.
THE ELECT ARE WHOSOEVER WILL; THE NON-ELECT ARE WHOSOEVER WON'T.

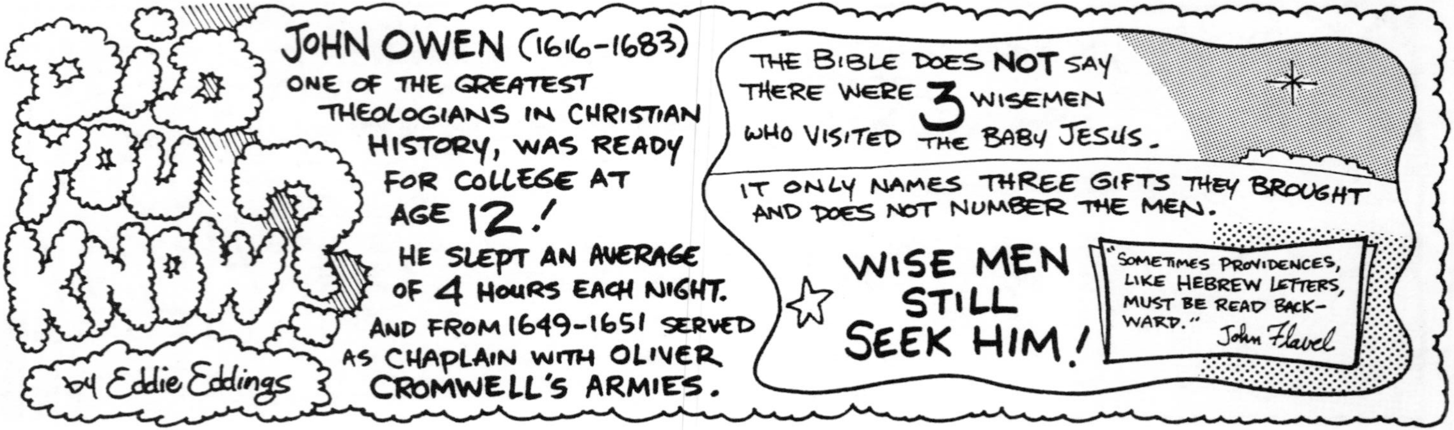
DID YOU KNOW?
by Eddie Eddings
JOHN OWEN (1616-1683) ONE OF THE GREATEST THEOLOGIANS IN CHRISTIAN HISTORY, WAS READY FOR COLLEGE AT AGE 12!
HE SLEPT AN AVERAGE OF 4 HOURS EACH NIGHT.
AND FROM 1649-1651 SERVED AS CHAPLAIN WITH OLIVER CROMWELL'S ARMIES.
THE BIBLE DOES NOT SAY THERE WERE 3 WISEMEN WHO VISITED THE BABY JESUS.
IT ONLY NAMES THREE GIFTS THEY BROUGHT AND DOES NOT NUMBER THE MEN.
WISE MEN STILL SEEK HIM!
"SOMETIMES PROVIDENCES, LIKE HEBREW LETTERS, MUST BE READ BACKWARD." John Flavel

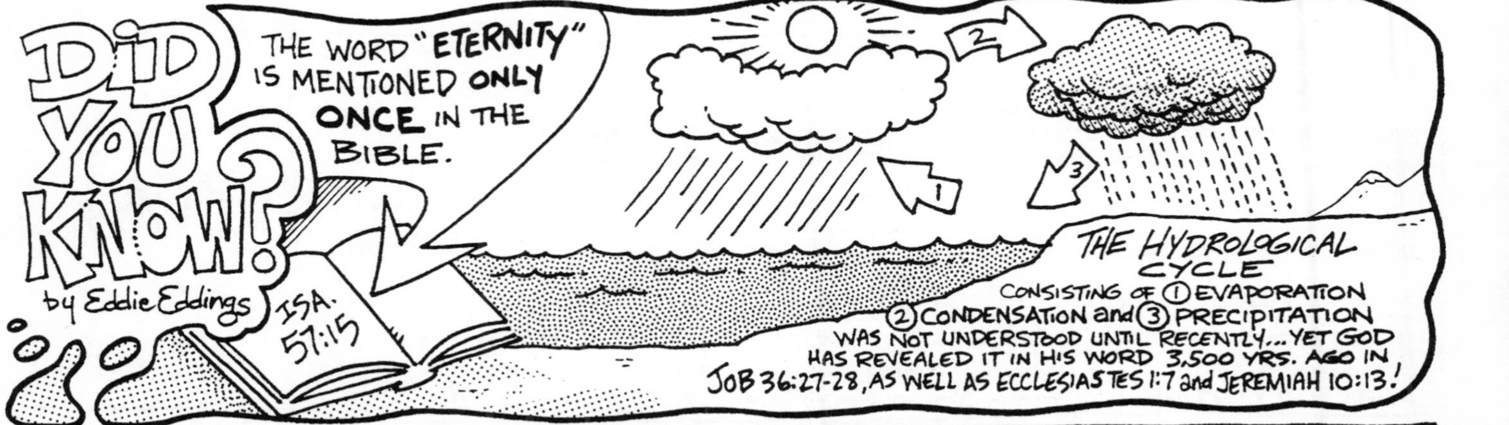
DID YOU KNOW?
by Eddie Eddings
THE WORD "ETERNITY" IS MENTIONED ONLY ONCE IN THE BIBLE.
ISA. 57:15
THE HYDROLOGICAL CYCLE
CONSISTING OF ① EVAPORATION ② CONDENSATION and ③ PRECIPITATION WAS NOT UNDERSTOOD UNTIL RECENTLY... YET GOD HAS REVEALED IT IN HIS WORD 3,500 YRS. AGO IN JOB 36:27-28, AS WELL AS ECCLESIASTES 1:7 and JEREMIAH 10:13!
1
2
3

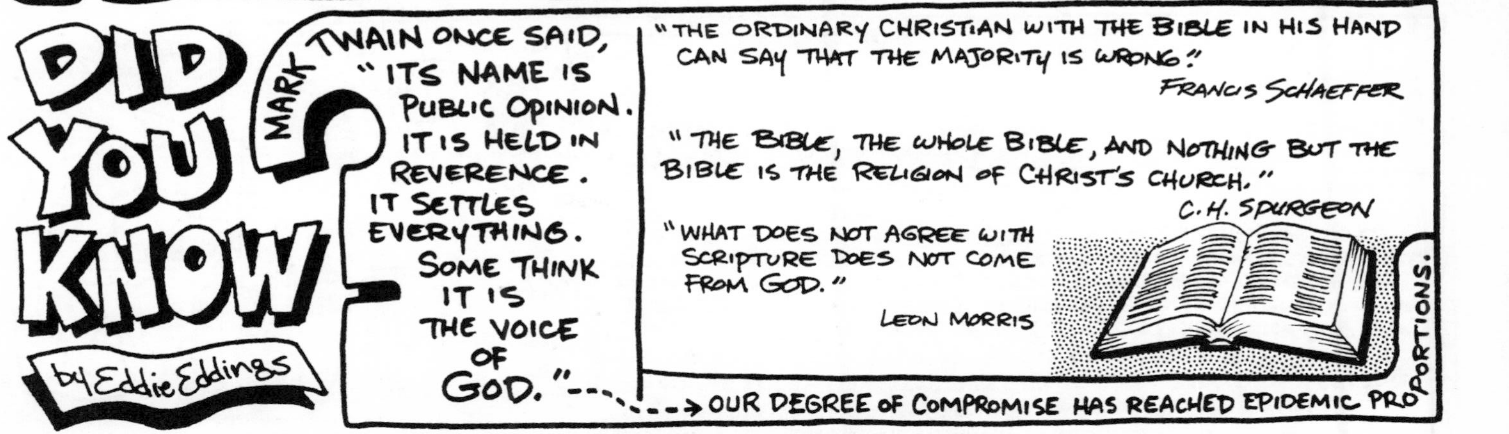
DID YOU KNOW
by Eddie Eddings
MARK TWAIN ONCE SAID, "ITS NAME IS PUBLIC OPINION. IT IS HELD IN REVERENCE. IT SETTLES EVERYTHING. SOME THINK IT IS THE VOICE OF GOD."
"THE ORDINARY CHRISTIAN WITH THE BIBLE IN HIS HAND CAN SAY THAT THE MAJORITY IS WRONG." FRANCIS SCHAEFFER
"THE BIBLE, THE WHOLE BIBLE, AND NOTHING BUT THE BIBLE IS THE RELIGION OF CHRIST'S CHURCH." C.H. SPURGEON
"WHAT DOES NOT AGREE WITH SCRIPTURE DOES NOT COME FROM GOD." LEON MORRIS
OUR DEGREE OF COMPROMISE HAS REACHED EPIDEMIC PROPORTIONS.

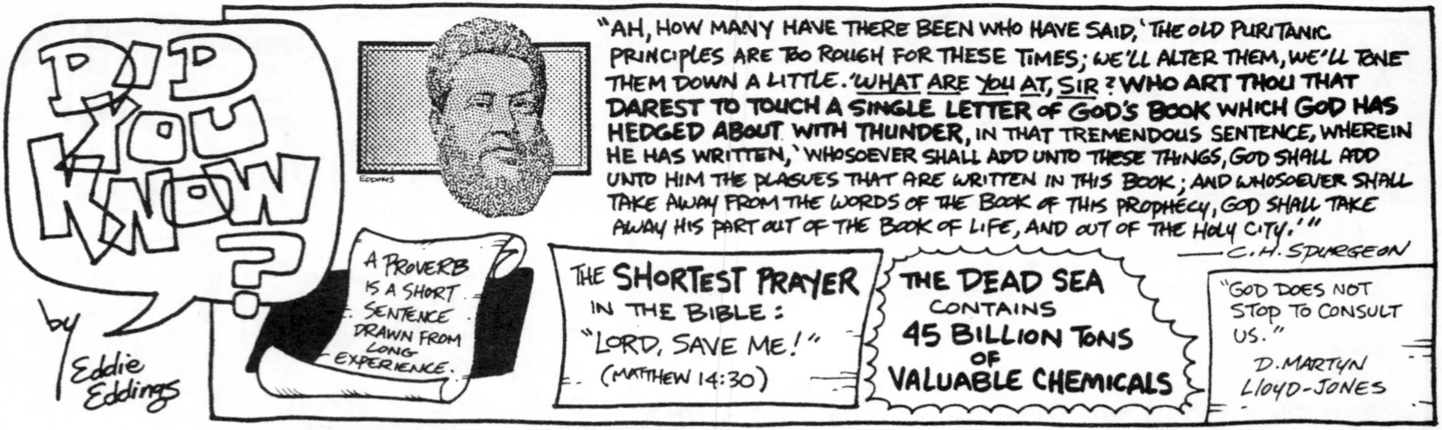

DID YOU KNOW?
by Eddie Eddings
"AH, HOW MANY HAVE THERE BEEN WHO HAVE SAID, 'THE OLD PURITANIC PRINCIPLES ARE TOO ROUGH FOR THESE TIMES; WE'LL ALTER THEM, WE'LL TONE THEM DOWN A LITTLE.' WHAT ARE YOU AT, SIR? WHO ART THOU THAT DAREST TO TOUCH A SINGLE LETTER OF GOD'S BOOK WHICH GOD HAS HEDGED ABOUT WITH THUNDER, IN THAT TREMENDOUS SENTENCE, WHEREIN HE HAS WRITTEN, 'WHOSOEVER SHALL ADD UNTO THESE THINGS, GOD SHALL ADD UNTO HIM THE PLAGUES THAT ARE WRITTEN IN THIS BOOK; AND WHOSOEVER SHALL TAKE AWAY FROM THE WORDS OF THE BOOK OF THIS PROPHECY, GOD SHALL TAKE AWAY HIS PART OUT OF THE BOOK OF LIFE, AND OUT OF THE HOLY CITY.'"
—C.H. SPURGEON
A PROVERB IS A SHORT SENTENCE DRAWN FROM LONG EXPERIENCE.
THE SHORTEST PRAYER IN THE BIBLE: "LORD, SAVE ME!" (MATTHEW 14:30)
THE DEAD SEA CONTAINS 45 BILLION TONS OF VALUABLE CHEMICALS
"GOD DOES NOT STOP TO CONSULT US."
D. MARTYN LLOYD-JONES

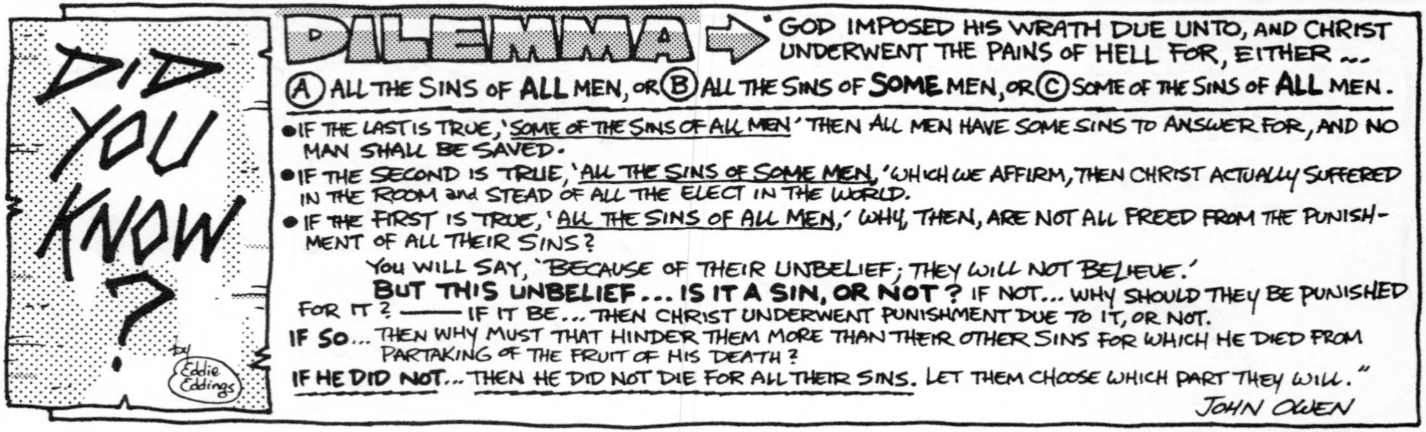

DID YOU KNOW?
by Eddie Eddings
DILEMMA
"GOD IMPOSED HIS WRATH DUE UNTO, AND CHRIST UNDERWENT THE PAINS OF HELL FOR, EITHER...
(A) ALL THE SINS OF ALL MEN, OR (B) ALL THE SINS OF SOME MEN, OR (C) SOME OF THE SINS OF ALL MEN.
• IF THE LAST IS TRUE, 'SOME OF THE SINS OF ALL MEN' THEN ALL MEN HAVE SOME SINS TO ANSWER FOR, AND NO MAN SHALL BE SAVED.
• IF THE SECOND IS TRUE, 'ALL THE SINS OF SOME MEN,' WHICH WE AFFIRM, THEN CHRIST ACTUALLY SUFFERED IN THE ROOM and STEAD OF ALL THE ELECT IN THE WORLD.
• IF THE FIRST IS TRUE, 'ALL THE SINS OF ALL MEN,' WHY, THEN, ARE NOT ALL FREED FROM THE PUNISHMENT OF ALL THEIR SINS?
YOU WILL SAY, 'BECAUSE OF THEIR UNBELIEF; THEY WILL NOT BELIEVE.'
BUT THIS UNBELIEF... IS IT A SIN, OR NOT? IF NOT... WHY SHOULD THEY BE PUNISHED FOR IT? —— IF IT BE... THEN CHRIST UNDERWENT PUNISHMENT DUE TO IT, OR NOT.
IF SO... THEN WHY MUST THAT HINDER THEM MORE THAN THEIR OTHER SINS FOR WHICH HE DIED FROM PARTAKING OF THE FRUIT OF HIS DEATH?
IF HE DID NOT... THEN HE DID NOT DIE FOR ALL THEIR SINS. LET THEM CHOOSE WHICH PART THEY WILL."
JOHN OWEN

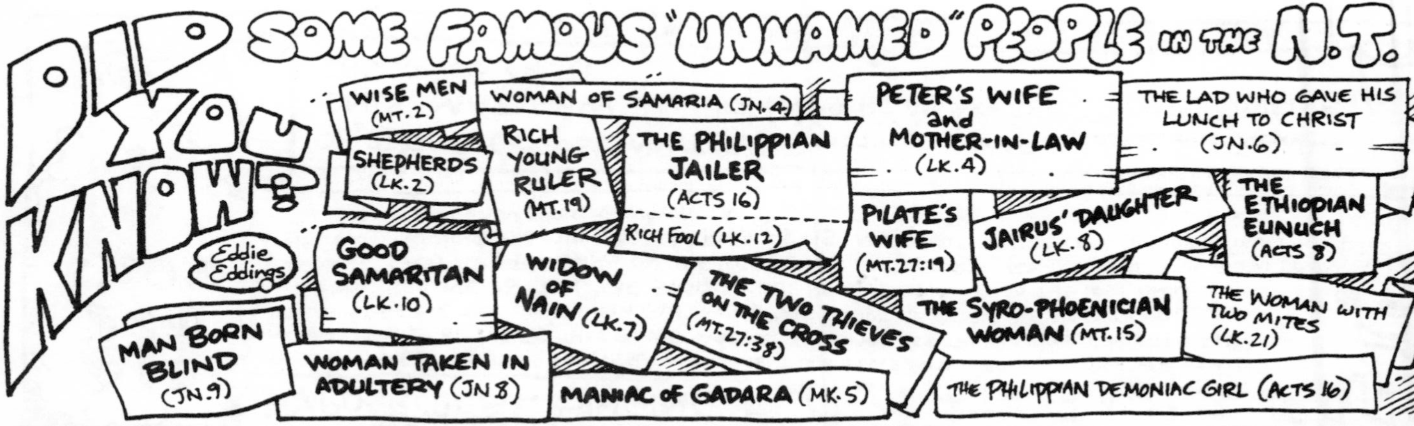
DID YOU KNOW?
Eddie Eddings
SOME FAMOUS "UNNAMED" PEOPLE IN THE N.T.
WISE MEN (MT. 2)
SHEPHERDS (LK. 2)
WOMAN OF SAMARIA (JN. 4)
RICH YOUNG RULER (MT. 19)
THE PHILIPPIAN JAILER (ACTS 16)
RICH FOOL (LK. 12)
PETER'S WIFE and MOTHER-IN-LAW (LK. 4)
THE LAD WHO GAVE HIS LUNCH TO CHRIST (JN. 6)
PILATE'S WIFE (MT. 27:19)
JAIRUS' DAUGHTER (LK. 8)
THE ETHIOPIAN EUNUCH (ACTS 8)
GOOD SAMARITAN (LK. 10)
WIDOW OF NAIN (LK. 7)
THE TWO THIEVES ON THE CROSS (MT. 27:38)
THE SYRO-PHOENICIAN WOMAN (MT. 15)
THE WOMAN WITH TWO MITES (LK. 21)
MAN BORN BLIND (JN. 9)
WOMAN TAKEN IN ADULTERY (JN 8)
MANIAC OF GADARA (MK. 5)
THE PHILIPPIAN DEMONIAC GIRL (ACTS 16)

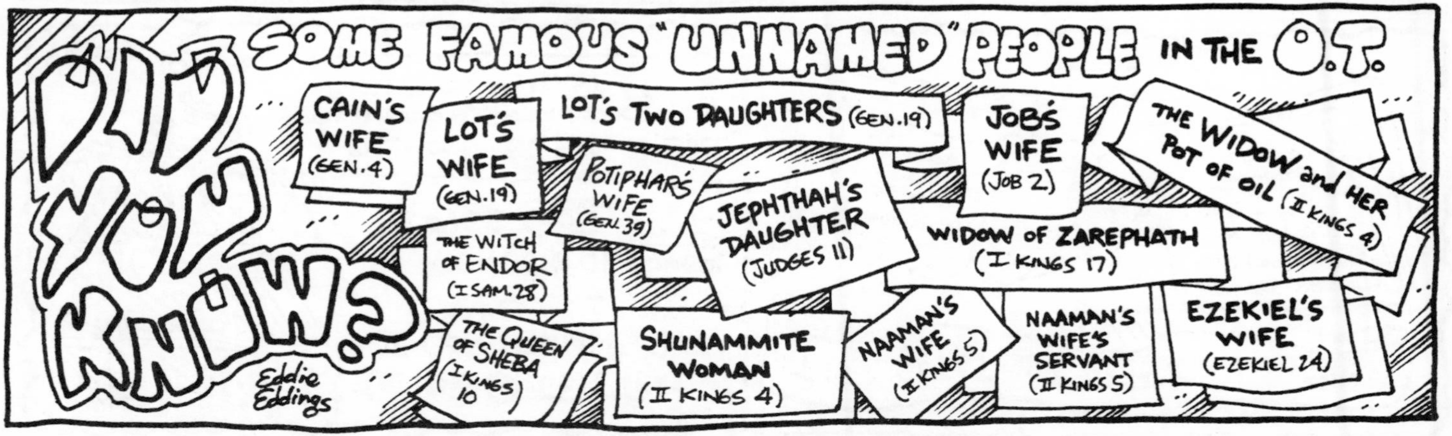
DID YOU KNOW?
Eddie Eddings
SOME FAMOUS "UNNAMED" PEOPLE IN THE O.T.
CAIN'S WIFE (GEN. 4)
LOT'S WIFE (GEN. 19)
LOT'S TWO DAUGHTERS (GEN. 19)
POTIPHAR'S WIFE (GEN. 39)
JOB'S WIFE (JOB 2)
THE WIDOW and HER POT OF OIL (II KINGS 4)
THE WITCH OF ENDOR (I SAM. 28)
JEPHTHAH'S DAUGHTER (JUDGES 11)
WIDOW OF ZAREPHATH (I KINGS 17)
THE QUEEN OF SHEBA (I KINGS 10)
SHUNAMMITE WOMAN (II KINGS 4)
NAAMAN'S WIFE (II KINGS 5)
NAAMAN'S WIFE'S SERVANT (II KINGS 5)
EZEKIEL'S WIFE (EZEKIEL 24)

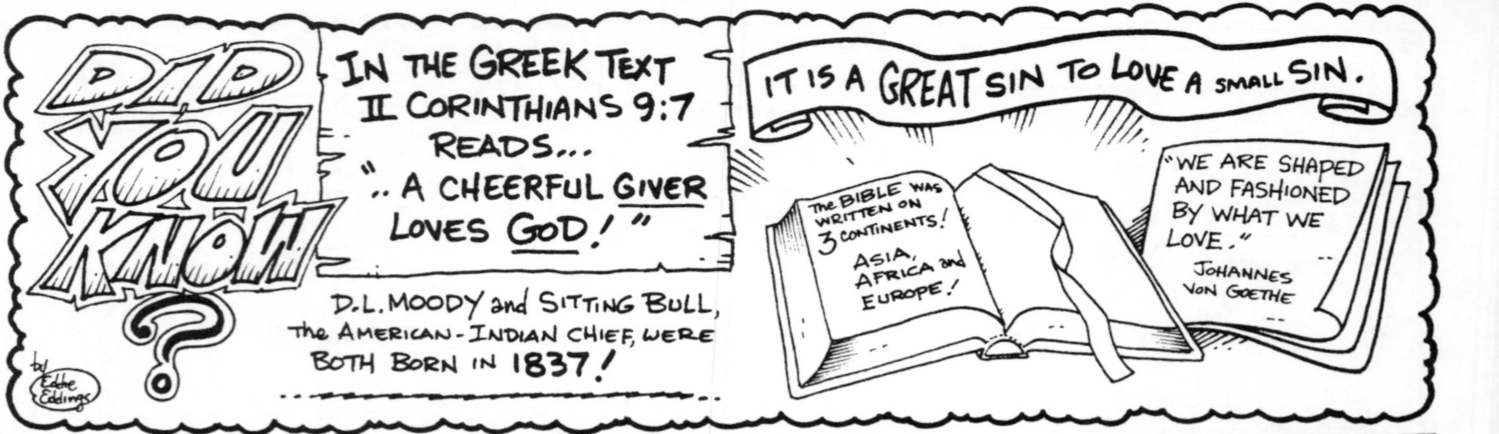
DID YOU KNOW?
by Eddie Eddings
IN THE GREEK TEXT II CORINTHIANS 9:7 READS... "... A CHEERFUL GIVER LOVES GOD!"
D.L. MOODY and SITTING BULL, the AMERICAN-INDIAN CHIEF, WERE BOTH BORN IN 1837!
IT IS A GREAT SIN TO LOVE A SMALL SIN.
The BIBLE WAS WRITTEN ON 3 CONTINENTS! ASIA, AFRICA and EUROPE!
"WE ARE SHAPED AND FASHIONED BY WHAT WE LOVE." JOHANNES VON GOETHE

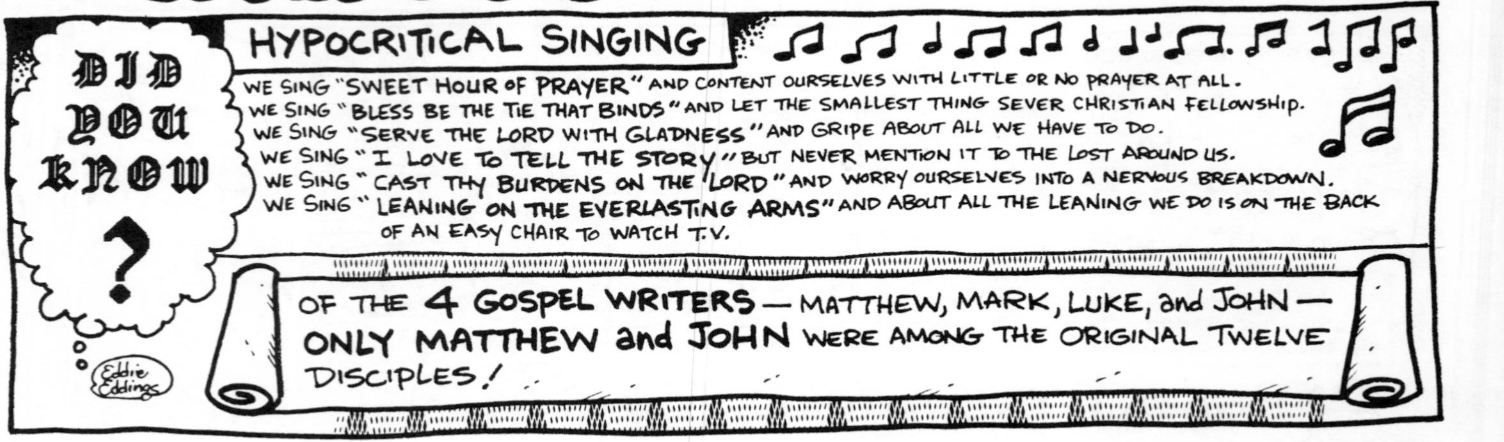
DID YOU KNOW?
Eddie Eddings
HYPOCRITICAL SINGING
WE SING "SWEET HOUR OF PRAYER" AND CONTENT OURSELVES WITH LITTLE OR NO PRAYER AT ALL.
WE SING "BLESS BE THE TIE THAT BINDS" AND LET THE SMALLEST THING SEVER CHRISTIAN FELLOWSHIP.
WE SING "SERVE THE LORD WITH GLADNESS" AND GRIPE ABOUT ALL WE HAVE TO DO.
WE SING "I LOVE TO TELL THE STORY" BUT NEVER MENTION IT TO THE LOST AROUND US.
WE SING "CAST THY BURDENS ON THE LORD" AND WORRY OURSELVES INTO A NERVOUS BREAKDOWN.
WE SING "LEANING ON THE EVERLASTING ARMS" AND ABOUT ALL THE LEANING WE DO IS ON THE BACK OF AN EASY CHAIR TO WATCH T.V.
OF THE 4 GOSPEL WRITERS — MATTHEW, MARK, LUKE, and JOHN — ONLY MATTHEW and JOHN WERE AMONG THE ORIGINAL TWELVE DISCIPLES!

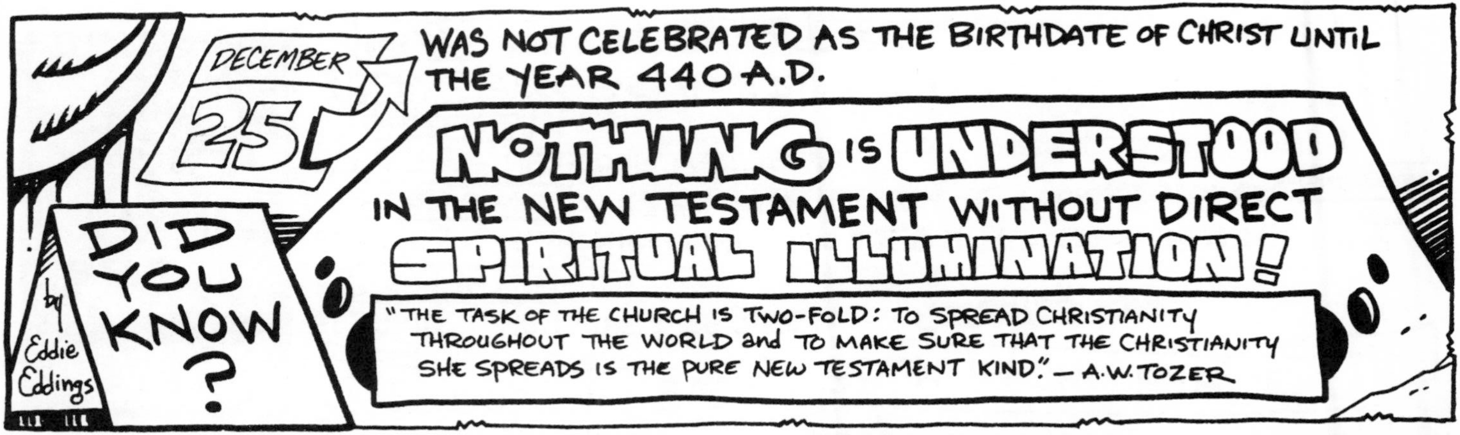
DID YOU KNOW ?
by Eddie Eddings
DECEMBER 25
WAS NOT CELEBRATED AS THE BIRTHDATE OF CHRIST UNTIL THE YEAR 440 A.D.
NOTHING IS UNDERSTOOD IN THE NEW TESTAMENT WITHOUT DIRECT SPIRITUAL ILLUMINATION!
"THE TASK OF THE CHURCH IS TWO-FOLD: TO SPREAD CHRISTIANITY THROUGHOUT THE WORLD and TO MAKE SURE THAT THE CHRISTIANITY SHE SPREADS IS THE PURE NEW TESTAMENT KIND." — A.W. TOZER

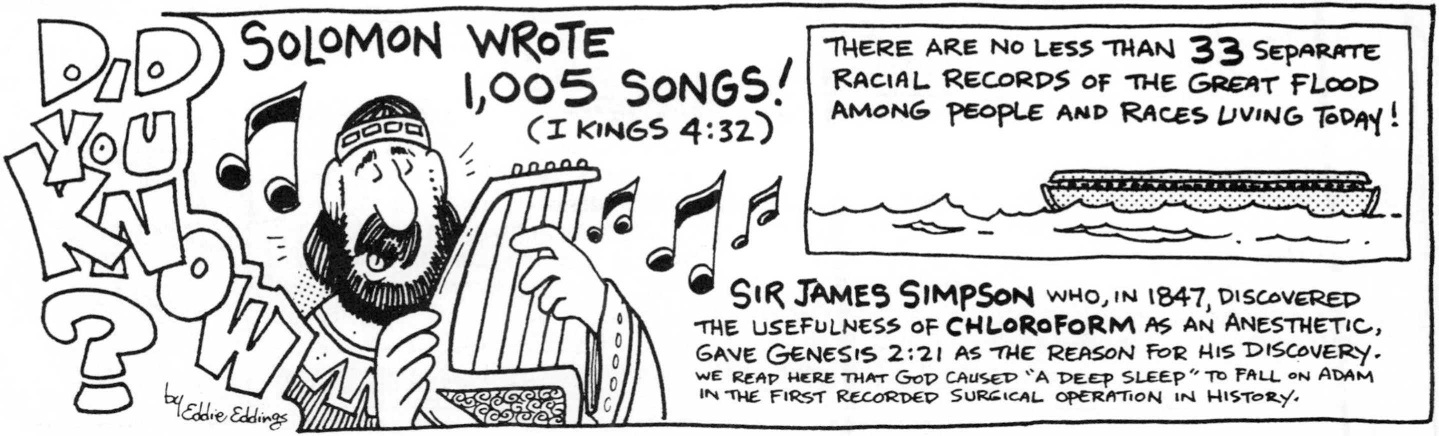
DID YOU KNOW?
by Eddie Eddings
SOLOMON WROTE 1,005 SONGS! (I KINGS 4:32)
THERE ARE NO LESS THAN 33 SEPARATE RACIAL RECORDS OF THE GREAT FLOOD AMONG PEOPLE AND RACES LIVING TODAY!
SIR JAMES SIMPSON WHO, IN 1847, DISCOVERED THE USEFULNESS OF CHLOROFORM AS AN ANESTHETIC, GAVE GENESIS 2:21 AS THE REASON FOR HIS DISCOVERY. WE READ HERE THAT GOD CAUSED "A DEEP SLEEP" TO FALL ON ADAM IN THE FIRST RECORDED SURGICAL OPERATION IN HISTORY.

Did You Know?

by Eddie Eddings

J. VERNON McGEE COMMENTING ON **PSALM 11:5** ("BUT THE WICKED AND HIM THAT LOVETH VIOLENCE HIS SOUL HATETH."): "IF YOU THINK GOD IS JUST LOVEY-DOVEY, YOU HAD BETTER READ THIS AND SOME OF THE OTHER PSALMS AGAIN. GOD HATES THE WICKED WHO HOLD ON TO THEIR WICKEDNESS. I DON'T THINK GOD LOVES THE DEVIL. I THINK GOD HATES HIM AND HE HATES THOSE WHO HAVE NO INTENTION OF TURNING TO GOD. FRANKLY, I DON'T LIKE THIS DISTINCTION THAT I HEAR TODAY THAT, 'GOD LOVES THE SINNER, BUT HE HATES THE SIN.' ... IF YOU PERSIST IN YOUR SIN AND CONTINUE IN THAT SIN, YOU ARE THE ENEMY OF GOD. AND GOD IS YOUR ENEMY... GOD WILL SAVE YOU IF YOU TURN TO HIM AND FORSAKE YOUR INIQUITY. UNTIL THEN, MAY I SAY, GOD IS NOT A LOVEY-DOVEY, SENTIMENTAL, OLD GENTLEMAN FROM GEORGIA!"

—C.H. SPURGEON

"DEFEND the BIBLE? I MIGHT AS WELL TRY TO DEFEND A LION!"

CHRIST IN EVERY BOOK IN THE BIBLE!

IN **SAMUEL** HE IS THE **DESPISED** and **REJECTED KING.**
I SAM. 16-19

IN **KINGS** and **CHRONICLES** HE IS THE **LORD OF HEAVEN** and **EARTH.**
ENTIRE BOOKS

IN **EZRA** and **NEHEMIAH** HE IS OUR **RESTORER.** ENTIRE BOOKS

IN **ESTHER** HE IS OUR **MORDECAI.**
CHAPTER 10

IN **JOB** HE IS OUR **RISEN** and **RETURNING REDEEMER.**
19:25

DID YOU KNOW?

By Eddie Eddings

DID YOU KNOW?

By Eddie Eddings

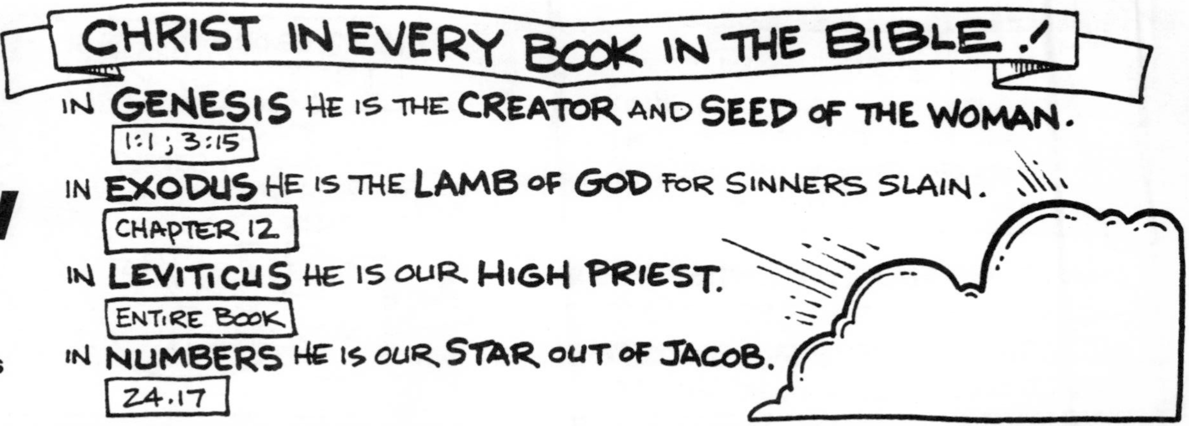

CHRIST IN EVERY BOOK IN THE BIBLE!
IN GENESIS HE IS THE CREATOR AND SEED OF THE WOMAN.
1:1; 3:15
IN EXODUS HE IS THE LAMB OF GOD FOR SINNERS SLAIN.
CHAPTER 12
IN LEVITICUS HE IS OUR HIGH PRIEST.
ENTIRE BOOK
IN NUMBERS HE IS OUR STAR OUT OF JACOB.
24.17

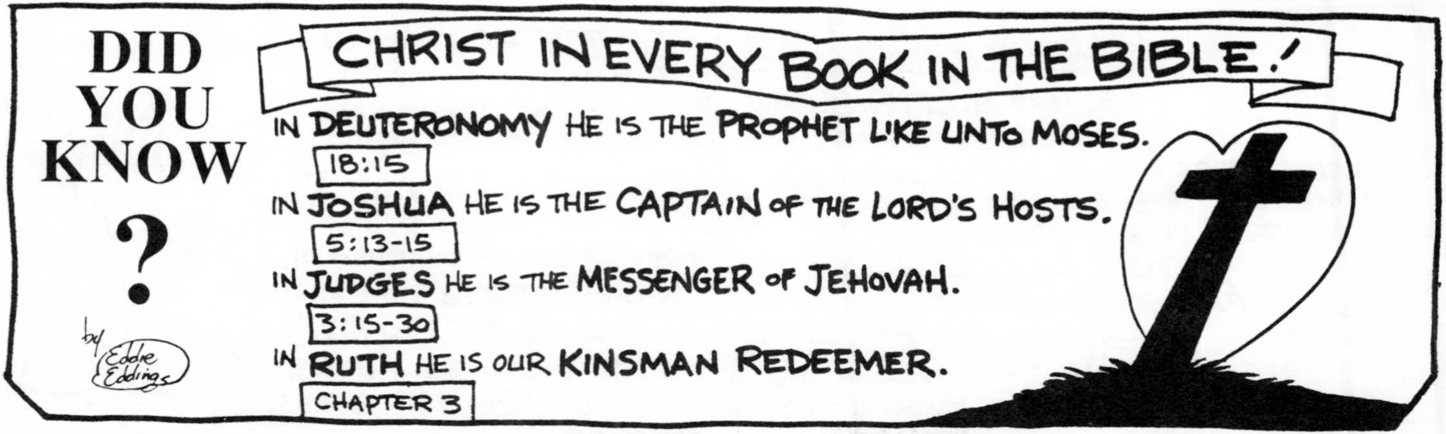

DID YOU KNOW?
by Eddie Eddings
CHRIST IN EVERY BOOK IN THE BIBLE!
IN DEUTERONOMY HE IS THE PROPHET LIKE UNTO MOSES.
18:15
IN JOSHUA HE IS THE CAPTAIN OF THE LORD'S HOSTS.
5:13-15
IN JUDGES HE IS THE MESSENGER OF JEHOVAH.
3:15-30
IN RUTH HE IS OUR KINSMAN REDEEMER.
CHAPTER 3

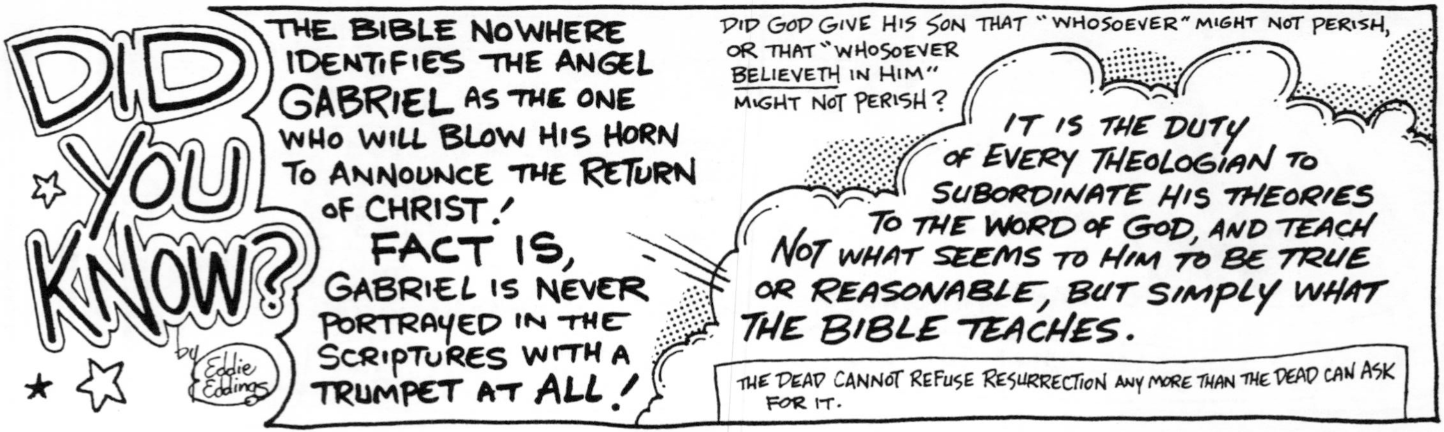
DID YOU KNOW?
by Eddie Eddings
THE BIBLE NOWHERE IDENTIFIES THE ANGEL GABRIEL AS THE ONE WHO WILL BLOW HIS HORN TO ANNOUNCE THE RETURN OF CHRIST!
FACT IS,
GABRIEL IS NEVER PORTRAYED IN THE SCRIPTURES WITH A TRUMPET AT ALL!
DID GOD GIVE HIS SON THAT "WHOSOEVER" MIGHT NOT PERISH, OR THAT "WHOSOEVER BELIEVETH IN HIM" MIGHT NOT PERISH?
IT IS THE DUTY OF EVERY THEOLOGIAN TO SUBORDINATE HIS THEORIES TO THE WORD OF GOD, AND TEACH NOT WHAT SEEMS TO HIM TO BE TRUE OR REASONABLE, BUT SIMPLY WHAT THE BIBLE TEACHES.
THE DEAD CANNOT REFUSE RESURRECTION ANY MORE THAN THE DEAD CAN ASK FOR IT.

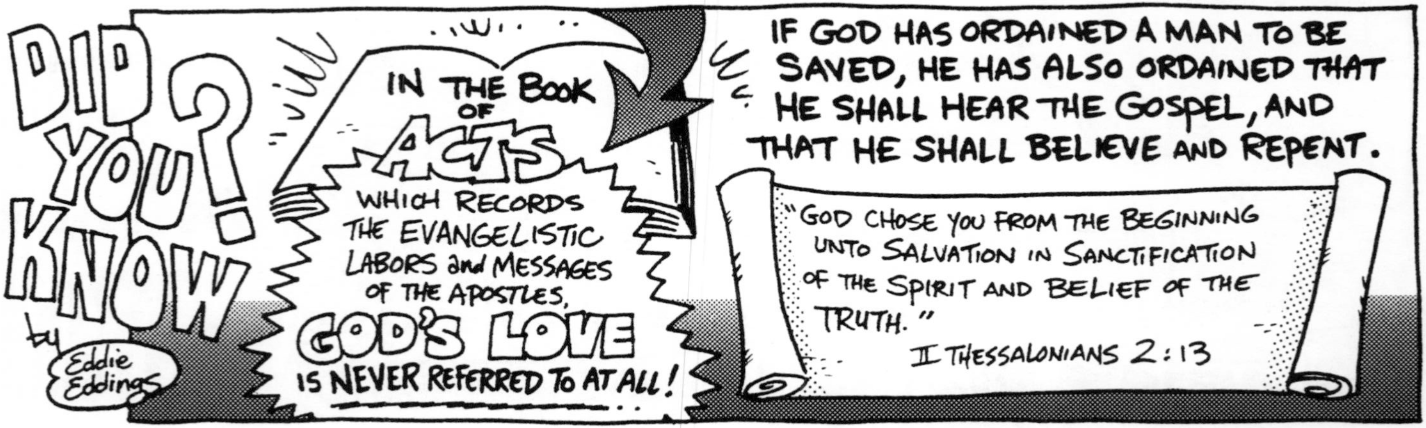
DID YOU KNOW?!
by Eddie Eddings
IN THE BOOK OF ACTS WHICH RECORDS THE EVANGELISTIC LABORS and MESSAGES OF THE APOSTLES, GOD'S LOVE IS NEVER REFERRED TO AT ALL!
IF GOD HAS ORDAINED A MAN TO BE SAVED, HE HAS ALSO ORDAINED THAT HE SHALL HEAR THE GOSPEL, AND THAT HE SHALL BELIEVE AND REPENT.
"GOD CHOSE YOU FROM THE BEGINNING UNTO SALVATION IN SANCTIFICATION OF THE SPIRIT AND BELIEF OF THE TRUTH."
II THESSALONIANS 2:13

DID YOU KNOW ?

BY EDDIE EDDINGS

THE GREATEST SOLOIST IN THE UNIVERSE!

JESUS!

HEBREWS 2:12, JESUS IS TALKING TO THE FATHER and HE SAYS, "I WILL DECLARE THY NAME UNTO MY BRETHREN, IN THE MIDST OF THE CHURCH WILL I SING PRAISE UNTO THEE."

OF THE 27 BOOKS of the New Testament, PAUL WROTE AT LEAST 13, POSSIBLY 14, IF HE WROTE HEBREWS.

BUT LUKE

WROTE MORE WORDS OF THE NEW TESTAMENT THAN DID PAUL.

MOSES SPENT

40 YEARS THINKING HE WAS SOMEBODY

40 YEARS LEARNING HE WAS NOBODY

40 YEARS DISCOVERING WHAT GOD CAN DO WITH A NOBODY

(See HEBREWS 11:23-29)

MARTIN LUTHER SAID: "I PREACH AS THOUGH CHRIST WAS CRUCIFIED YESTERDAY; ROSE AGAIN FROM THE DEAD TODAY; AND IS COMING BACK TO EARTH TOMORROW!"

DID YOU KNOW ?

BY EDDIE EDDINGS

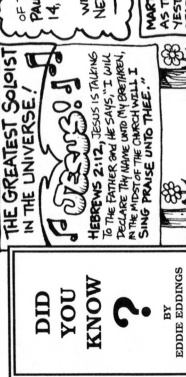

CHRIST IN EVERY BOOK IN THE BIBLE!

IN I PETER HE IS THE THEME OF OLD TESTAMENT PROPHECY. 1:10-11

IN II PETER HE IS THE LONG SUFFERING SAVIOR. 3:9

IN I JOHN HE IS THE WORD OF LIFE. 1:1

IN II JOHN HE IS THE TARGET OF THE ANTI-CHRIST. V.7

IN III JOHN HE IS THE PERSONIFICATION OF TRUTH. V.3-4

IN JUDE HE IS THE BELIEVER'S SECURITY. V.24-25

IN REVELATION HE IS THE KING OF KINGS and LORD OF LORDS. 19:11-16

BEHIND and BENEATH THE BIBLE, ABOVE and BEYOND THE BIBLE, IS THE GOD OF THE BIBLE.

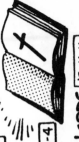

DID YOU KNOW?

by Eddie Eddings

SCRIPTURE IS THE LIBRARY OF THE HOLY SPIRIT.

QUARANTINING CONTAGIOUS DISEASES: (LEVITICUS 13:45,46.) The BIBLE IS THE ONLY ANCIENT BOOK IN ALL THE WORLD THAT DEMANDS THIS PRACTICE.

HOLY BIBLE

THERE IS SOMETHING WRONG WITH A PERSON'S SPIRITUAL APPETITE WHEN YOU HAVE TO BEG THEM TO EAT.

WHAT IS CALLED THE "WIDOW'S MITE" IS, IN THE GOSPEL ACCOUNTS, ACTUALLY TWO MITES! BOTH COPPER COINS STILL ADD UP TO LESS THAN ONE PENNY. (MARK 12:41-44; LUKE 21:1-4).

CHRIST IN EVERY BOOK IN THE BIBLE!

IN MATTHEW HE IS THE KING OF THE JEWS. 2:1

IN MARK HE IS THE SERVANT OF JEHOVAH. ENTIRE BOOK

IN LUKE HE IS THE PERFECT SON OF MAN. 3:38; 4:1-13

IN JOHN HE IS THE SON OF GOD. 1:1

IN ACTS HE IS THE ASCENDED LORD. 1:8-9

IN ROMANS HE IS OUR RIGHTEOUSNESS. 3:22

IN I CORINTHIANS HE IS THE FIRST-FRUITS FROM AMONG THE DEAD. 15:20

IN II CORINTHIANS HE IS MADE SIN FOR US. 5:21

IN GALATIANS HE IS THE END OF THE LAW. 3:10 and 3:13

IN EPHESIANS HE IS OUR ARMOR. 6:11-18

ΔΙΔ ΨΟΥ ΚΝΟΩ?

By Εδδιε Εδδινγσ

82

DID YOU KNOW ?

BY EDDIE EDDINGS

CHRIST IN EVERY BOOK IN THE BIBLE!

IN PHILIPPIANS HE IS THE SUPPLIER OF EVERY NEED. 4:19
IN COLOSSIANS HE IS THE PREEMINENT ONE. 1:18
IN I THESSALONIANS HE IS OUR RETURNING LORD. 4:15-18
IN II THESSALONIANS HE IS THE WORLD'S RETURNING JUDGE. 1:7-9
IN I TIMOTHY HE IS THE MEDIATOR. 2:5
IN II TIMOTHY HE IS THE BESTOWER OF CROWNS. 4:8
IN TITUS HE IS OUR GREAT GOD and SAVIOR. 2:13
IN PHILEMON HE IS THE FATHER'S PARTNER. V. 17-19
IN HEBREWS HE IS THE REST OF FAITH and FULFILLER OF TYPES. 9; 11; 12:1-2
IN JAMES HE IS THE LORD OF SABAOTH. 5:4

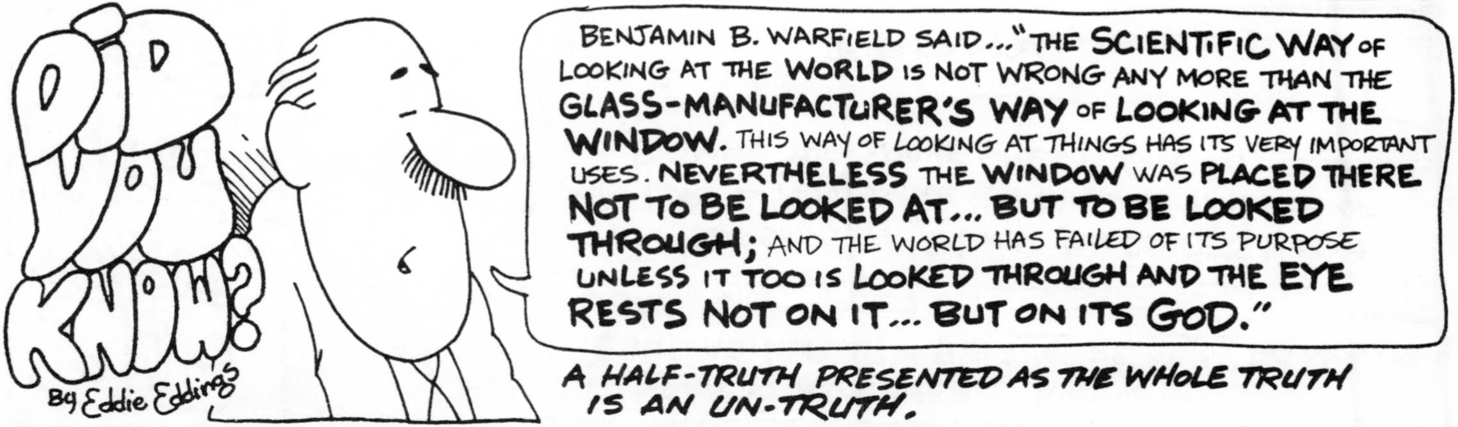
DID YOU KNOW?
By Eddie Eddings
BENJAMIN B. WARFIELD SAID..."THE SCIENTIFIC WAY OF LOOKING AT THE WORLD IS NOT WRONG ANY MORE THAN THE GLASS-MANUFACTURER'S WAY OF LOOKING AT THE WINDOW. THIS WAY OF LOOKING AT THINGS HAS ITS VERY IMPORTANT USES. NEVERTHELESS THE WINDOW WAS PLACED THERE NOT TO BE LOOKED AT... BUT TO BE LOOKED THROUGH; AND THE WORLD HAS FAILED OF ITS PURPOSE UNLESS IT TOO IS LOOKED THROUGH AND THE EYE RESTS NOT ON IT... BUT ON ITS GOD."

A HALF-TRUTH PRESENTED AS THE WHOLE TRUTH IS AN UN-TRUTH.

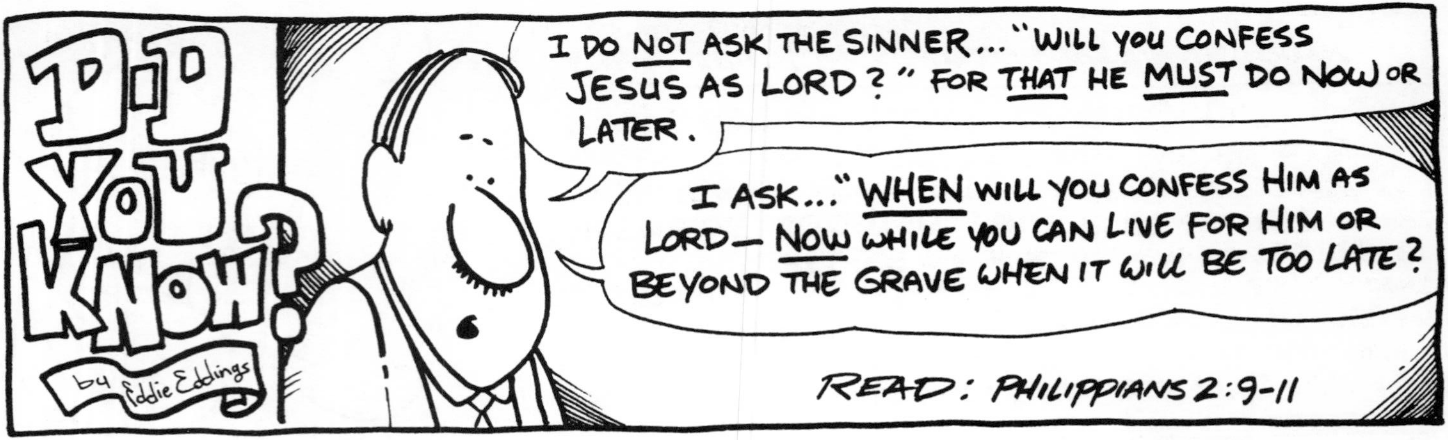
DID YOU KNOW?
by Eddie Eddings
I DO NOT ASK THE SINNER... "WILL YOU CONFESS JESUS AS LORD?" FOR THAT HE MUST DO NOW OR LATER.
I ASK... "WHEN WILL YOU CONFESS HIM AS LORD — NOW WHILE YOU CAN LIVE FOR HIM OR BEYOND THE GRAVE WHEN IT WILL BE TOO LATE?
READ: PHILIPPIANS 2:9-11

DID YOU KNOW ?

By Eddie Eddings

THE MOST FAMOUS SERMON EVER PREACHED IN AMERICA CAME FROM DEUTERONOMY 32:25, "THEIR FOOT SHALL SLIDE IN DUE SEASON."

THIS IS ONE OF THE MOST FAMOUS SERMONS EVER PREACHED IN THE WORLD AND IS PROBABLY THE MOST-REPRINTED!

PREACHERS REFER TO IT OFTEN IN THEIR SERMONS... BUT FEW CHRISTIANS TODAY HAVE ACTUALLY READ IT... PREACHED JULY 8, 1741, BY JONATHAN EDWARDS ——→ IT WAS ENTITLED..."**SINNERS IN THE HANDS OF AN ANGRY GOD.**"

WHEN EDWARDS DELIVERED IT, AN INTENSELY **POWERFUL REVIVAL BROKE OUT IN THE MIDDLE OF THE MESSAGE**. PEOPLE BEGAN MOANING AND SCREAMING FOR MERCY AS EDWARDS **READ HIS MANUSCRIPT**. THEY WERE UNDER DEEP CONVICTION FOR THEIR SINS AND SAW THAT THEY DESERVED HELL. **THIS WAS NO EXAMPLE OF A CHEAP 'PREACHER' PLAYING ON MEN'S EMOTIONS — THIS WAS THE WORK OF GOD!** READING THE ACCOUNTS OF IT STIRS THE HEART, and READING THE SERMON CONVICTS THE HEART. **ALL CHRISTIANS AND NON-CHRISTIANS SHOULD READ IT and HEED IT!**

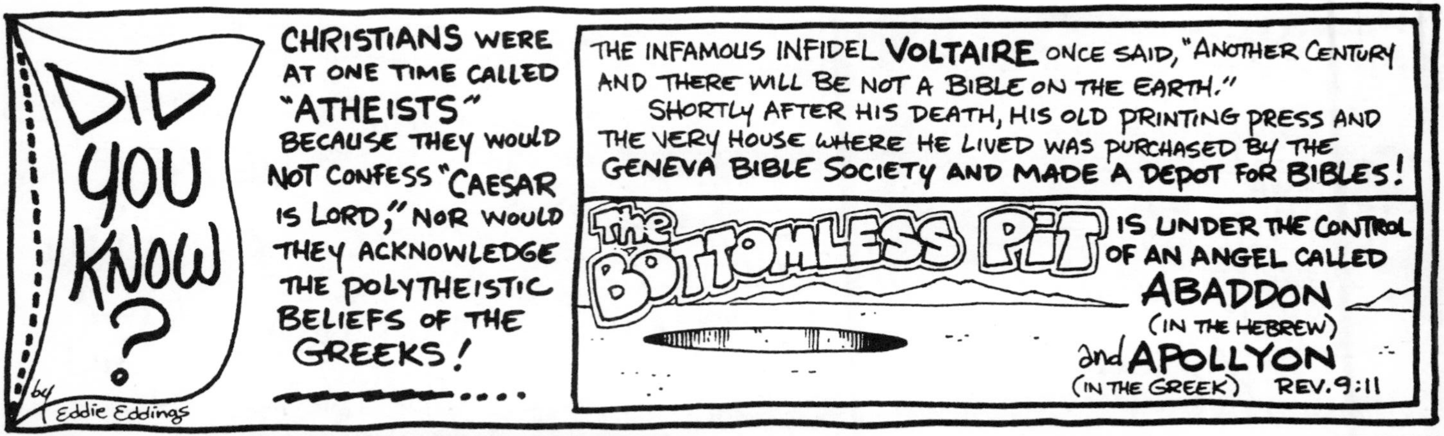
DID YOU KNOW?
by Eddie Eddings
CHRISTIANS WERE AT ONE TIME CALLED "ATHEISTS" BECAUSE THEY WOULD NOT CONFESS "CAESAR IS LORD," NOR WOULD THEY ACKNOWLEDGE THE POLYTHEISTIC BELIEFS OF THE GREEKS!
THE INFAMOUS INFIDEL VOLTAIRE ONCE SAID, "ANOTHER CENTURY AND THERE WILL BE NOT A BIBLE ON THE EARTH."
SHORTLY AFTER HIS DEATH, HIS OLD PRINTING PRESS AND THE VERY HOUSE WHERE HE LIVED WAS PURCHASED BY THE GENEVA BIBLE SOCIETY AND MADE A DEPOT FOR BIBLES!
The BOTTOMLESS PIT IS UNDER THE CONTROL OF AN ANGEL CALLED ABADDON (IN THE HEBREW) and APOLLYON (IN THE GREEK) REV. 9:11

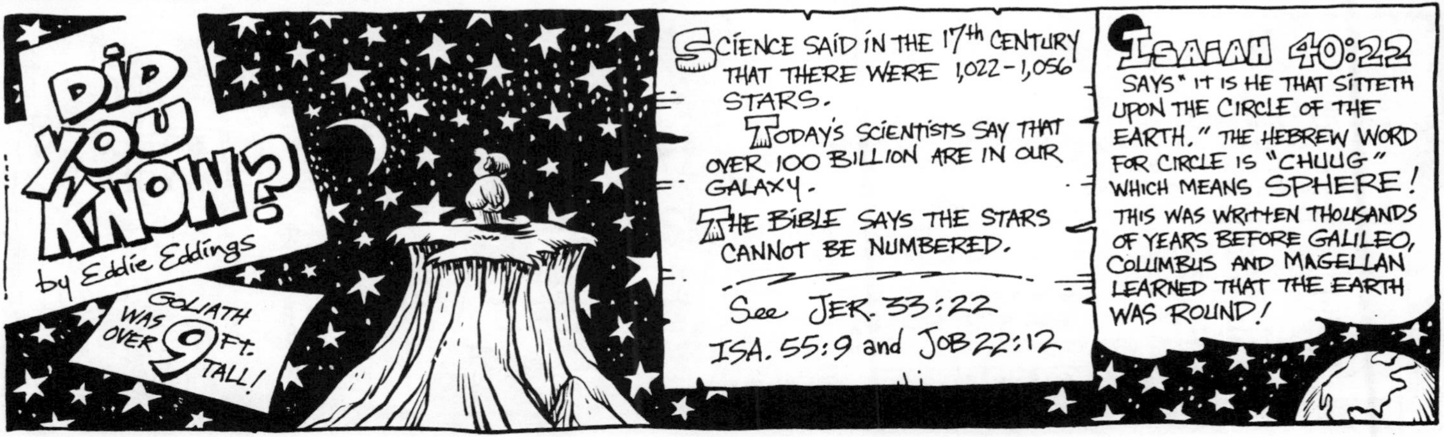
DID YOU KNOW?
by Eddie Eddings
GOLIATH WAS OVER 9 FT. TALL!
SCIENCE SAID IN THE 17th CENTURY THAT THERE WERE 1,022-1,056 STARS.
TODAY'S SCIENTISTS SAY THAT OVER 100 BILLION ARE IN OUR GALAXY.
THE BIBLE SAYS THE STARS CANNOT BE NUMBERED.
See JER. 33:22
ISA. 55:9 and JOB 22:12
ISAIAH 40:22 SAYS "IT IS HE THAT SITTETH UPON THE CIRCLE OF THE EARTH." THE HEBREW WORD FOR CIRCLE IS "CHUUG" WHICH MEANS SPHERE!
THIS WAS WRITTEN THOUSANDS OF YEARS BEFORE GALILEO, COLUMBUS AND MAGELLAN LEARNED THAT THE EARTH WAS ROUND!

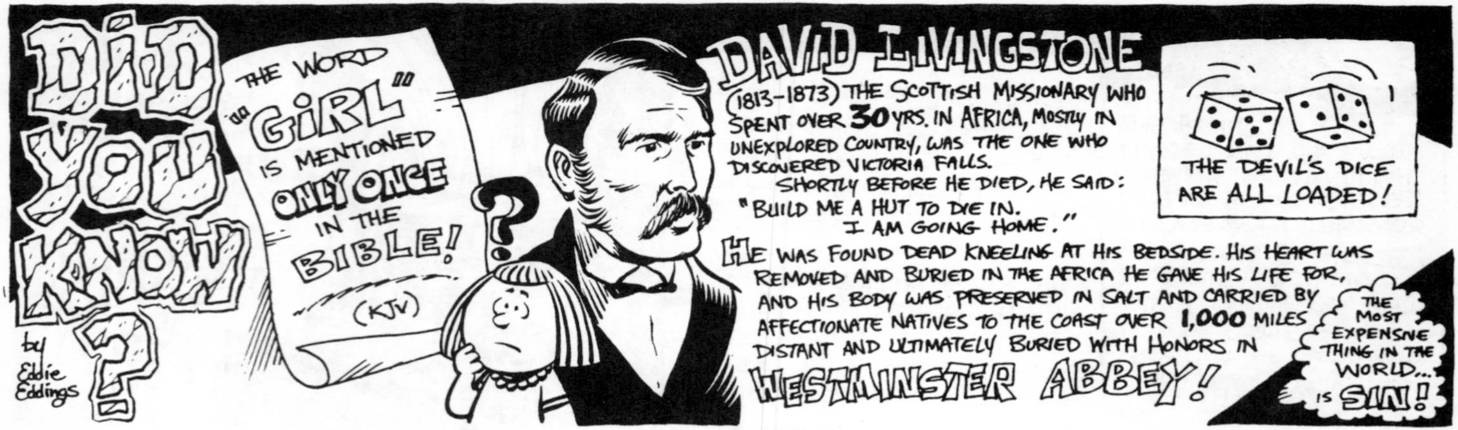
DID YOU KNOW?
by Eddie Eddings
THE WORD "GIRL" IS MENTIONED ONLY ONCE IN THE BIBLE! (KJV)
DAVID LIVINGSTONE
(1813-1873) THE SCOTTISH MISSIONARY WHO SPENT OVER 30 YRS. IN AFRICA, MOSTLY IN UNEXPLORED COUNTRY, WAS THE ONE WHO DISCOVERED VICTORIA FALLS.
SHORTLY BEFORE HE DIED, HE SAID: "BUILD ME A HUT TO DIE IN. I AM GOING HOME."
HE WAS FOUND DEAD KNEELING AT HIS BEDSIDE. HIS HEART WAS REMOVED AND BURIED IN THE AFRICA HE GAVE HIS LIFE FOR, AND HIS BODY WAS PRESERVED IN SALT AND CARRIED BY AFFECTIONATE NATIVES TO THE COAST OVER 1,000 MILES DISTANT AND ULTIMATELY BURIED WITH HONORS IN WESTMINSTER ABBEY!
THE DEVIL'S DICE ARE ALL LOADED!
THE MOST EXPENSIVE THING IN THE WORLD... IS SIN!

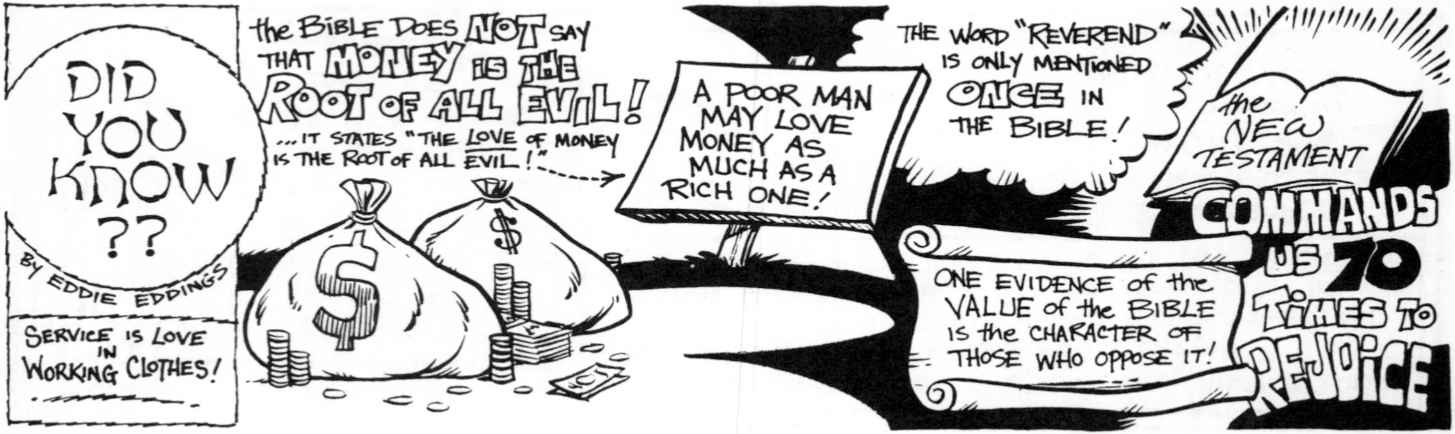
DID YOU KNOW ??
BY EDDIE EDDINGS
SERVICE IS LOVE IN WORKING CLOTHES!
the BIBLE DOES NOT SAY THAT MONEY IS THE ROOT OF ALL EVIL!
...IT STATES "THE LOVE OF MONEY IS THE ROOT OF ALL EVIL!"
A POOR MAN MAY LOVE MONEY AS MUCH AS A RICH ONE!
THE WORD "REVEREND" IS ONLY MENTIONED ONCE IN THE BIBLE!
the NEW TESTAMENT COMMANDS US 70 TIMES TO REJOICE
ONE EVIDENCE of the VALUE of the BIBLE is the CHARACTER OF THOSE WHO OPPOSE IT!

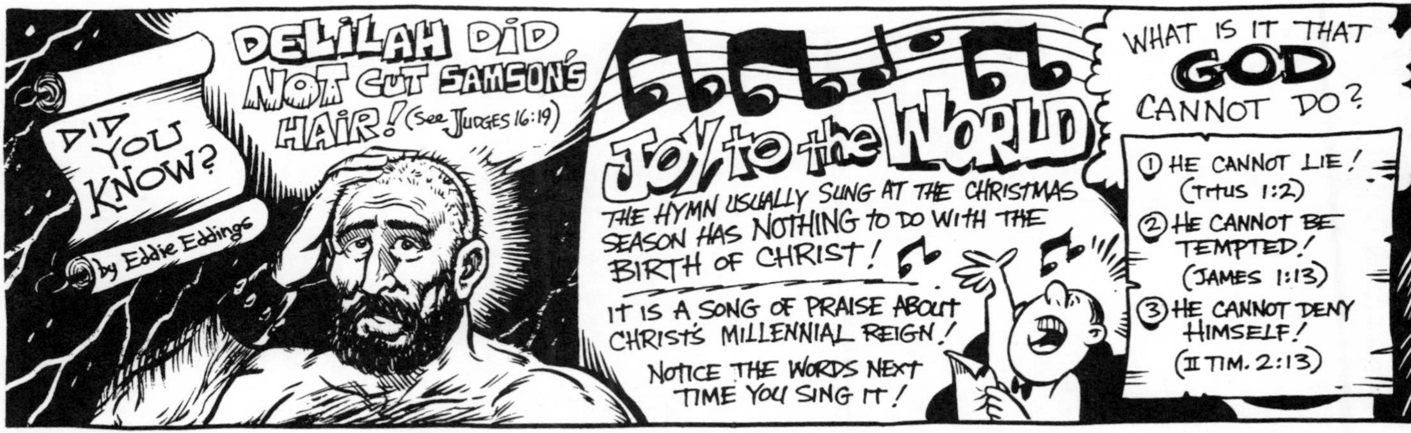
DID YOU KNOW?
by Eddie Eddings
DELILAH DID NOT CUT SAMSON'S HAIR! (See JUDGES 16:19)
JOY to the WORLD
THE HYMN USUALLY SUNG AT THE CHRISTMAS SEASON HAS NOTHING TO DO WITH THE BIRTH OF CHRIST!
IT IS A SONG OF PRAISE ABOUT CHRIST'S MILLENNIAL REIGN!
NOTICE THE WORDS NEXT TIME YOU SING IT!
WHAT IS IT THAT GOD CANNOT DO?
① HE CANNOT LIE! (TITUS 1:2)
② HE CANNOT BE TEMPTED! (JAMES 1:13)
③ HE CANNOT DENY HIMSELF! (II TIM. 2:13)

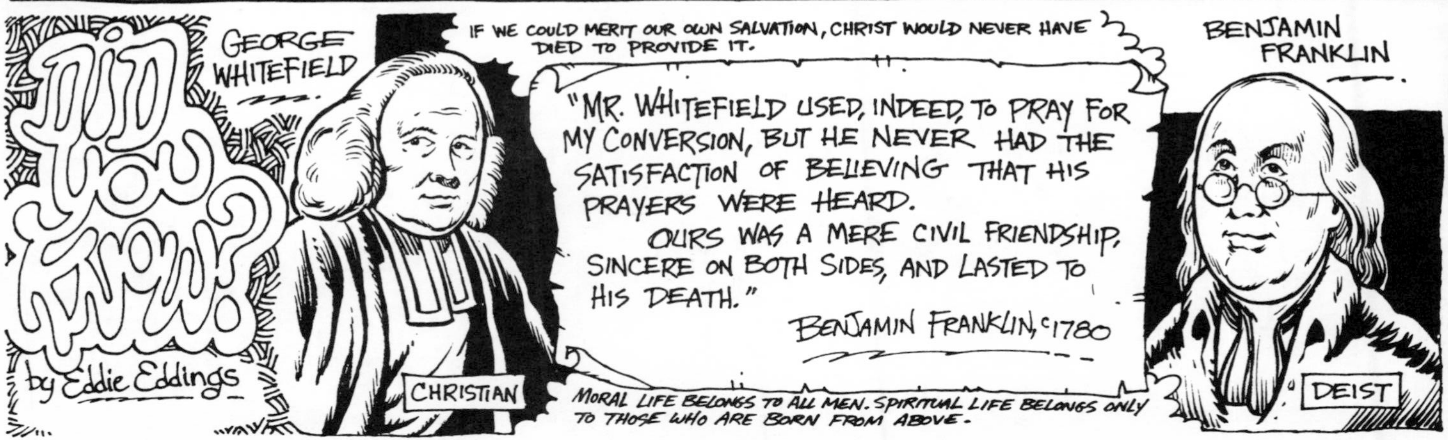
DID YOU KNOW?
by Eddie Eddings
GEORGE WHITEFIELD
CHRISTIAN
IF WE COULD MERIT OUR OWN SALVATION, CHRIST WOULD NEVER HAVE DIED TO PROVIDE IT.
"MR. WHITEFIELD USED, INDEED, TO PRAY FOR MY CONVERSION, BUT HE NEVER HAD THE SATISFACTION OF BELIEVING THAT HIS PRAYERS WERE HEARD.
OURS WAS A MERE CIVIL FRIENDSHIP, SINCERE ON BOTH SIDES, AND LASTED TO HIS DEATH."
BENJAMIN FRANKLIN, c1780
BENJAMIN FRANKLIN
DEIST
MORAL LIFE BELONGS TO ALL MEN. SPIRITUAL LIFE BELONGS ONLY TO THOSE WHO ARE BORN FROM ABOVE.

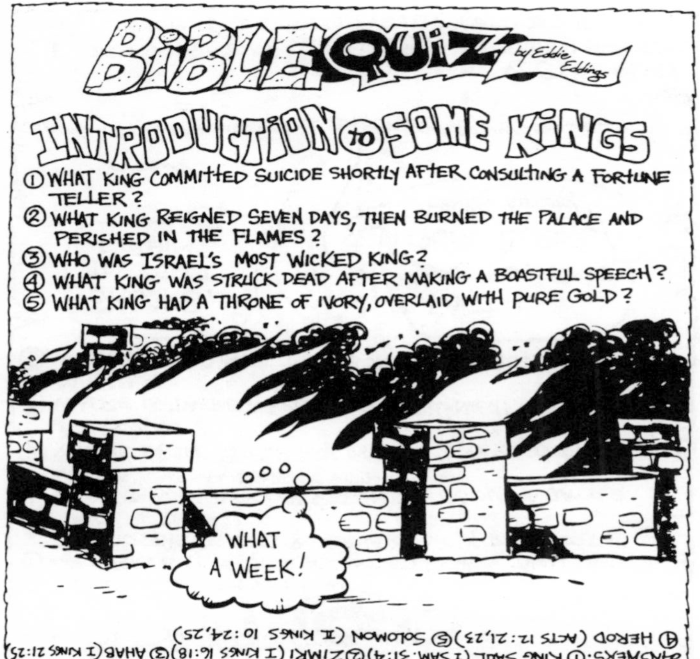
BIBLE QUIZ
by Eddie Eddings
INTRODUCTION to SOME KINGS
① WHAT KING COMMITTED SUICIDE SHORTLY AFTER CONSULTING A FORTUNE TELLER?
② WHAT KING REIGNED SEVEN DAYS, THEN BURNED THE PALACE AND PERISHED IN THE FLAMES?
③ WHO WAS ISRAEL'S MOST WICKED KING?
④ WHAT KING WAS STRUCK DEAD AFTER MAKING A BOASTFUL SPEECH?
⑤ WHAT KING HAD A THRONE OF IVORY, OVERLAID WITH PURE GOLD?
WHAT A WEEK!
ANSWERS: ① KING SAUL (I SAM. 31:4) ② ZIMRI (I KINGS 16:18) ③ AHAB (I KINGS 21:25) ④ HEROD (ACTS 12:21,23) ⑤ SOLOMON (II KINGS 10:24,25)

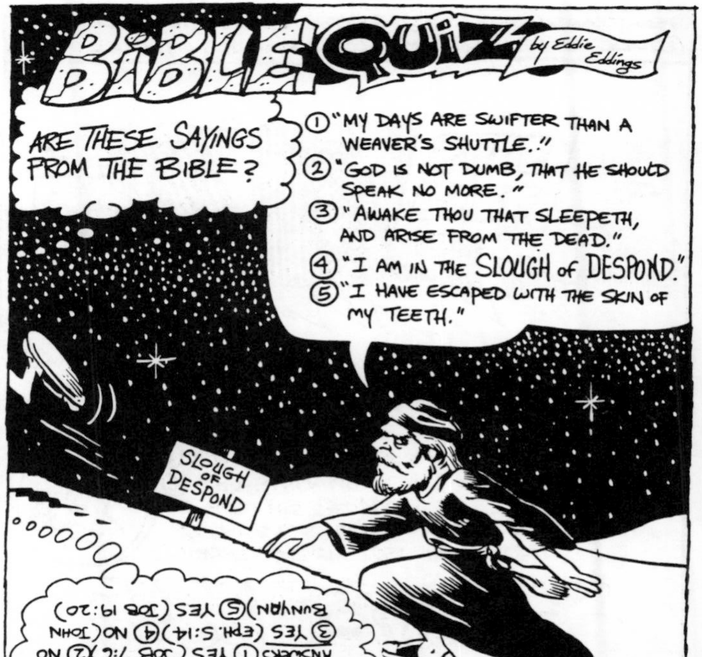
BIBLE QUIZ
by Eddie Eddings
ARE THESE SAYINGS FROM THE BIBLE?
① "MY DAYS ARE SWIFTER THAN A WEAVER'S SHUTTLE."
② "GOD IS NOT DUMB, THAT HE SHOULD SPEAK NO MORE."
③ "AWAKE THOU THAT SLEEPETH, AND ARISE FROM THE DEAD."
④ "I AM IN THE SLOUGH of DESPOND."
⑤ "I HAVE ESCAPED WITH THE SKIN OF MY TEETH."
SLOUGH OF DESPOND
ANSWERS ① YES (JOB 7:6) ② NO ③ YES (EPH. 5:14) ④ NO (JOHN BUNYAN) ⑤ YES (JOB 19:20)

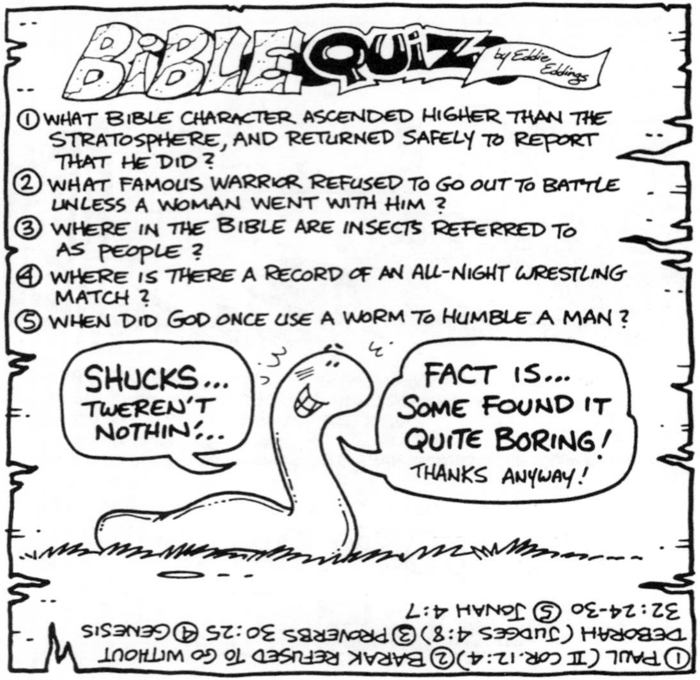
BIBLE QUIZ
by Eddie Eddings
① WHAT BIBLE CHARACTER ASCENDED HIGHER THAN THE STRATOSPHERE, AND RETURNED SAFELY TO REPORT THAT HE DID?
② WHAT FAMOUS WARRIOR REFUSED TO GO OUT TO BATTLE UNLESS A WOMAN WENT WITH HIM?
③ WHERE IN THE BIBLE ARE INSECTS REFERRED TO AS PEOPLE?
④ WHERE IS THERE A RECORD OF AN ALL-NIGHT WRESTLING MATCH?
⑤ WHEN DID GOD ONCE USE A WORM TO HUMBLE A MAN?
SHUCKS... TWEREN'T NOTHIN'!...
FACT IS... SOME FOUND IT QUITE BORING! THANKS ANYWAY!
① PAUL (II COR. 12:4) ② BARAK REFUSED TO GO WITHOUT DEBORAH (JUDGES 4:8) ③ PROVERBS 30:25 ④ GENESIS 32:24-30 ⑤ JONAH 4:7

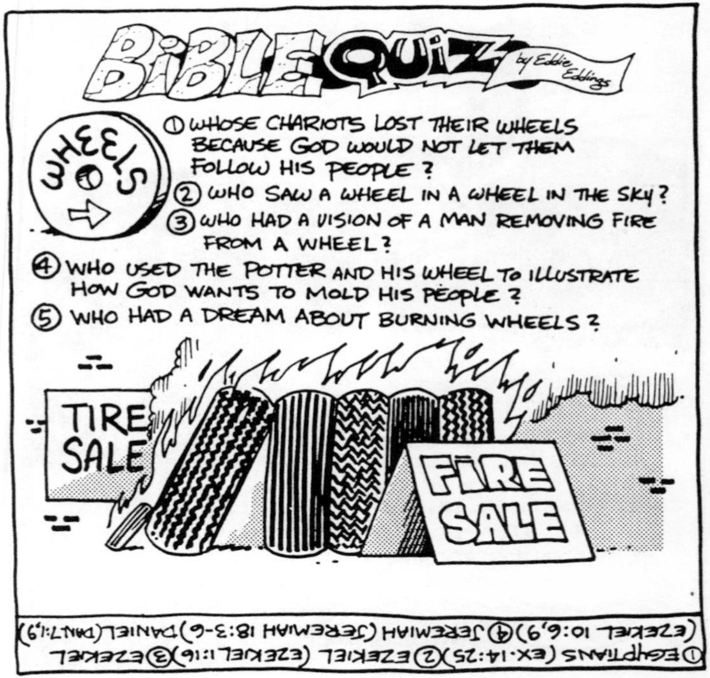
BIBLE QUIZ
by Eddie Eddings
WHEELS
① WHOSE CHARIOTS LOST THEIR WHEELS BECAUSE GOD WOULD NOT LET THEM FOLLOW HIS PEOPLE?
② WHO SAW A WHEEL IN A WHEEL IN THE SKY?
③ WHO HAD A VISION OF A MAN REMOVING FIRE FROM A WHEEL?
④ WHO USED THE POTTER AND HIS WHEEL TO ILLUSTRATE HOW GOD WANTS TO MOLD HIS PEOPLE?
⑤ WHO HAD A DREAM ABOUT BURNING WHEELS?
TIRE SALE
FIRE SALE
① EGYPTIANS (EX. 14:25) ② EZEKIEL (EZEKIEL 1:16) ③ EZEKIEL (EZEKIEL 10:6,9) ④ JEREMIAH (JEREMIAH 18:3-6) DANIEL (DAN. 7:1,9)

BIBLE QUIZ by Eddie Eddings

WHAT'S YOUR I.Q. ON FAMOUS PROVERBS?

① WHOSE WAY IS "RIGHT IN HIS OWN EYES"?
② WHOSE WAY IS DESCRIBED AS "HARD"?
③ WHAT PROVERB TELLS WHAT TO DO "WHEN SINNERS ENTICE THEE"?
④ TO WHAT INSECTS ARE SLUGGARDS ADMONISHED TO GO FOR INSTRUCTION?
⑤ WHAT IS IT THAT IS "CRUEL AS THE GRAVE"?

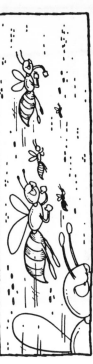

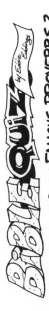

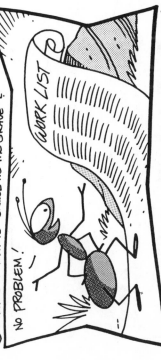

NO PROBLEM!
WORK LIST

① THE FOOL'S (PROV. 12:15) ② "THE WAY OF THE TRANSGRESSORS" (PROV. 13:15) ③ "CONSENT THOU NOT" (PROV. 1:10) ④ THE ANTS (PROV. 6:6-8) ⑤ JEALOUSY (SONG OF SOLOMON 8:6)

BIBLE QUIZ by Eddie Eddings

"STRICTLY MILITARY"

① WHAT WERE THE FIRST CITIES DESTROYED BY AN AERIAL BLAST?
② NAME A FAMOUS BIBLE CHARACTER WHO WON A GREAT BATTLE BY KEEPING HIS HANDS LIFTED TO GOD.
③ ON WHAT OCCASION DID GOD SEND HORNETS OUT AGAINST AN ARMY AND SCATTER THEM?
④ RECALL AN INSTANCE WHEN GOD DESTROYED AN ENEMY ARMY BY DROWNING EVERY ONE OF THEM.
⑤ WHO WILL LEAD IN THE WAR TO END ALL WARS?

① ...RAH (GEN. 19:24-28) ② MOSES (EXOD. 17:11) ③ IN THE DEFEAT OF THE AMORITES (JOSHUA 24:12) ④ THE DESTRUCTION OF PHARAOH'S ARMY IN THE RED SEA (EXOD. 14) ⑤ THE SON OF GOD (REV. 19:11-21; 20:1-3).

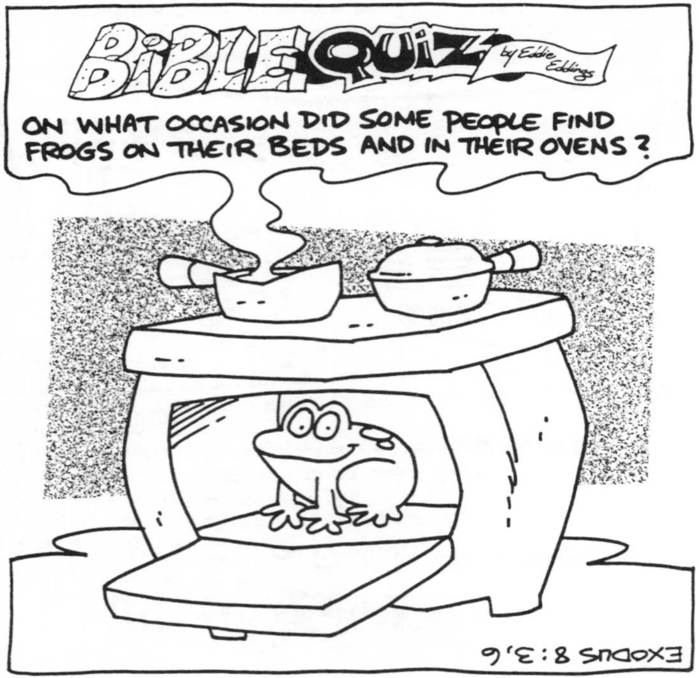
BIBLE QUIZ
by Eddie Eddings
ON WHAT OCCASION DID SOME PEOPLE FIND FROGS ON THEIR BEDS AND IN THEIR OVENS?
EXODUS 8:3,6

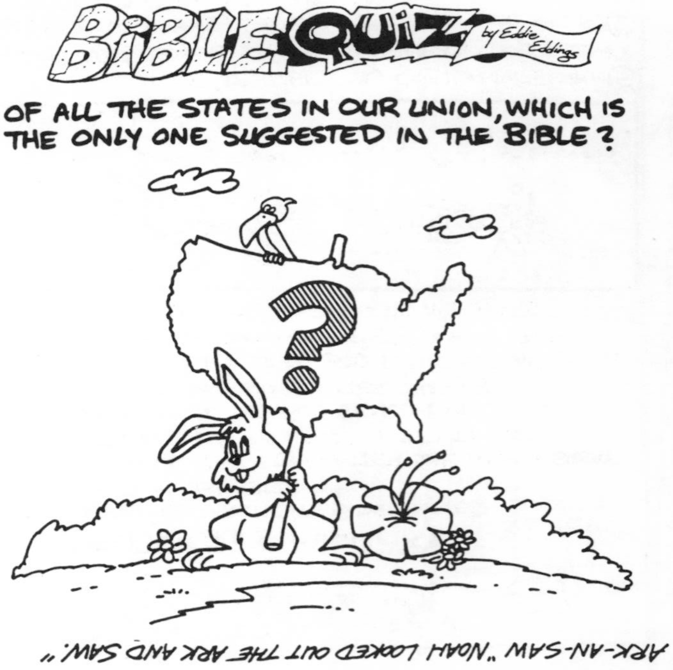
BIBLE QUIZ
by Eddie Eddings
OF ALL THE STATES IN OUR UNION, WHICH IS THE ONLY ONE SUGGESTED IN THE BIBLE?
ARK-AN-SAW "NOAH LOOKED OUT THE ARK AND SAW."

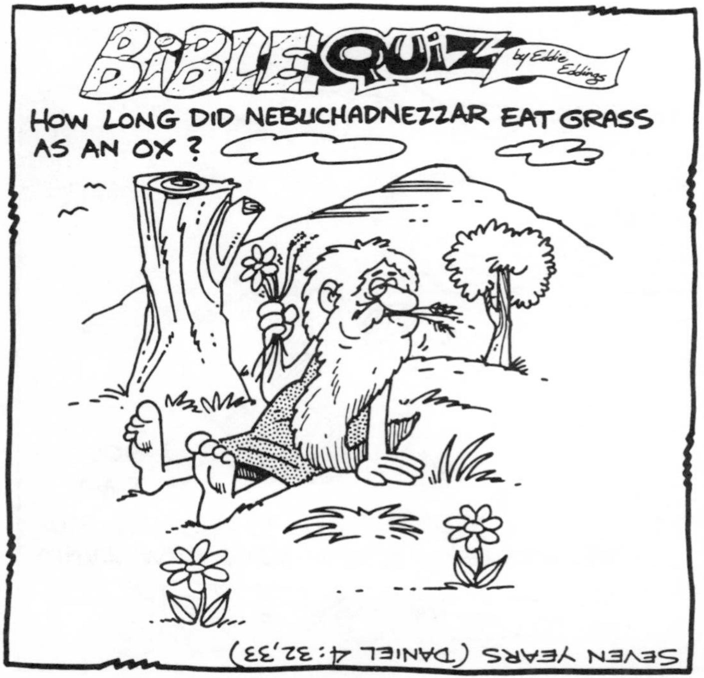
BIBLE QUIZ
by Eddie Eddings
HOW LONG DID NEBUCHADNEZZAR EAT GRASS AS AN OX ?
SEVEN YEARS (DANIEL 4:32,33)

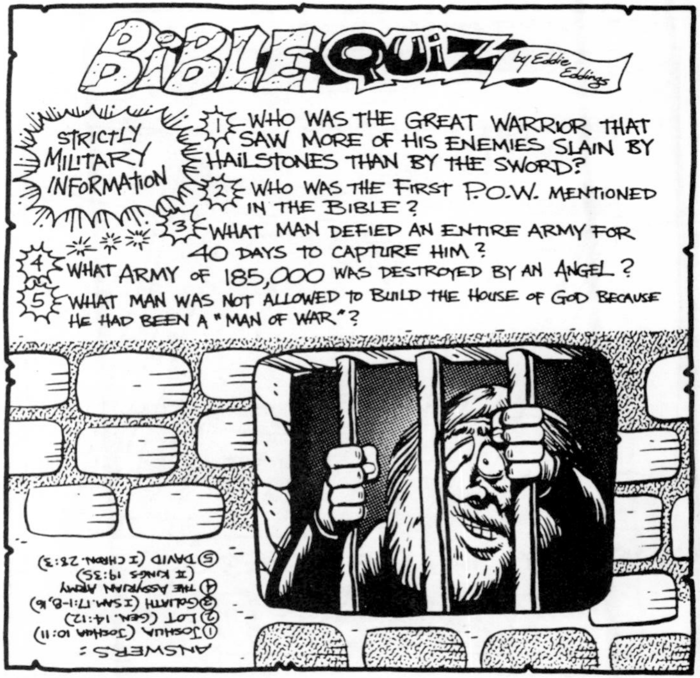
BIBLE QUIZ
by Eddie Eddings
STRICTLY MILITARY INFORMATION
1 WHO WAS THE GREAT WARRIOR THAT SAW MORE OF HIS ENEMIES SLAIN BY HAILSTONES THAN BY THE SWORD?
2 WHO WAS THE FIRST P.O.W. MENTIONED IN THE BIBLE ?
3 WHAT MAN DEFIED AN ENTIRE ARMY FOR 40 DAYS TO CAPTURE HIM ?
4 WHAT ARMY OF 185,000 WAS DESTROYED BY AN ANGEL ?
5 WHAT MAN WAS NOT ALLOWED TO BUILD THE HOUSE OF GOD BECAUSE HE HAD BEEN A "MAN OF WAR"?
ANSWERS:
① JOSHUA (JOSHUA 10:11)
② LOT (GEN. 14:12)
③ GOLIATH (I SAM. 17:1-8, 16)
④ THE ASSYRIAN ARMY (II KINGS 19:35)
⑤ DAVID (I CHRON. 28:3)

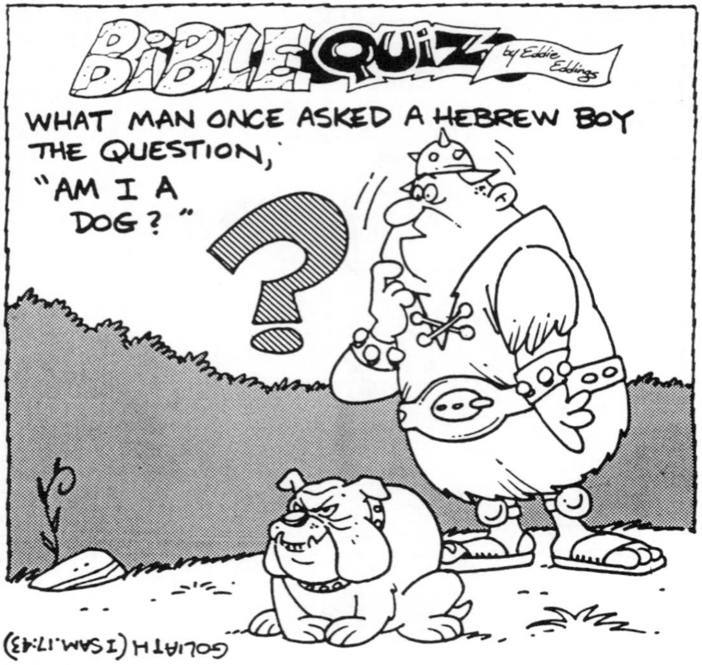
BIBLE QUIZ by Eddie Eddings
WHAT MAN ONCE ASKED A HEBREW BOY THE QUESTION, "AM I A DOG?"
GOLIATH (I SAM. 17:43)

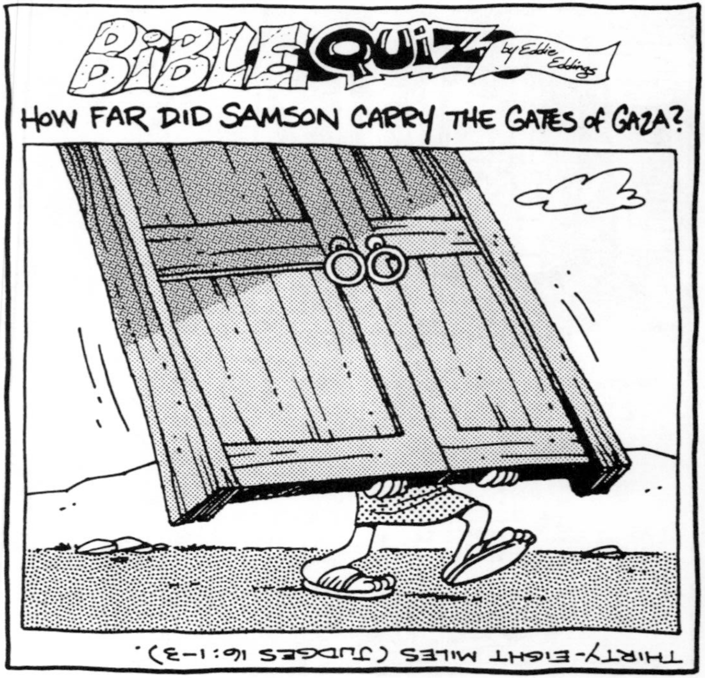
BIBLE QUIZ by Eddie Eddings
HOW FAR DID SAMSON CARRY THE GATES of GAZA?
THIRTY-EIGHT MILES (JUDGES 16:1-3).

BIBLE QUIZ by Eddie Eddings

THINK TWICE!

① HOW MANY TIMES IS THE DEAD SEA MENTIONED IN THE BIBLE?
② WHOSE DAUGHTER WAS NOAH?
③ WHAT WAS THE LARGEST CATCH OF FISH RECORDED IN THE BIBLE?
④ WHICH WAS THE OLDER BROTHER — MOSES OR AARON?
⑤ WHAT BIBLE CHARACTER WAS GIVEN A "HAM" AT THE AGE OF 99 YEARS?

A DEAD "C"!

① NONE. IT WAS CALLED "SALT SEA", MENTIONED NINE TIMES, AS SUCH.
② ZELOPHEHAD'S (NUM. 26:33) ③ 153 (JOHN 21:11) ④ AARON
(EX. 7:7) ⑤ ABRAM-ham (GEN. 17:5).

BIBLE QUIZ by Eddie Eddings

PERSON, PLACE, OR THING?
CHECK THE PROPER IDENTITY OF EACH NAME:

	PERSON	PLACE	THING
① ZOBEBAH	☐	☐	☐
② REHUM	☐	☐	☐
③ NISAN	☐	☐	☐
④ HUZZAB	☐	☐	☐
⑤ SAREPTA	☐	☐	☐

YOUR NAME HUZZAB?
— NO...IT'S T.BONE!
YOUR NAME NISAN?
— NO...IT'S BUD!
PLEASED TO MEET YOU.
— LIKEWISE!

① PERSON (I. CHRON. 4:8) ② PERSON (EZRA 2:2) ③ THING (MONTH) (NEH. 2:1) ④ PLACE (NAH. 2:7) ⑤ PLACE (LUKE 4:26)

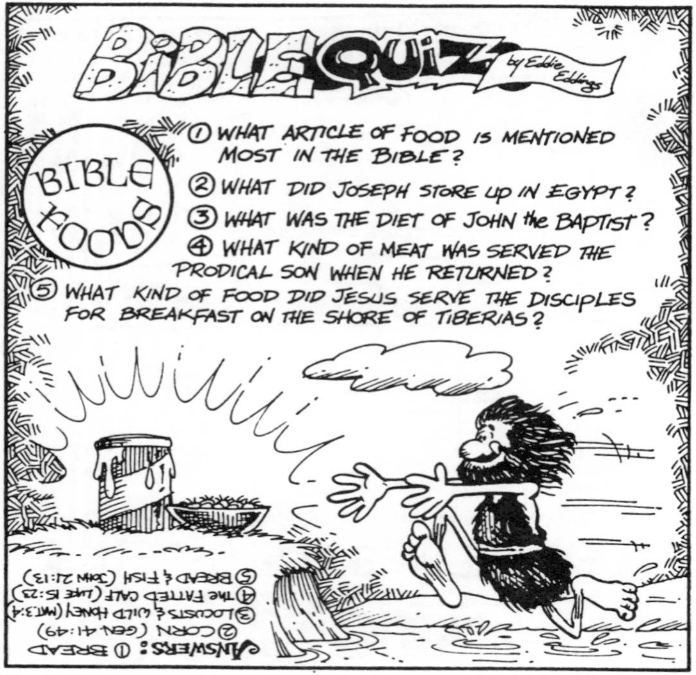
BIBLE QUIZ
by Eddie Eddings
BIBLE FOODS
① WHAT ARTICLE OF FOOD IS MENTIONED MOST IN THE BIBLE?
② WHAT DID JOSEPH STORE UP IN EGYPT?
③ WHAT WAS THE DIET OF JOHN the BAPTIST?
④ WHAT KIND OF MEAT WAS SERVED THE PRODIGAL SON WHEN HE RETURNED?
⑤ WHAT KIND OF FOOD DID JESUS SERVE THE DISCIPLES FOR BREAKFAST ON THE SHORE OF TIBERIAS?
ANSWERS: ① BREAD
② CORN (GEN. 41:49)
③ LOCUSTS & WILD HONEY (MAT. 3:4)
④ THE FATTED CALF (LUKE 15:23)
⑤ BREAD & FISH (JOHN 21:13)

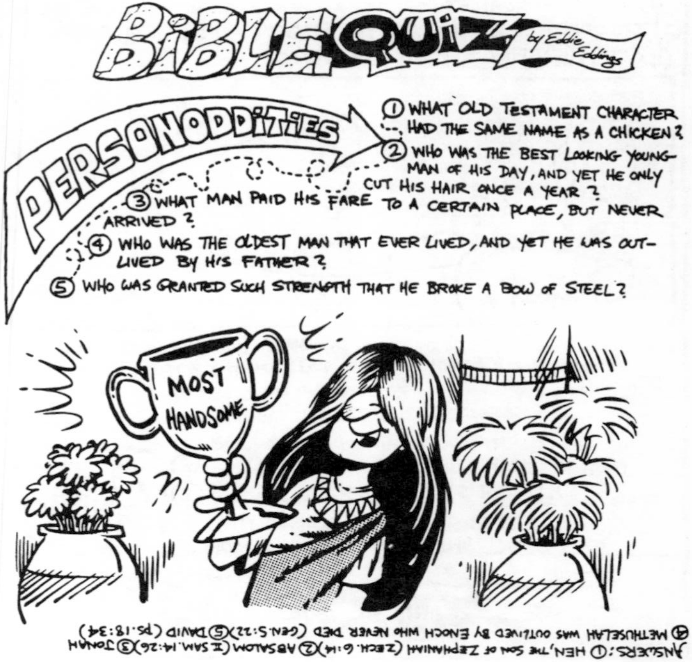
BIBLE QUIZ
by Eddie Eddings
PERSONODDITIES
① WHAT OLD TESTAMENT CHARACTER HAD THE SAME NAME AS A CHICKEN?
② WHO WAS THE BEST LOOKING YOUNG-MAN OF HIS DAY, AND YET HE ONLY CUT HIS HAIR ONCE A YEAR?
③ WHAT MAN PAID HIS FARE TO A CERTAIN PLACE, BUT NEVER ARRIVED?
④ WHO WAS THE OLDEST MAN THAT EVER LIVED, AND YET HE WAS OUT-LIVED BY HIS FATHER?
⑤ WHO WAS GRANTED SUCH STRENGTH THAT HE BROKE A BOW OF STEEL?
MOST HANDSOME
ANSWERS: ① HEN, THE SON OF ZEPHANIAH (ZECH. 6:14) ② ABSALOM (II SAM. 14:26) ③ JONAH
④ METHUSELAH WAS OUTLIVED BY ENOCH WHO NEVER DIED (GEN. 5:22) ⑤ DAVID (PS. 18:34)

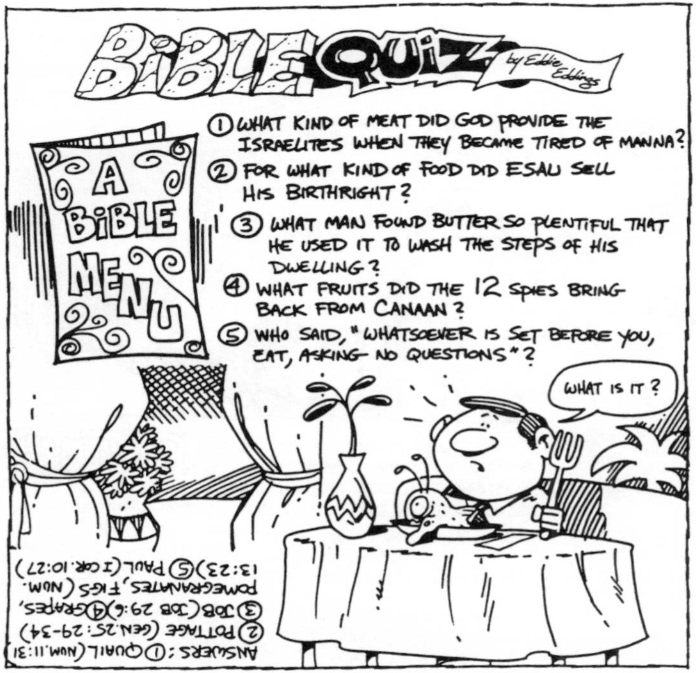
BIBLE QUIZ
by Eddie Eddings
A BIBLE MENU
① WHAT KIND OF MEAT DID GOD PROVIDE THE ISRAELITES WHEN THEY BECAME TIRED OF MANNA?
② FOR WHAT KIND OF FOOD DID ESAU SELL HIS BIRTHRIGHT?
③ WHAT MAN FOUND BUTTER SO PLENTIFUL THAT HE USED IT TO WASH THE STEPS OF HIS DWELLING?
④ WHAT FRUITS DID THE 12 SPIES BRING BACK FROM CANAAN?
⑤ WHO SAID, "WHATSOEVER IS SET BEFORE YOU, EAT, ASKING NO QUESTIONS"?
WHAT IS IT?
ANSWERS: ① QUAIL (NUM. 11:31) ② POTTAGE (GEN. 25:29-34) ③ JOB (JOB 29:6) ④ GRAPES, POMEGRANATES, FIGS (NUM. 13:23) ⑤ PAUL (I COR. 10:27)

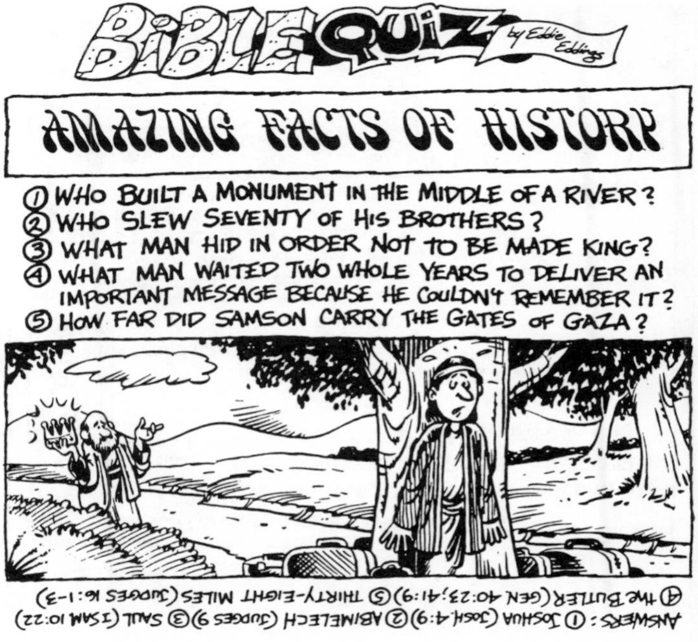
BIBLE QUIZ
by Eddie Eddings
AMAZING FACTS OF HISTORY
① WHO BUILT A MONUMENT IN THE MIDDLE OF A RIVER?
② WHO SLEW SEVENTY OF HIS BROTHERS?
③ WHAT MAN HID IN ORDER NOT TO BE MADE KING?
④ WHAT MAN WAITED TWO WHOLE YEARS TO DELIVER AN IMPORTANT MESSAGE BECAUSE HE COULDN'T REMEMBER IT?
⑤ HOW FAR DID SAMSON CARRY THE GATES OF GAZA?
ANSWERS: ① JOSHUA (JOSH. 4:9) ② ABIMELECH (JUDGES 9) ③ SAUL (I SAM. 10:22) ④ THE BUTLER (GEN. 40:23; 41:9) ⑤ THIRTY-EIGHT MILES (JUDGES 16:1-3)

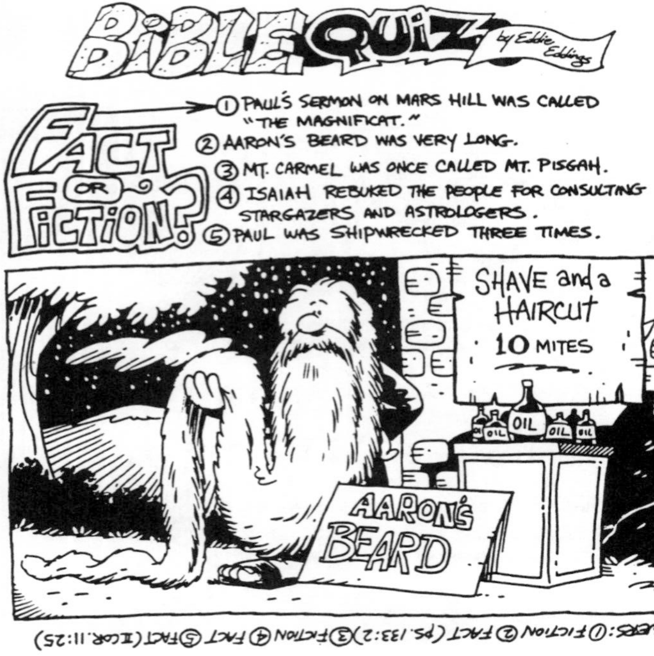
BIBLE QUIZ
by Eddie Eddings
FACT OR FICTION?
① PAUL'S SERMON ON MARS HILL WAS CALLED "THE MAGNIFICAT."
② AARON'S BEARD WAS VERY LONG.
③ MT. CARMEL WAS ONCE CALLED MT. PISGAH.
④ ISAIAH REBUKED THE PEOPLE FOR CONSULTING STARGAZERS AND ASTROLOGERS.
⑤ PAUL WAS SHIPWRECKED THREE TIMES.
SHAVE and a HAIRCUT 10 MITES
OIL
AARON'S BEARD
ANSWERS: ① FICTION ② FACT (PS. 133:2) ③ FICTION ④ FACT ⑤ FACT (II COR. 11:25)

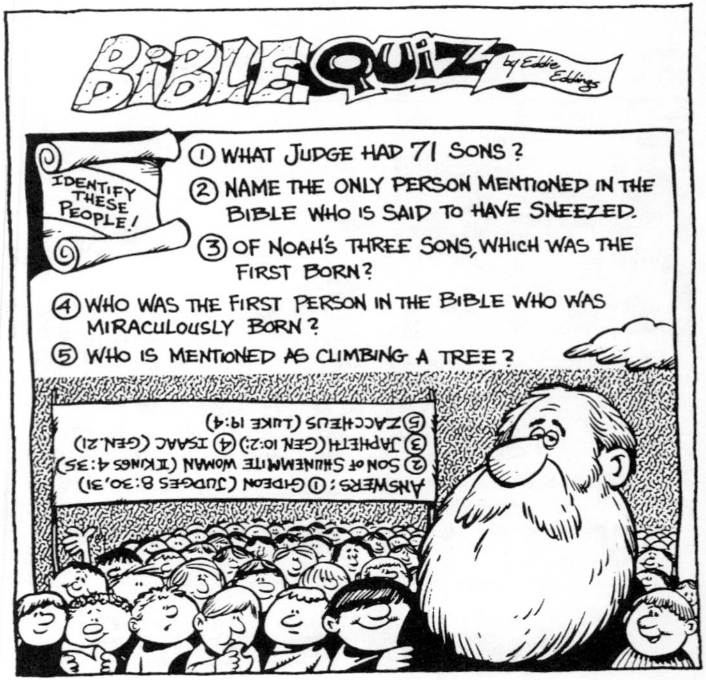
BIBLE QUIZ
by Eddie Eddings
IDENTIFY THESE PEOPLE!
① WHAT JUDGE HAD 71 SONS?
② NAME THE ONLY PERSON MENTIONED IN THE BIBLE WHO IS SAID TO HAVE SNEEZED.
③ OF NOAH'S THREE SONS, WHICH WAS THE FIRST BORN?
④ WHO WAS THE FIRST PERSON IN THE BIBLE WHO WAS MIRACULOUSLY BORN?
⑤ WHO IS MENTIONED AS CLIMBING A TREE?
ANSWERS: ① GIDEON (JUDGES 8:30,31)
② SON of SHUNEMMITE WOMAN (II KINGS 4:35)
③ JAPHETH (GEN. 10:21) ④ ISAAC (GEN. 21)
⑤ ZACCHEUS (LUKE 19:4)

BIBLE QUIZ
by Eddie Eddings

FACT or FICTION

1. SOLOMON WROTE MORE THAN 1000 SONGS.
2. KING OG SLEPT ON AN IRON BED THIRTEEN FEET LONG.
3. JOSHUA and CALEB WERE BROTHERS.
4. THE TOWN of BEERSHEBA WAS NAMED FOR THE QUEEN of SHEBA.
5. SOLOMON'S ISLAND WAS NAMED AFTER KING SOLOMON.

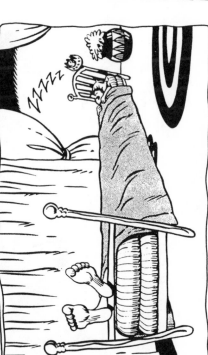

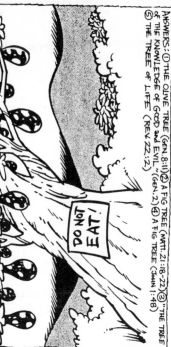

ZZZZZ

ANSWERS: (1) FACT (I KINGS 4:32) (2) FACT (DEUT. 3:11) (3) FICTION (4) FICTION (5) FACT

BIBLE QUIZ
by Eddie Eddings

FAMOUS TREES OF THE BIBLE

1. AFTER NOAH HAD SENT THE DOVE OUT FROM THE ARK THE SECOND TIME, FROM WHAT KIND OF TREE DID SHE BRING A LEAF?
2. WHAT KIND OF TREE, WHEN FOUND TO BE FRUITLESS, WITHERED AT THE COMMAND OF JESUS?
3. THE FRUIT OF WHAT TREE WERE ADAM and EVE FORBIDDEN TO EAT?
4. UNDER WHAT KIND OF TREE DID JESUS FIRST SEE NATHANAEL?
5. WHAT TREE MENTIONED AS BEING IN THE GARDEN of EDEN WILL ALSO GROW IN THE ETERNAL CITY of THE NEW JERUSALEM?

DO NOT EAT!

ANSWERS: (1) THE OLIVE TREE (GEN. 8:11) (2) A FIG TREE (MATT. 21:18-22) (3) "THE TREE of THE KNOWLEDGE of GOOD and EVIL" (GEN. 2) (4) A FIG TREE (JOHN 1:48) (5) THE TREE of LIFE (REV. 22:2)

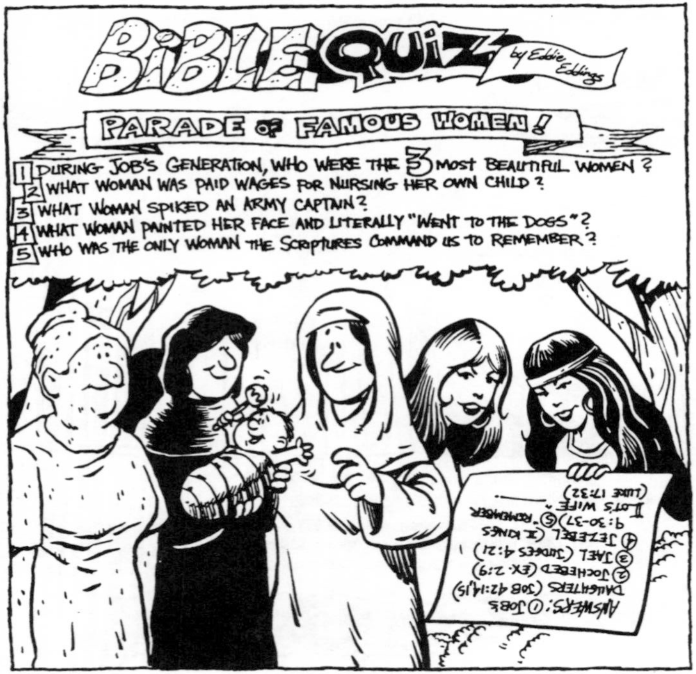
BIBLE QUIZ
by Eddie Eddings
PARADE OF FAMOUS WOMEN!
1 DURING JOB'S GENERATION, WHO WERE THE 3 MOST BEAUTIFUL WOMEN?
2 WHAT WOMAN WAS PAID WAGES FOR NURSING HER OWN CHILD?
3 WHAT WOMAN SPIKED AN ARMY CAPTAIN?
4 WHAT WOMAN PAINTED HER FACE AND LITERALLY "WENT TO THE DOGS"?
5 WHO WAS THE ONLY WOMAN THE SCRIPTURES COMMAND US TO REMEMBER?
ANSWERS: ① JOB'S DAUGHTERS (JOB 42:14,15) ② JOCHEBED (EX. 2:9) ③ JAEL (JUDGES 4:21) ④ JEZEBEL (II KINGS 9:30-37) ⑤ "REMEMBER LOT'S WIFE" (LUKE 17:32)

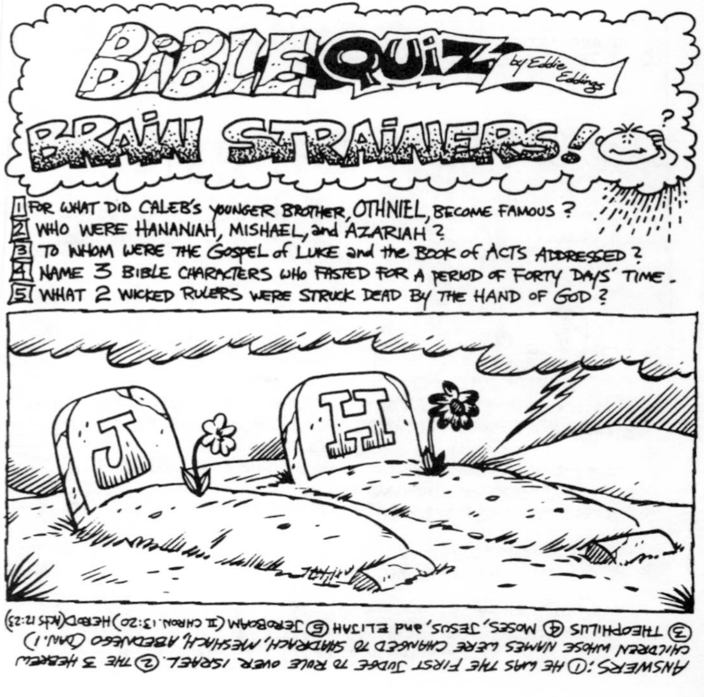
BIBLE QUIZ
by Eddie Eddings
BRAIN STRAINERS!
1 FOR WHAT DID CALEB'S YOUNGER BROTHER, OTHNIEL, BECOME FAMOUS?
2 WHO WERE HANANIAH, MISHAEL, and AZARIAH?
3 TO WHOM WERE THE GOSPEL of LUKE and the BOOK of ACTS ADDRESSED?
4 NAME 3 BIBLE CHARACTERS WHO FASTED FOR A PERIOD OF FORTY DAYS' TIME.
5 WHAT 2 WICKED RULERS WERE STRUCK DEAD BY THE HAND OF GOD?
J
H
ANSWERS: ① HE WAS THE FIRST JUDGE TO RULE OVER ISRAEL. ② THE 3 HEBREW CHILDREN WHOSE NAMES WERE CHANGED TO SHADRACH, MESHACH, ABEDNEGO (DAN. 1) ③ THEOPHILUS ④ MOSES, JESUS, and ELIJAH ⑤ JEROBOAM (II CHRON. 13:20) HEROD (ACTS 12:23)

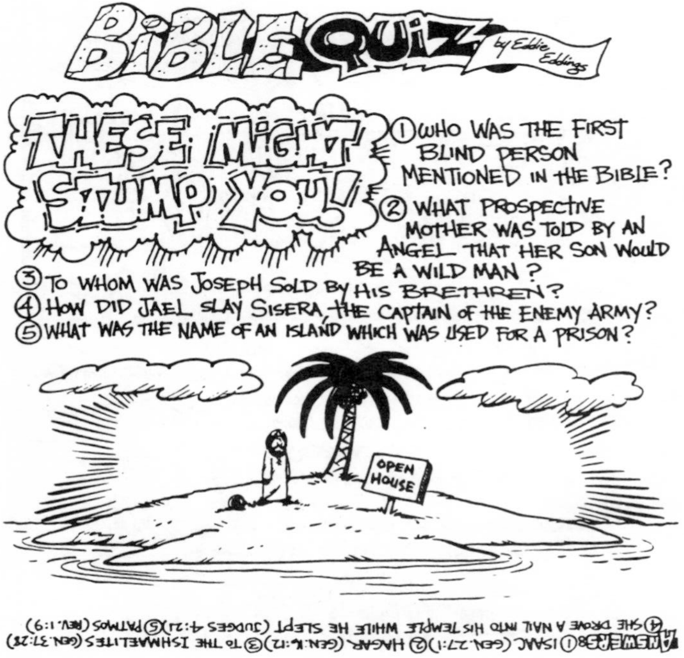
BIBLE QUIZ
by Eddie Eddings
THESE MIGHT STUMP YOU!
(1) WHO WAS THE FIRST BLIND PERSON MENTIONED IN THE BIBLE?
(2) WHAT PROSPECTIVE MOTHER WAS TOLD BY AN ANGEL THAT HER SON WOULD BE A WILD MAN?
(3) TO WHOM WAS JOSEPH SOLD BY HIS BRETHREN?
(4) HOW DID JAEL SLAY SISERA, THE CAPTAIN OF THE ENEMY ARMY?
(5) WHAT WAS THE NAME OF AN ISLAND WHICH WAS USED FOR A PRISON?
OPEN HOUSE
ANSWERS: (1) ISAAC (GEN. 27:1) (2) HAGAR (GEN. 16:12) (3) TO THE ISHMAELITES (GEN. 37:28)
(4) SHE DROVE A NAIL INTO HIS TEMPLE WHILE HE SLEPT (JUDGES 4:21) (5) PATMOS (REV. 1:9)

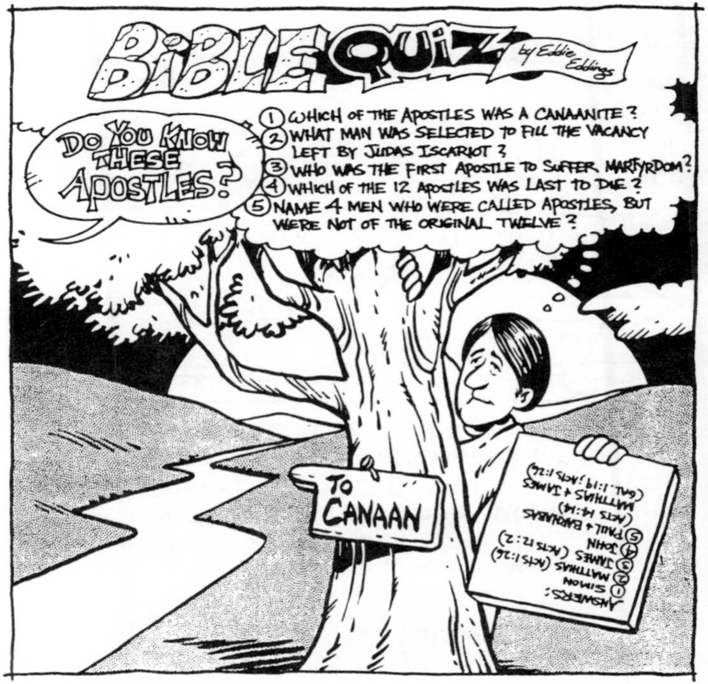
BIBLE QUIZ
by Eddie Eddings
DO YOU KNOW THESE APOSTLES?
(1) WHICH OF THE APOSTLES WAS A CANAANITE?
(2) WHAT MAN WAS SELECTED TO FILL THE VACANCY LEFT BY JUDAS ISCARIOT?
(3) WHO WAS THE FIRST APOSTLE TO SUFFER MARTYRDOM?
(4) WHICH OF THE 12 APOSTLES WAS LAST TO DIE?
(5) NAME 4 MEN WHO WERE CALLED APOSTLES, BUT WERE NOT OF THE ORIGINAL TWELVE?
TO CANAAN
ANSWERS:
(1) SIMON
(2) MATTHIAS (ACTS 1:26)
(3) JAMES (ACTS 12:2)
(4) JOHN
(5) PAUL + BARNABAS (ACTS 14:14) MATTHIAS + JAMES (GAL. 1:19; ACTS 1:26)

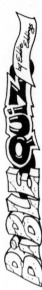

BIBLE QUIZ by Eddie Eddings

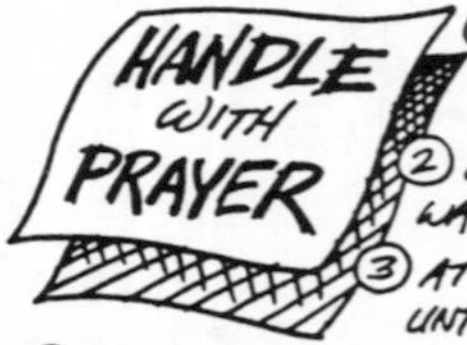
HANDLE
WITH
PRAYER

① TO WHOM DID JESUS TELL HIS DISCIPLES TO ADDRESS THEIR PRAYERS?
② WHAT MAN, AFTER A PERIOD OF INSANITY, WAS RESTORED HIS REASON WHILE PRAYING?
③ AT WHAT THREE TIMES DID DAVID CRY UNTO THE LORD EACH DAY?
④ WHO WERE THE TWO MEN WHO HELD MOSES' ARMS IN PRAYER DURING THE BATTLE WITH THE AMALEKITES?
⑤ WHAT IS THE ONE THING PAUL SAYS WE SHOULD DO "WITHOUT CEASING"?

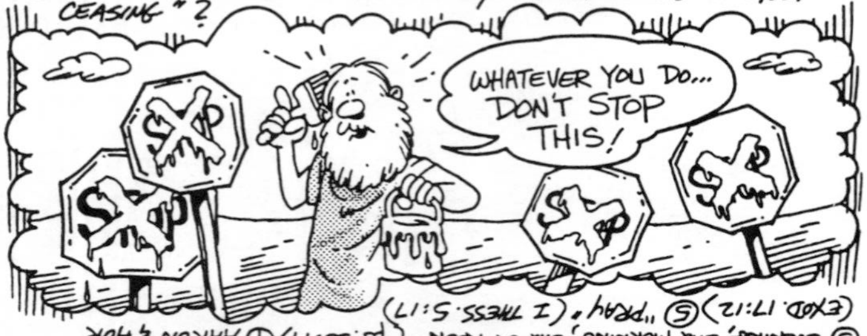
WHATEVER YOU DO... DON'T STOP THIS!

ANSWERS: ① "OUR FATHER" (MATT. 6:9) ② KING NEBUCHADNEZZAR (DAN. 4) ③ "EVENING, and MORNING, and at NOON" (PS. 55:17) ④ AARON & HUR (EXOD. 17:12) ⑤ "PRAY" (I THESS. 5:17)

BIBLE QUIZ by Eddie Eddings

① WHAT WAS THE FIRST QUESTION PHARAOH ASKED JACOB WHEN HE MET HIM IN EGYPT?
② WHO WAS THE FIRST MAN WHO DID NOT HAVE TO DIE?
③ WHO OFFICIATED AT MOSES' FUNERAL?
④ WHAT IS THE LARGEST CITY MENTIONED IN THE BIBLE?
⑤ NAME THREE NOTED ANGELS MENTIONED IN THE BIBLE.

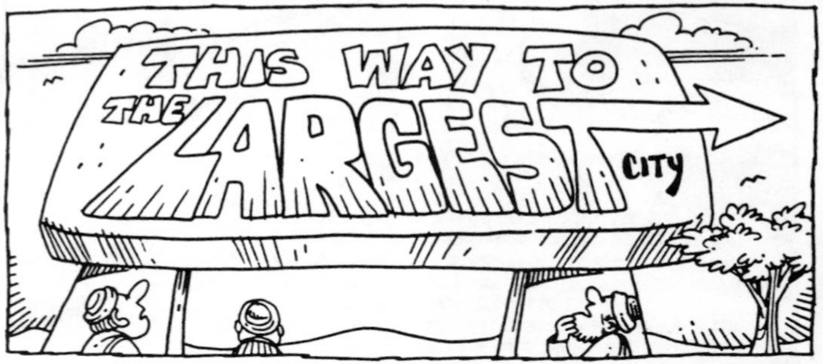
THIS WAY TO THE LARGEST CITY

ANSWERS: ① "HOW OLD ARE YOU?" (GEN. 47:8) ② ENOCH (GEN. 5:24) ③ GOD (DEUT. 34) ④ THE NEW JERUSALEM (ABOUT 1,400 MILES IN EVERY DIRECTION) — (REVELATION 21) ⑤ GABRIEL, MICHAEL, LUCIFER

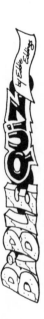

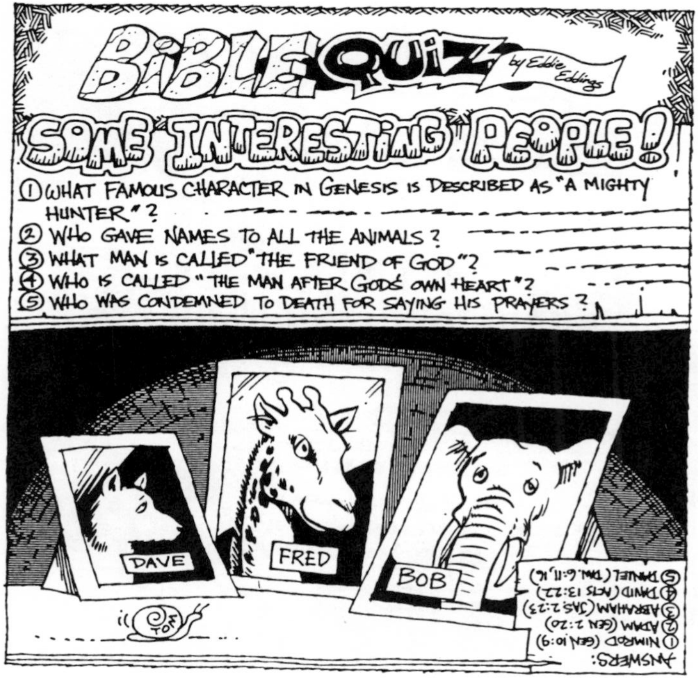
BIBLE QUIZ
by Eddie Eddings
SOME INTERESTING PEOPLE!
① WHAT FAMOUS CHARACTER IN GENESIS IS DESCRIBED AS "A MIGHTY HUNTER"?
② WHO GAVE NAMES TO ALL THE ANIMALS?
③ WHAT MAN IS CALLED "THE FRIEND OF GOD"?
④ WHO IS CALLED "THE MAN AFTER GOD'S OWN HEART"?
⑤ WHO WAS CONDEMNED TO DEATH FOR SAYING HIS PRAYERS?
DAVE
FRED
BOB
TOF
ANSWERS:
① NIMROD (GEN.10:9)
② ADAM (GEN 2:20)
③ ABRAHAM (JAS.2:23)
④ DAVID (ACTS 13:22)
⑤ DANIEL (DAN.6:11,16)

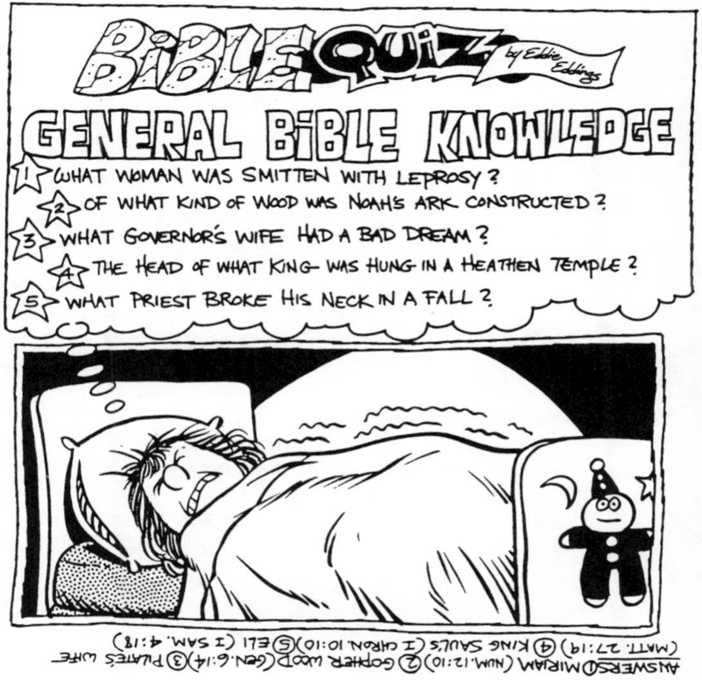
BIBLE QUIZ
by Eddie Eddings
GENERAL BIBLE KNOWLEDGE
1 WHAT WOMAN WAS SMITTEN WITH LEPROSY?
2 OF WHAT KIND OF WOOD WAS NOAH'S ARK CONSTRUCTED?
3 WHAT GOVERNOR'S WIFE HAD A BAD DREAM?
4 THE HEAD OF WHAT KING WAS HUNG IN A HEATHEN TEMPLE?
5 WHAT PRIEST BROKE HIS NECK IN A FALL?
ANSWERS ① MIRIAM (NUM.12:10) ② GOPHER WOOD (GEN.6:14) ③ PILATE'S WIFE (MATT. 27:19) ④ KING SAUL'S (I CHRON.10:10) ⑤ ELI (I SAM. 4:18)

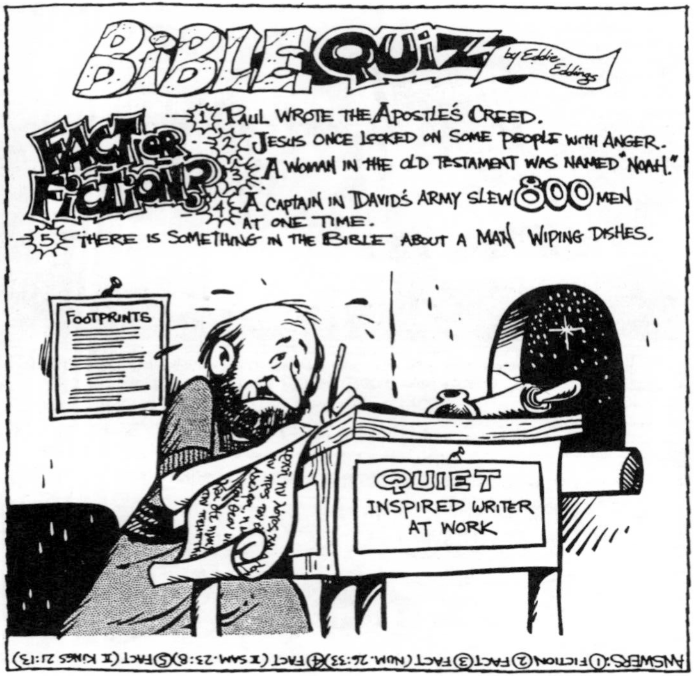
BIBLE QUIZ
by Eddie Eddings
FACT OR FICTION?
1 PAUL WROTE THE APOSTLE'S CREED.
2 JESUS ONCE LOOKED ON SOME PEOPLE WITH ANGER.
3 A WOMAN IN THE OLD TESTAMENT WAS NAMED "NOAH."
4 A CAPTAIN IN DAVID'S ARMY SLEW 800 MEN AT ONE TIME.
5 THERE IS SOMETHING IN THE BIBLE ABOUT A MAN WIPING DISHES.
FOOTPRINTS
QUIET
INSPIRED WRITER AT WORK
ANSWERS: 1 FICTION 2 FACT 3 FACT (NUM. 26:33) 4 FACT (II SAM. 23:8) 5 FACT (II KINGS 21:13)

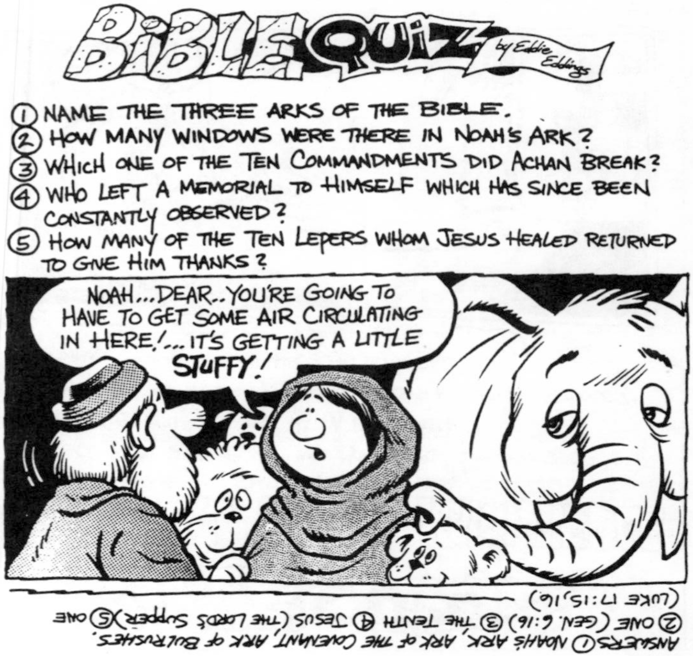
BIBLE QUIZ
by Eddie Eddings
1 NAME THE THREE ARKS OF THE BIBLE.
2 HOW MANY WINDOWS WERE THERE IN NOAH'S ARK?
3 WHICH ONE OF THE TEN COMMANDMENTS DID ACHAN BREAK?
4 WHO LEFT A MEMORIAL TO HIMSELF WHICH HAS SINCE BEEN CONSTANTLY OBSERVED?
5 HOW MANY OF THE TEN LEPERS WHOM JESUS HEALED RETURNED TO GIVE HIM THANKS?
NOAH...DEAR..YOU'RE GOING TO HAVE TO GET SOME AIR CIRCULATING IN HERE!...IT'S GETTING A LITTLE STUFFY!
ANSWERS 1 NOAH'S ARK, ARK OF THE COVENANT, ARK OF BULRUSHES. 2 ONE (GEN. 6:16) 3 THE TENTH 4 JESUS (THE LORD'S SUPPER) 5 ONE (LUKE 17:15,16)

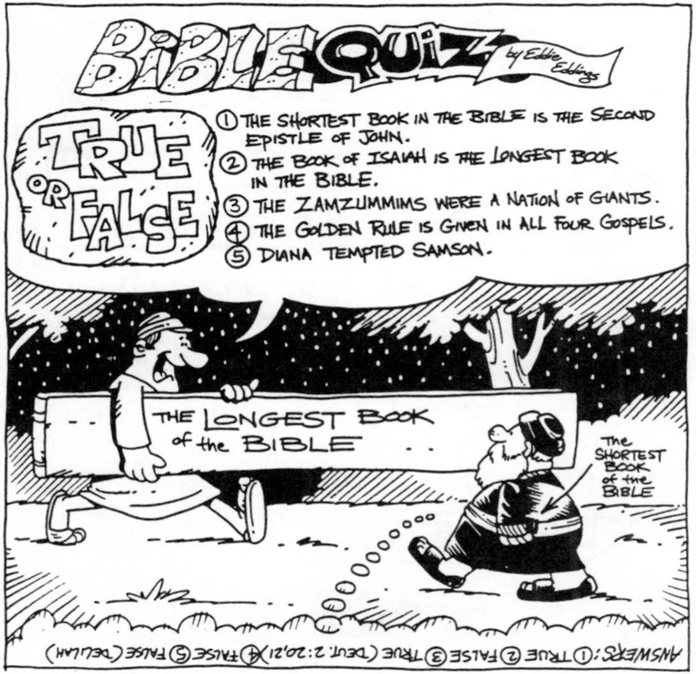
BIBLE QUIZ
by Eddie Eddings
TRUE OR FALSE
① THE SHORTEST BOOK IN THE BIBLE IS THE SECOND EPISTLE OF JOHN.
② THE BOOK OF ISAIAH IS THE LONGEST BOOK IN THE BIBLE.
③ THE ZAMZUMMIMS WERE A NATION OF GIANTS.
④ THE GOLDEN RULE IS GIVEN IN ALL FOUR GOSPELS.
⑤ DIANA TEMPTED SAMSON.
THE LONGEST BOOK of the BIBLE
The SHORTEST BOOK of the BIBLE
ANSWERS: ① TRUE ② FALSE ③ TRUE (DEUT. 2:20,21) ④ FALSE ⑤ FALSE (DELILAH)

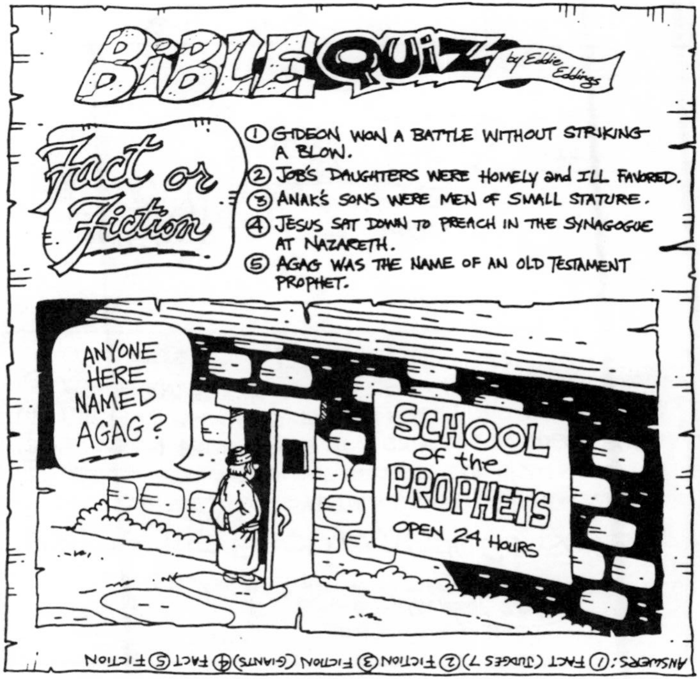
BIBLE QUIZ
by Eddie Eddings
Fact or Fiction
① GIDEON WON A BATTLE WITHOUT STRIKING A BLOW.
② JOB'S DAUGHTERS WERE HOMELY and ILL FAVORED.
③ ANAK'S SONS WERE MEN OF SMALL STATURE.
④ JESUS SAT DOWN TO PREACH IN THE SYNAGOGUE AT NAZARETH.
⑤ AGAG WAS THE NAME OF AN OLD TESTAMENT PROPHET.
ANYONE HERE NAMED AGAG?
SCHOOL of the PROPHETS
OPEN 24 HOURS
ANSWERS: ① FACT (JUDGES 7) ② FICTION ③ FICTION (GIANTS) ④ FACT ⑤ FICTION

BIBLE QUIZ by Eddie Eddings

HOUSE

① ________ RECEIVED JESUS INTO HER HOUSE (LUKE 10:38).

② ________, THE MOTHER OF JOHN, HELD A PRAYER MEETING IN HER HOUSE (ACTS 12:12).

③ ________ AND ________ HAD A CHURCH IN THEIR HOUSE (ROMANS 16:3-5).

④ ________ HAD A HOUSE NEXT DOOR TO A SYNAGOGUE (ACTS 18:7).

⑤ ________ BUILT A HOUSE OVERLAID WITH GOLD (I KINGS 6:21-22).

HONEY, DO YOU THINK WE COULD OVERLAY OUR HOUSE WITH GOLD TOMORROW? ...PLEASE...

① MARTHA ② MARY ③ PRISCILLA and AQUILLA ④ JUSTUS ⑤ SOLOMON

BIBLE QUIZ by Eddie Eddings

MATCH THE FOOD WITH THE CONSUMER

① DAVID GAVE AN EGYPTIAN (I SAM. 30:11-12)

② JESUS ATE AFTER HE AROSE (LUKE 24:42)

③ SAMSON FOUND THIS IN A CARCASE (JUDGES 14:8)

④ GIDEON BROUGHT TO AN ANGEL (JUDGES 6:19-20)

⑤ ABRAHAM BROUGHT TO HEAVENLY VISITORS (GENESIS 18:8)

E
RAISINS
A
BUTTER
B
HONEY
C
BROTH
D

① - A ② - E ③ - C ④ - D ⑤ - B

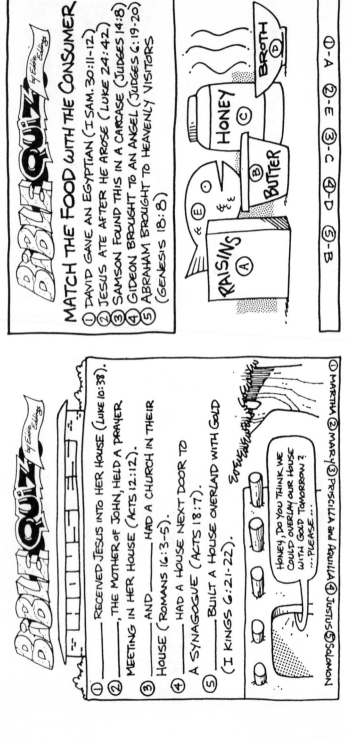

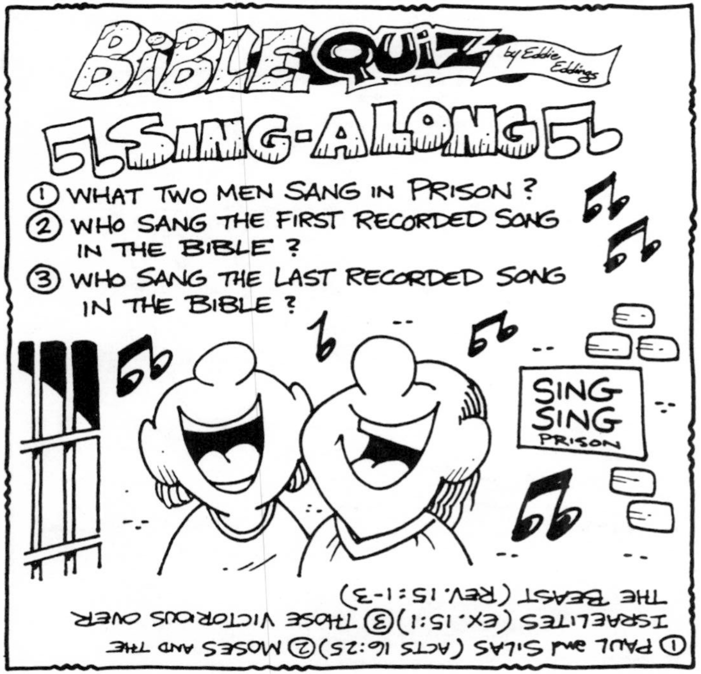
BIBLE QUIZ by Eddie Eddings
SING-ALONG
① WHAT TWO MEN SANG IN PRISON ?
② WHO SANG THE FIRST RECORDED SONG IN THE BIBLE ?
③ WHO SANG THE LAST RECORDED SONG IN THE BIBLE ?
SING SING PRISON
① PAUL and SILAS (ACTS 16:25) ② MOSES AND THE ISRAELITES (EX. 15:1) ③ THOSE VICTORIOUS OVER THE BEAST (REV. 15:1-3)

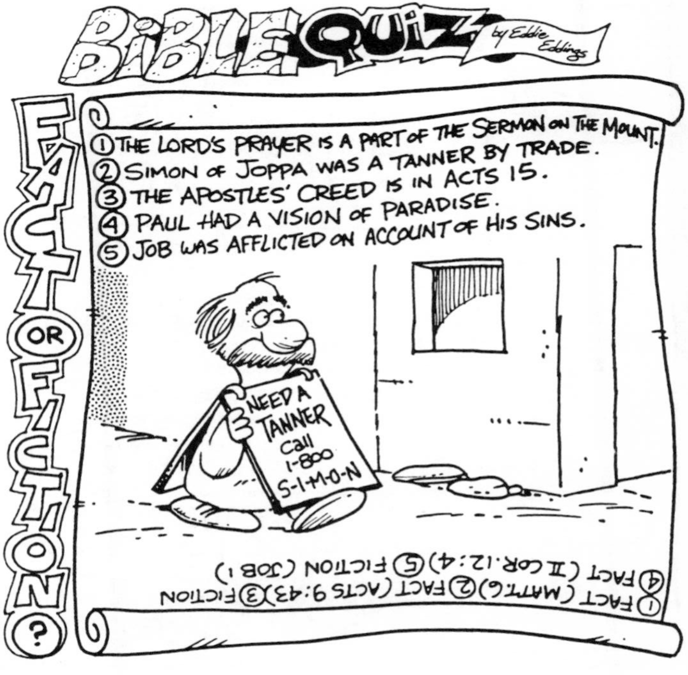
BIBLE QUIZ by Eddie Eddings
FACT OR FICTION ?
① THE LORD'S PRAYER IS A PART OF THE SERMON ON THE MOUNT.
② SIMON OF JOPPA WAS A TANNER BY TRADE.
③ THE APOSTLES' CREED IS IN ACTS 15.
④ PAUL HAD A VISION OF PARADISE.
⑤ JOB WAS AFFLICTED ON ACCOUNT OF HIS SINS.
NEED A TANNER Call 1-800 S-I-M-O-N
① FACT (MATT. 6) ② FACT (ACTS 9:43) ③ FICTION ④ FACT (II COR. 12:4) ⑤ FICTION (JOB 1)

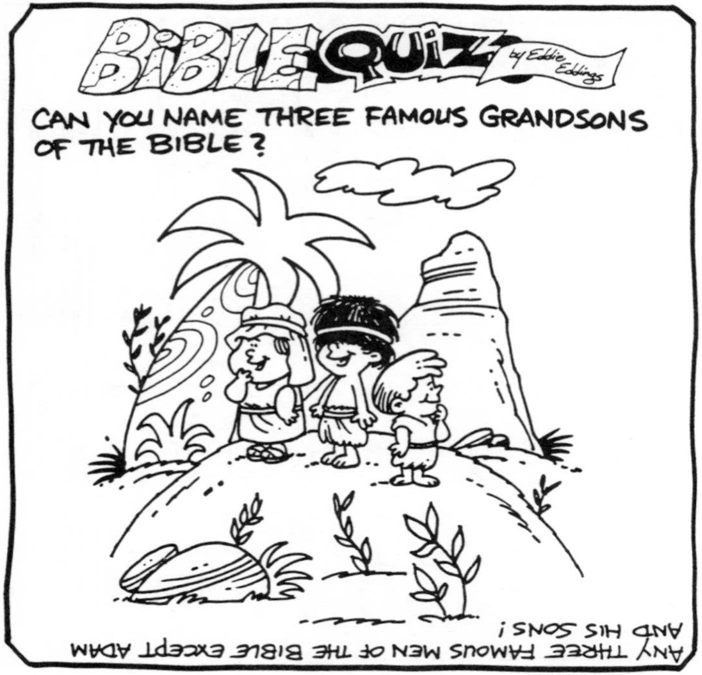
BIBLE QUIZ
by Eddie Eddings
CAN YOU NAME THREE FAMOUS GRANDSONS OF THE BIBLE?
ANY THREE FAMOUS MEN OF THE BIBLE EXCEPT ADAM AND HIS SONS!

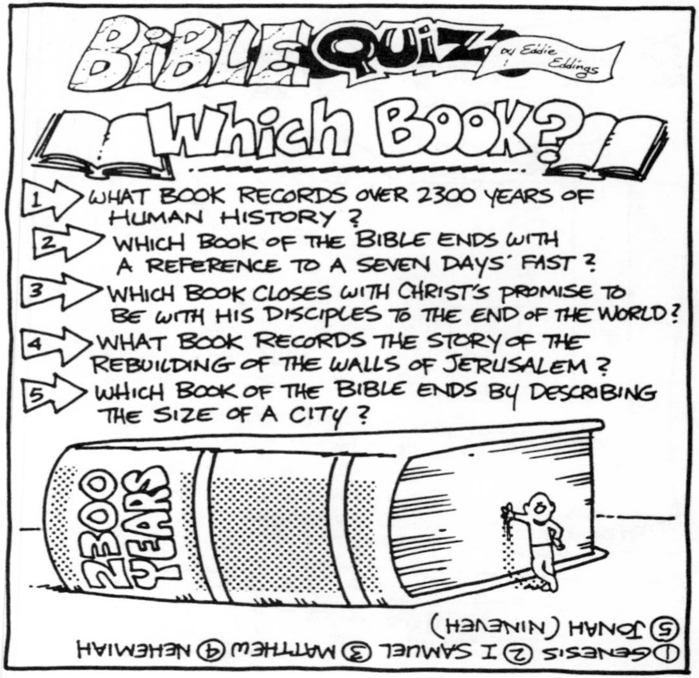
BIBLE QUIZ
by Eddie Eddings
Which Book?
1 WHAT BOOK RECORDS OVER 2300 YEARS OF HUMAN HISTORY?
2 WHICH BOOK OF THE BIBLE ENDS WITH A REFERENCE TO A SEVEN DAYS' FAST?
3 WHICH BOOK CLOSES WITH CHRIST'S PROMISE TO BE WITH HIS DISCIPLES TO THE END OF THE WORLD?
4 WHAT BOOK RECORDS THE STORY OF THE REBUILDING OF THE WALLS OF JERUSALEM?
5 WHICH BOOK OF THE BIBLE ENDS BY DESCRIBING THE SIZE OF A CITY?
2300 YEARS
① GENESIS ② I SAMUEL ③ MATTHEW ④ NEHEMIAH ⑤ JONAH (NINEVEH)

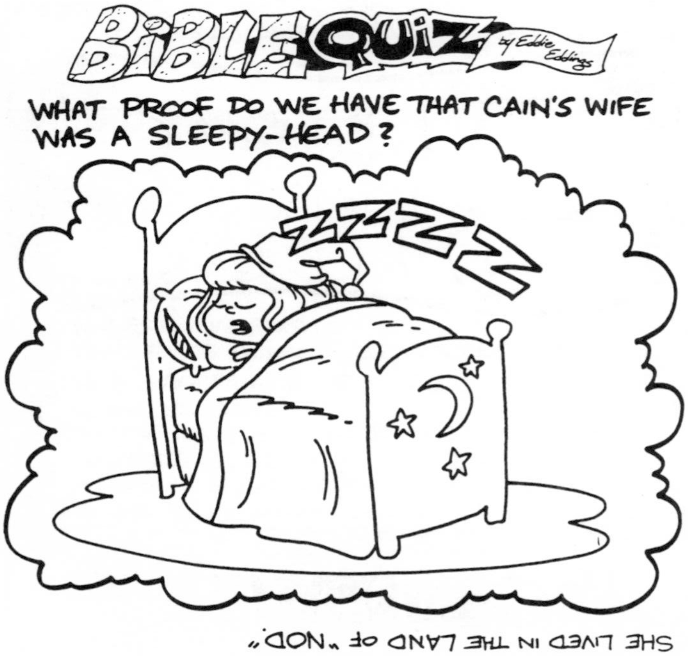
BIBLE QUIZ by Eddie Eddings
WHAT PROOF DO WE HAVE THAT CAIN'S WIFE WAS A SLEEPY-HEAD?
ZZZZZ
SHE LIVED IN THE LAND OF "NOD."

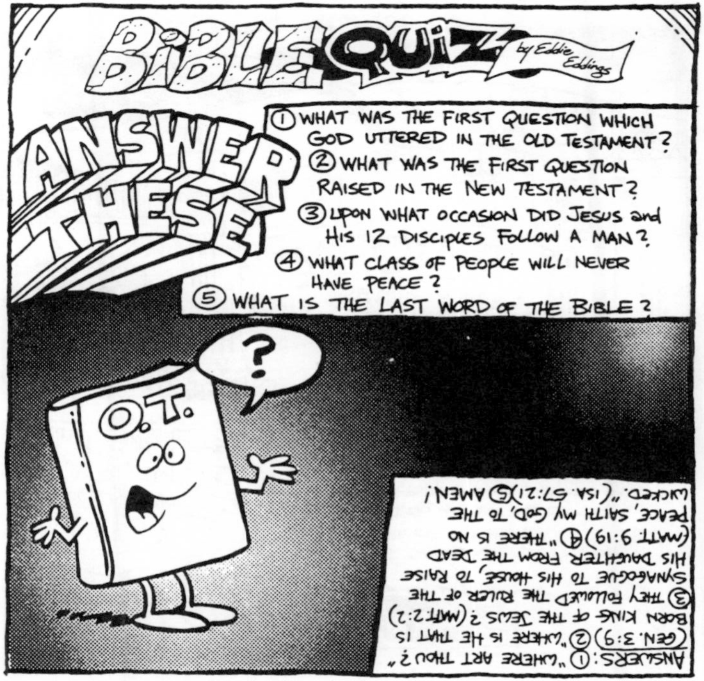
BIBLE QUIZ by Eddie Eddings
ANSWER THESE
① WHAT WAS THE FIRST QUESTION WHICH GOD UTTERED IN THE OLD TESTAMENT?
② WHAT WAS THE FIRST QUESTION RAISED IN THE NEW TESTAMENT?
③ UPON WHAT OCCASION DID JESUS and HIS 12 DISCIPLES FOLLOW A MAN?
④ WHAT CLASS OF PEOPLE WILL NEVER HAVE PEACE?
⑤ WHAT IS THE LAST WORD OF THE BIBLE?
?
O.T.
ANSWERS: ① "WHERE ART THOU?" (GEN. 3:9) ② "WHERE IS HE THAT IS BORN KING OF THE JEWS?" (MATT. 2:2) ③ THEY FOLLOWED THE RULER OF THE SYNAGOGUE TO HIS HOUSE, TO RAISE HIS DAUGHTER FROM THE DEAD (MATT. 9:19) ④ "THERE IS NO PEACE, SAITH MY GOD, TO THE WICKED." (ISA. 57:21) ⑤ AMEN!

BIBLE QUIZ
by Eddie Eddings

1. WHAT MAN'S BIOGRAPHY IS GIVEN IN ONE VERSE OF THE OLD TESTAMENT?
2. WHO WAS THE FIRST GREAT CIRCUIT-RIDING PREACHER MENTIONED IN THE BIBLE?
3. WHO WAS THE LAST OF THE JUDGES AND THE FIRST OF THE PROPHETS?
4. WHAT MAN NAMED HIS WIFE?
5. WHAT BIBLE FATHER WAS SPEECHLESS WHEN HIS SON WAS BORN?

① ENOCH (GEN. 5:24) ② SAMUEL (I SAM. 7:16) ③ SAMUEL ④ ADAM (GEN. 3:20) ⑤ ZACHARIAS (LUKE 1:20)

BIBLE QUIZ
by Eddie Eddings

TRUE OR FALSE?

① JACOB DREAMED THAT HE WALKED UP and DOWN A LADDER THAT REACHED TO HEAVEN.
② THE BOOK OF TITUS HAS BUT ONE CHAPTER.
③ A GREAT MANY PEOPLE WERE CONVERTED AT ATHENS WHEN PAUL PREACHED THERE.
④ DAVID WAS THE FIRST KING OF ISRAEL
⑤ THE PEOPLE OF NAZARETH WERE CALLED NAZARITES.

COME TO THE GREATER ATHENS CRUSADE
HEAR PAUL PREACH
COME ONE COME ALL!

ANSWERS: ALL ARE FALSE!

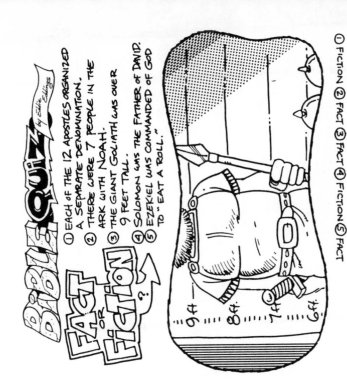

BIBLE QUIZ by Eddie Eddings

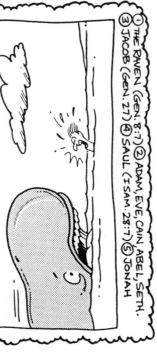

1. WHICH ONE OF THE TWO BIRDS — RAVEN and DOVE — DID NOT RETURN TO THE ARK WHEN NOAH SENT THEM FORTH?
2. WHO WERE THE FIVE PERSONS MENTIONED IN THE BIBLE WHO NEVER HAD A GRANDFATHER?
3. WHAT MAN ONCE CHEATED HIS BLIND FATHER?
4. WHAT KING WENT TO A WITCH FOR ADVICE?
5. WHAT MAN WAS LITERALLY DOWN IN THE MOUTH, BUT STILL, HE CAME OUT ALL RIGHT?

(1) THE RAVEN (GEN. 8:7) (2) ADAM, EVE, CAIN, ABEL, SETH. (3) JACOB (GEN. 27) (4) SAUL (I SAM. 28:7) (5) JONAH

BIBLE QUIZ by Eddie Eddings

FACT OR FICTION?

1. EACH OF THE 12 APOSTLES ORGANIZED A SEPARATE DENOMINATION.
2. THERE WERE 7 PEOPLE IN THE ARK WITH NOAH.
3. THE GIANT GOLIATH WAS OVER 9 FEET TALL.
4. SOLOMON WAS THE FATHER OF DAVID.
5. EZEKIEL WAS COMMANDED OF GOD TO "EAT A ROLL."

9 ft
8 ft.
7 ft
6 ft.

(1) FICTION (2) FACT (3) FACT (4) FICTION (5) FACT

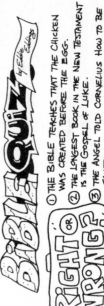

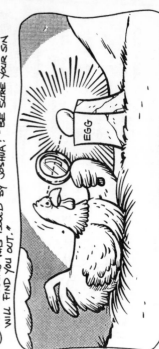

BIBLE QUIZ by Eddie Eddings

AMAZING HISTORICAL FACTS

1. WHAT MAN WAS DRAGGED OUT OF DANGER BY ANGELS?
2. WHAT MAN WENT TO HEAVEN IN A WHIRLWIND?
3. WHAT IS THE FIRST REFERENCE TO RAIN IN THE BIBLE?
4. WHAT RULER ISSUED A DECREE THAT ALL THE WORLD SHOULD BE TAXED?
5. WHAT PREACHER TURNED DOWN A GIFT OF TEN SUITS OF CLOTHES, AND MORE MONEY THAN HE COULD CARRY AWAY?

ANSWERS: ① LOT (GEN. 19:16) ② ELIJAH (II KINGS 2:11) ③ THE GREAT FLOOD (GEN. 7) ④ AUGUSTUS CAESAR (LUKE 2) ⑤ ELISHA (II KINGS 5:5,16)

BIBLE QUIZ by Eddie Eddings

RIGHT OR WRONG?

1. THE BIBLE TEACHES THAT THE CHICKEN WAS CREATED BEFORE THE EGG.
2. THE LONGEST BOOK IN THE NEW TESTAMENT IS THE GOSPEL OF LUKE.
3. THE ANGEL TOLD CORNELIUS HOW TO BE SAVED.
4. THERE IS NO REFERENCE IN THE BIBLE TO BUTTER.
5. THIS WARNING WAS ISSUED BY JOSHUA: "BE SURE YOUR SIN WILL FIND YOU OUT."

EGG

ANSWERS: ① RIGHT (GEN. 1:20,22) ② RIGHT ③ WRONG (ACTS 10) ④ WRONG (GEN. 18:8) ⑤ WRONG (MOSES—NUMBERS 32:23)

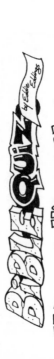

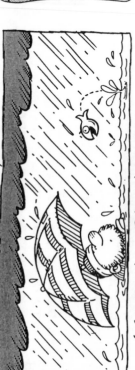

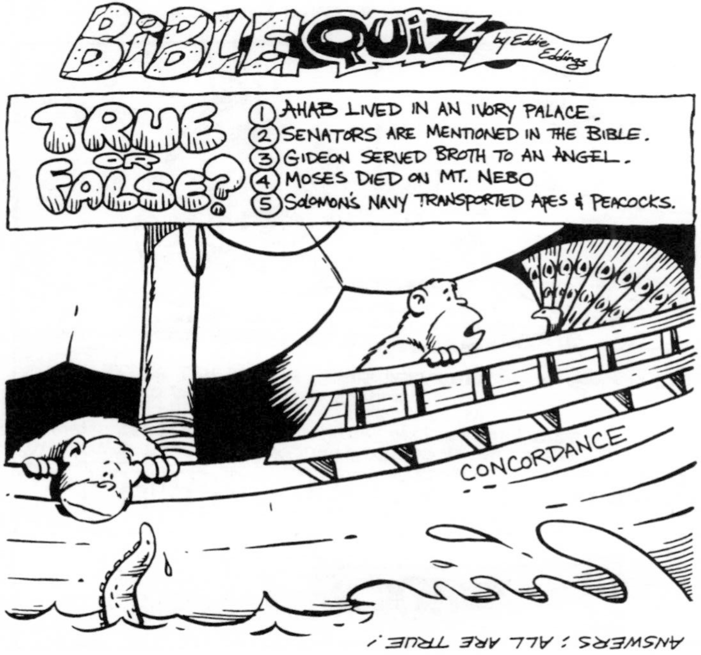
BIBLE QUIZ
by Eddie Eddings
TRUE OR FALSE?
① AHAB LIVED IN AN IVORY PALACE.
② SENATORS ARE MENTIONED IN THE BIBLE.
③ GIDEON SERVED BROTH TO AN ANGEL.
④ MOSES DIED ON MT. NEBO
⑤ SOLOMON'S NAVY TRANSPORTED APES & PEACOCKS.
CONCORDANCE
ANSWERS: ALL ARE TRUE!

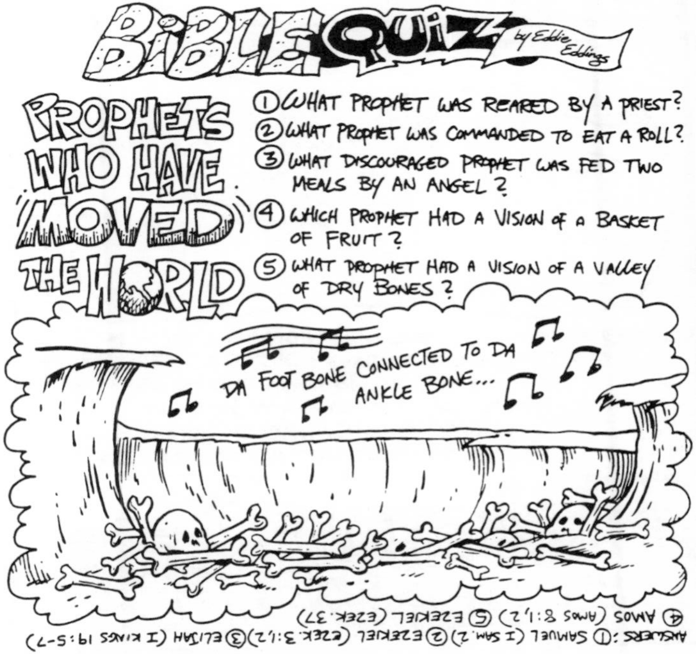
BIBLE QUIZ
by Eddie Eddings
PROPHETS WHO HAVE MOVED THE WORLD
① WHAT PROPHET WAS REARED BY A PRIEST?
② WHAT PROPHET WAS COMMANDED TO EAT A ROLL?
③ WHAT DISCOURAGED PROPHET WAS FED TWO MEALS BY AN ANGEL?
④ WHICH PROPHET HAD A VISION OF A BASKET OF FRUIT?
⑤ WHAT PROPHET HAD A VISION OF A VALLEY OF DRY BONES?
DA FOOT BONE CONNECTED TO DA ANKLE BONE...
ANSWERS: ① SAMUEL (I SAM. 2) ② EZEKIEL (EZEK. 3:1,2) ③ ELIJAH (I KINGS 19:5-7) ④ AMOS (AMOS 8:1,2) ⑤ EZEKIEL (EZEK. 37)

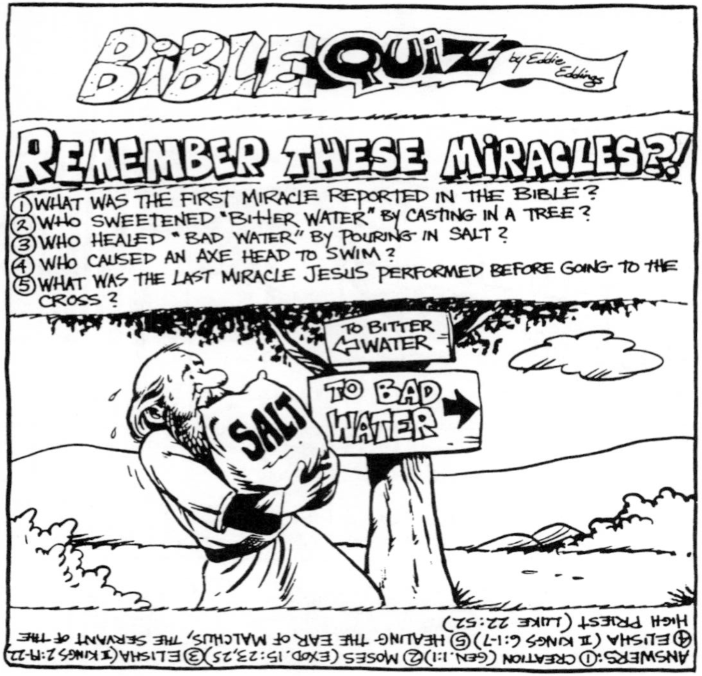
BIBLE QUIZ
by Eddie Eddings
REMEMBER THESE MIRACLES?!
① WHAT WAS THE FIRST MIRACLE REPORTED IN THE BIBLE?
② WHO SWEETENED "BITTER WATER" BY CASTING IN A TREE?
③ WHO HEALED "BAD WATER" BY POURING IN SALT?
④ WHO CAUSED AN AXE HEAD TO SWIM?
⑤ WHAT WAS THE LAST MIRACLE JESUS PERFORMED BEFORE GOING TO THE CROSS?
TO BITTER WATER
TO BAD WATER
SALT
ANSWERS: ① CREATION (GEN. 1:1) ② MOSES (EXOD. 15:23,25) ③ ELISHA (II KINGS 2:19-22) ④ ELISHA (II KINGS 6:1-7) ⑤ HEALING THE EAR OF MALCHUS, THE SERVANT OF THE HIGH PRIEST (LUKE 22:52)

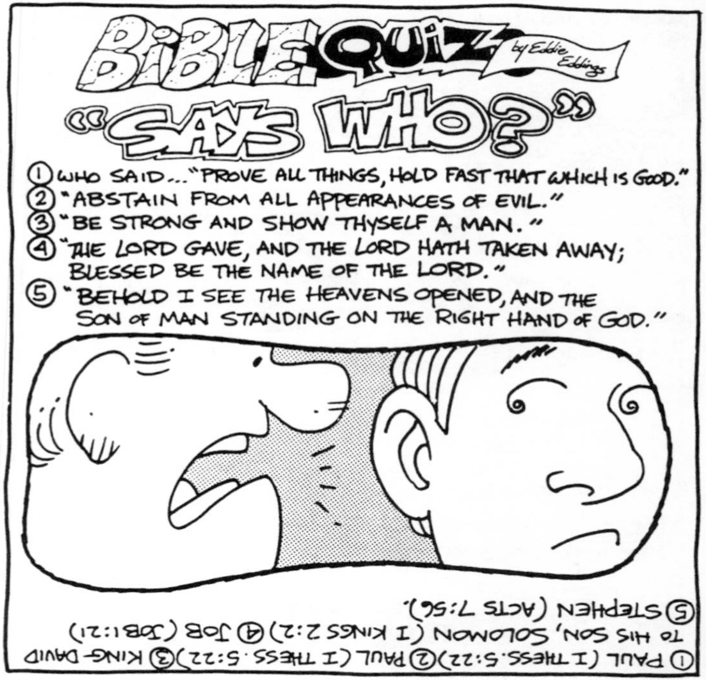
BIBLE QUIZ
by Eddie Eddings
"SAYS WHO?"
① WHO SAID... "PROVE ALL THINGS, HOLD FAST THAT WHICH IS GOOD."
② "ABSTAIN FROM ALL APPEARANCES OF EVIL."
③ "BE STRONG AND SHOW THYSELF A MAN."
④ "THE LORD GAVE, AND THE LORD HATH TAKEN AWAY; BLESSED BE THE NAME OF THE LORD."
⑤ "BEHOLD I SEE THE HEAVENS OPENED, AND THE SON OF MAN STANDING ON THE RIGHT HAND OF GOD."
① PAUL (I THESS. 5:22) ② PAUL (I THESS. 5:22) ③ KING DAVID TO HIS SON, SOLOMON (I KINGS 2:2) ④ JOB (JOB 1:21) ⑤ STEPHEN (ACTS 7:56).

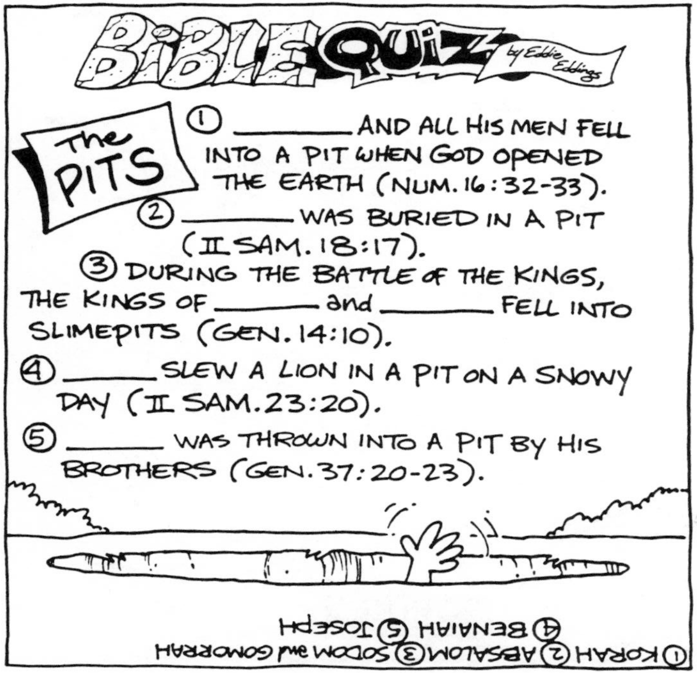
BIBLE QUIZ
by Eddie Eddings
The PITS
① _____ AND ALL HIS MEN FELL INTO A PIT WHEN GOD OPENED THE EARTH (NUM. 16:32-33).
② _____ WAS BURIED IN A PIT (II SAM. 18:17).
③ DURING THE BATTLE OF THE KINGS, THE KINGS OF _____ and _____ FELL INTO SLIMEPITS (GEN. 14:10).
④ _____ SLEW A LION IN A PIT ON A SNOWY DAY (II SAM. 23:20).
⑤ _____ WAS THROWN INTO A PIT BY HIS BROTHERS (GEN. 37:20-23).
① KORAH ② ABSALOM ③ SODOM and GOMORRAH ④ BENAIAH ⑤ JOSEPH

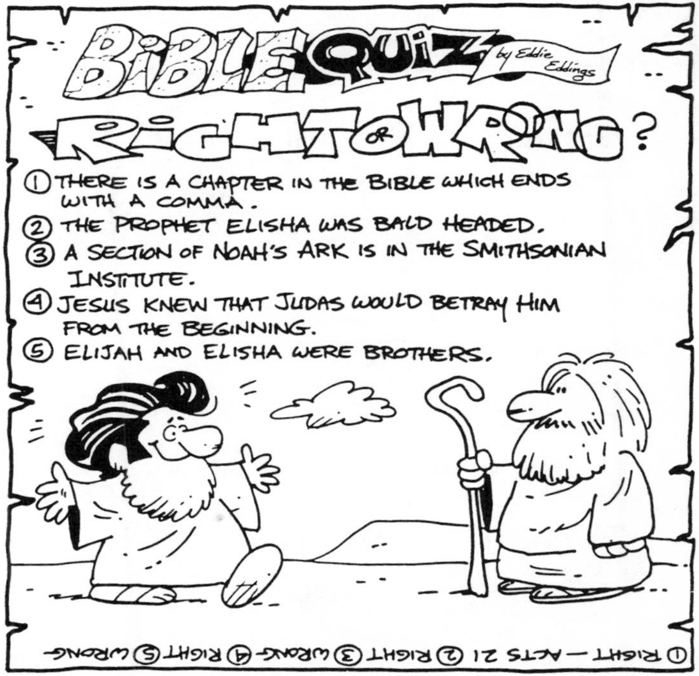
BIBLE QUIZ
by Eddie Eddings
RIGHT OR WRONG?
① THERE IS A CHAPTER IN THE BIBLE WHICH ENDS WITH A COMMA.
② THE PROPHET ELISHA WAS BALD HEADED.
③ A SECTION OF NOAH'S ARK IS IN THE SMITHSONIAN INSTITUTE.
④ JESUS KNEW THAT JUDAS WOULD BETRAY HIM FROM THE BEGINNING.
⑤ ELIJAH AND ELISHA WERE BROTHERS.
① RIGHT — ACTS 21 ② RIGHT ③ WRONG ④ RIGHT ⑤ WRONG

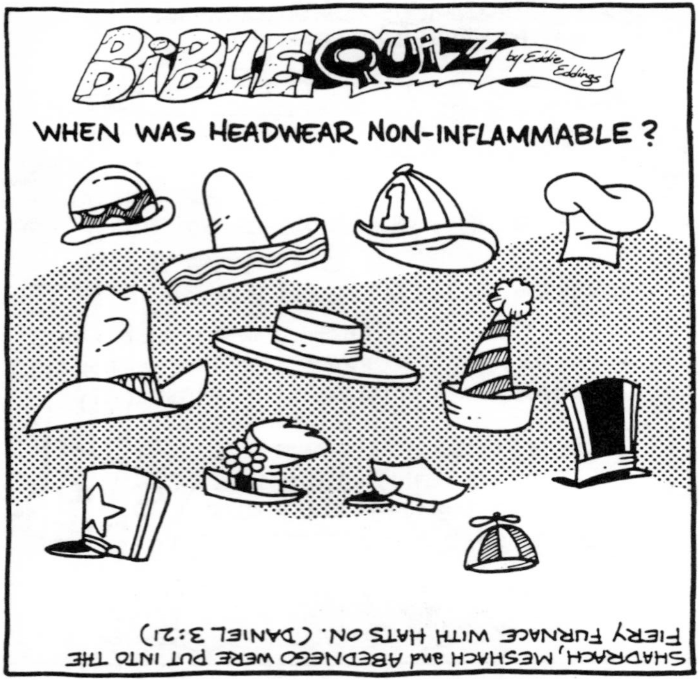
BIBLE QUIZ
by Eddie Eddings
WHEN WAS HEADWEAR NON-INFLAMMABLE?
1
SHADRACH, MESHACH and ABEDNEGO WERE PUT INTO THE FIERY FURNACE WITH HATS ON. (DANIEL 3:21)

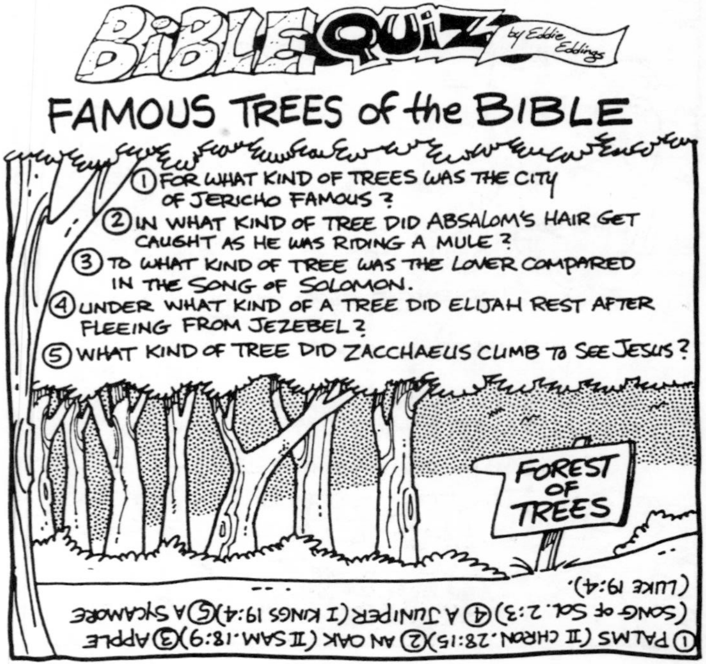
BIBLE QUIZ
by Eddie Eddings
FAMOUS TREES of the BIBLE
① FOR WHAT KIND OF TREES WAS THE CITY OF JERICHO FAMOUS?
② IN WHAT KIND OF TREE DID ABSALOM'S HAIR GET CAUGHT AS HE WAS RIDING A MULE?
③ TO WHAT KIND OF TREE WAS THE LOVER COMPARED IN THE SONG OF SOLOMON.
④ UNDER WHAT KIND OF A TREE DID ELIJAH REST AFTER FLEEING FROM JEZEBEL?
⑤ WHAT KIND OF TREE DID ZACCHAEUS CLIMB TO SEE JESUS?
FOREST OF TREES
① PALMS (II CHRON. 28:15) ② AN OAK (II SAM. 18:9) ③ APPLE (SONG of SOL. 2:3) ④ A JUNIPER (I KINGS 19:4) ⑤ A SYCAMORE (LUKE 19:4).

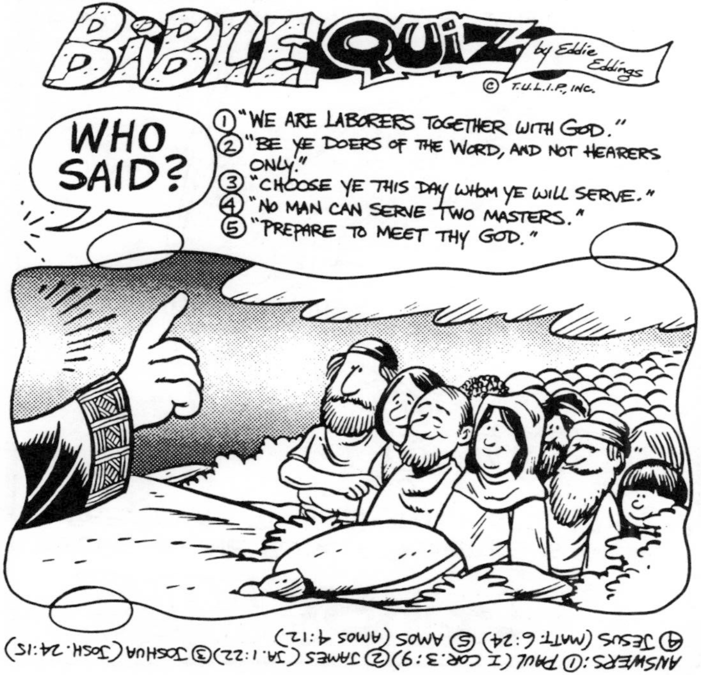
BIBLE QUIZ by Eddie Eddings
© T.U.L.I.P., INC.
WHO SAID?
① "WE ARE LABORERS TOGETHER WITH GOD."
② "BE YE DOERS OF THE WORD, AND NOT HEARERS ONLY."
③ "CHOOSE YE THIS DAY WHOM YE WILL SERVE."
④ "NO MAN CAN SERVE TWO MASTERS."
⑤ "PREPARE TO MEET THY GOD."
ANSWERS: ① PAUL (I COR. 3:9) ② JAMES (JA. 1:22) ③ JOSHUA (JOSH. 24:15)
④ JESUS (MATT. 6:24) ⑤ AMOS (AMOS 4:12)

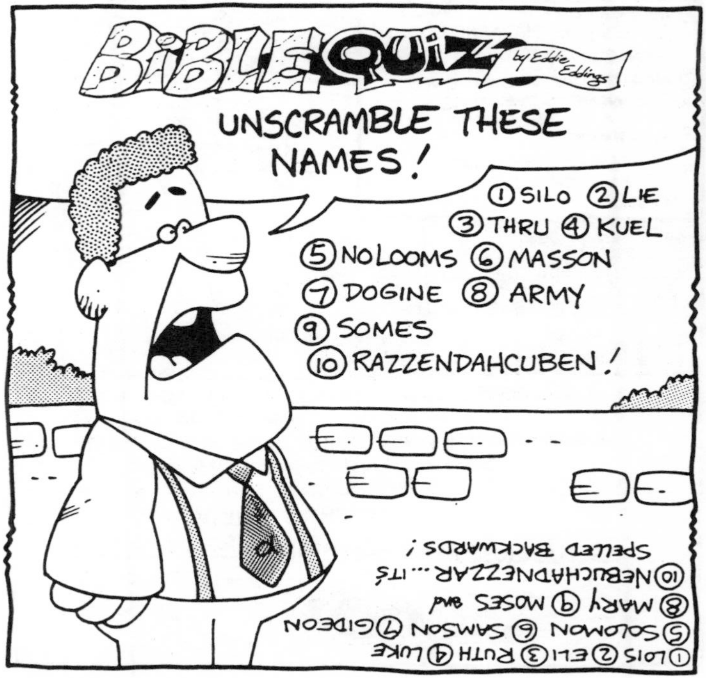
BIBLE QUIZ by Eddie Eddings
UNSCRAMBLE THESE NAMES!
① SILO ② LIE
③ THRU ④ KUEL
⑤ NOLOOMS ⑥ MASSON
⑦ DOGINE ⑧ ARMY
⑨ SOMES
⑩ RAZZENDAHCUBEN!
① LOIS ② ELI ③ RUTH ④ LUKE
⑤ SOLOMON ⑥ SAMSON ⑦ GIDEON
⑧ MARY ⑨ MOSES and
⑩ NEBUCHADNEZZAR... IT'S
SPELLED BACKWARDS!

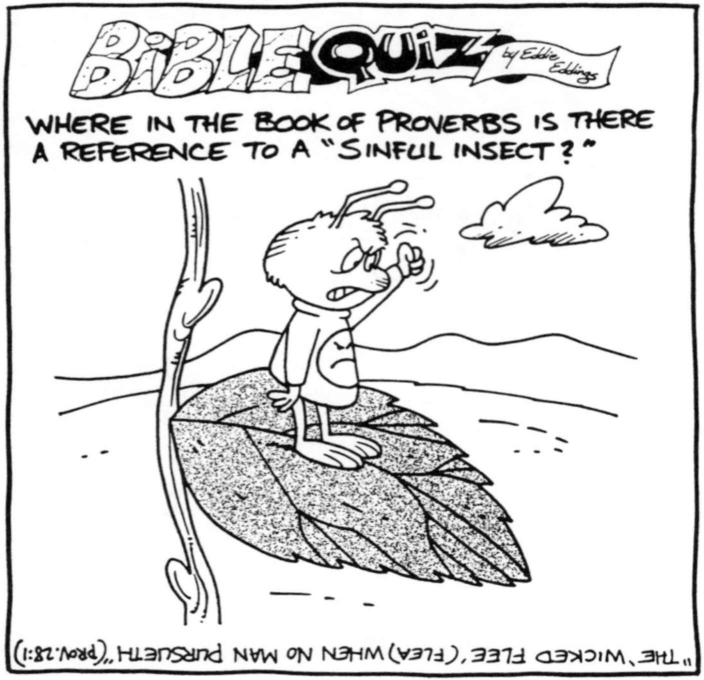
BIBLE QUIZ by Eddie Eddings
WHERE IN THE BOOK OF PROVERBS IS THERE A REFERENCE TO A "SINFUL INSECT?"
"THE 'WICKED FLEE' (FLEA) WHEN NO MAN PURSUETH" (PROV. 28:1)

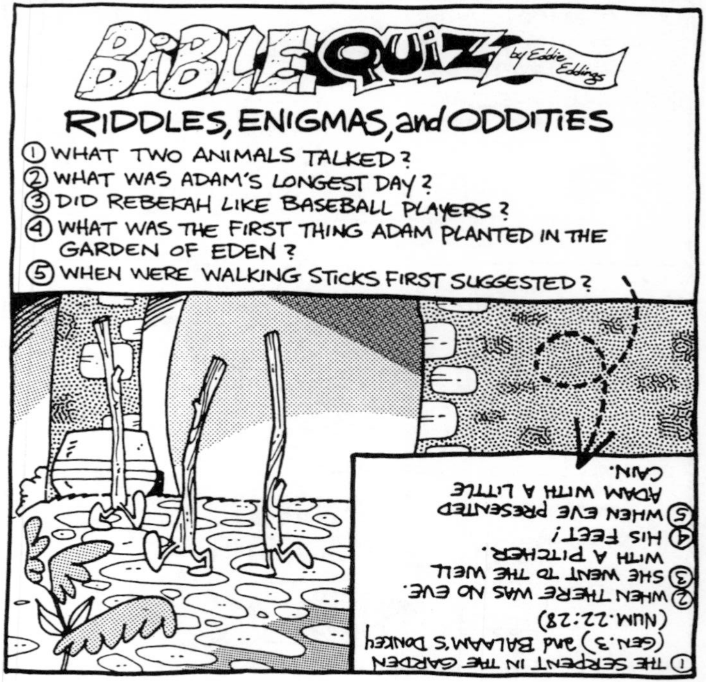
BIBLE QUIZ by Eddie Eddings
RIDDLES, ENIGMAS, and ODDITIES
① WHAT TWO ANIMALS TALKED?
② WHAT WAS ADAM'S LONGEST DAY?
③ DID REBEKAH LIKE BASEBALL PLAYERS?
④ WHAT WAS THE FIRST THING ADAM PLANTED IN THE GARDEN OF EDEN?
⑤ WHEN WERE WALKING STICKS FIRST SUGGESTED?
① THE SERPENT IN THE GARDEN (GEN. 3) and BALAAM'S DONKEY (NUM. 22:28)
② WHEN THERE WAS NO EVE.
③ SHE WENT TO THE WELL WITH A PITCHER.
④ HIS FEET!
⑤ WHEN EVE PRESENTED ADAM WITH A LITTLE CAIN.

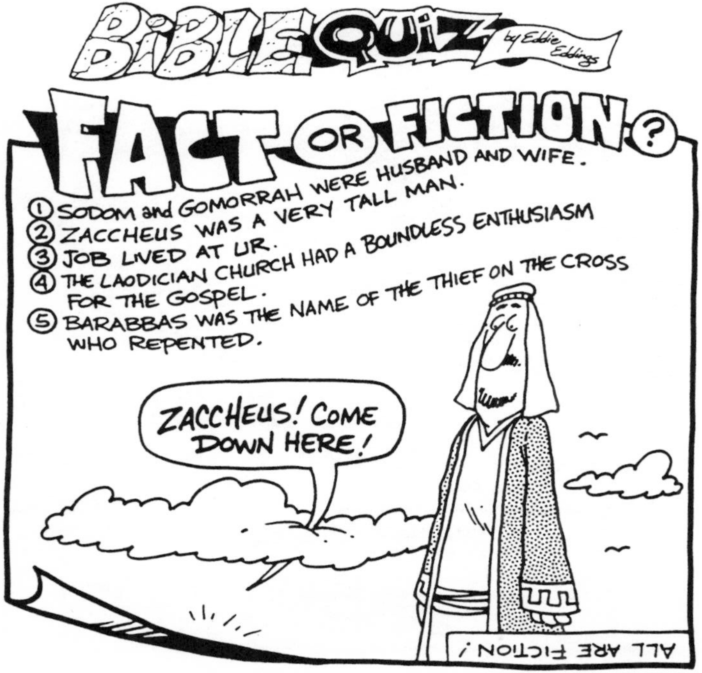
BIBLE QUIZ
by Eddie Eddings
FACT OR FICTION?
① SODOM and GOMORRAH WERE HUSBAND AND WIFE.
② ZACCHEUS WAS A VERY TALL MAN.
③ JOB LIVED AT UR.
④ THE LAODICIAN CHURCH HAD A BOUNDLESS ENTHUSIASM FOR THE GOSPEL.
⑤ BARABBAS WAS THE NAME OF THE THIEF ON THE CROSS WHO REPENTED.
ZACCHEUS! COME DOWN HERE!
ALL ARE FICTION!

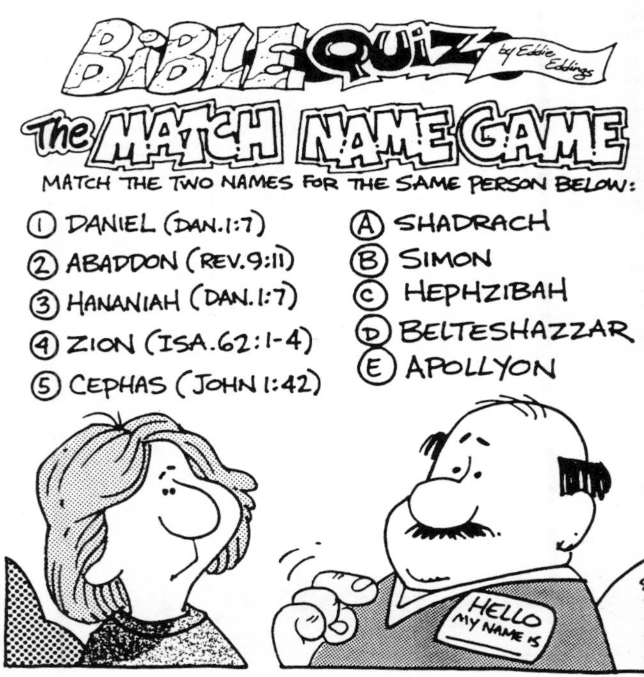
BIBLE QUIZ
by Eddie Eddings
The MATCH NAME GAME
MATCH THE TWO NAMES FOR THE SAME PERSON BELOW:
① DANIEL (DAN.1:7)
② ABADDON (REV.9:11)
③ HANANIAH (DAN.1:7)
④ ZION (ISA.62:1-4)
⑤ CEPHAS (JOHN 1:42)
Ⓐ SHADRACH
Ⓑ SIMON
Ⓒ HEPHZIBAH
Ⓓ BELTESHAZZAR
Ⓔ APOLLYON
HELLO MY NAME IS
1-D
2-E
3-A
4-C
5-B

BIBLE QUIZ by Eddie Eddings

TRUE OR FALSE

① ESAU WAS PROUD OF HIS BIRTHRIGHT.
② DEMETRIUS WAS A TRUE FRIEND TO PAUL.
③ THE LEVITES WERE THE TRIBE DEDICATED TO THE SERVICE OF THE LORD.
④ SOLOMAN HAD MORE WIVES THAN HE HAD HORSES.
⑤ THE GIANT GOLIATH WAS THE STRONGEST MAN WHO EVER LIVED.

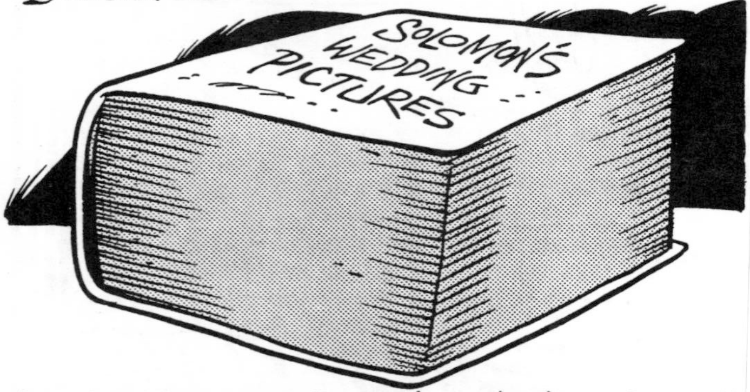
SOLOMON'S WEDDING PICTURES

ANSWERS: ① FALSE ("DESPISED" IT) ② FALSE ③ TRUE ④ FALSE ⑤ FALSE (SAMSON)

BIBLE QUIZ by Eddie Eddings

IT'S IN THE BIBLE!

① WHAT PEOPLE WERE FORCED TO DRINK PULVERIZED GOLD?
② WHAT BIBLE CHARACTER, ON A CERTAIN DAY EACH YEAR, REDUCED HIS WEIGHT BY 4 lbs.?
③ WHAT IS IT THAT GOD COMMANDED, BUT DID NOT PERMIT; IT WAS STARTED BUT NEVER COMPLETED?
④ HOW LONG DID NEBUCHADNEZZAR EAT GRASS LIKE AN OX?
⑤ THE MISPRONUNCIATION OF WHAT WORD COST THE LIVES OF 42,000 PEOPLE?

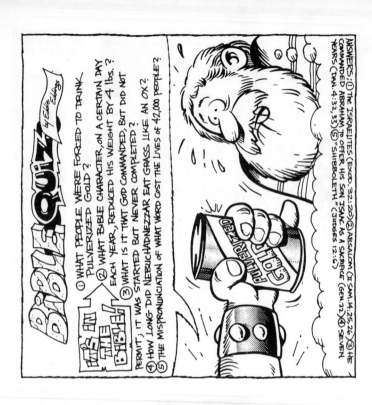

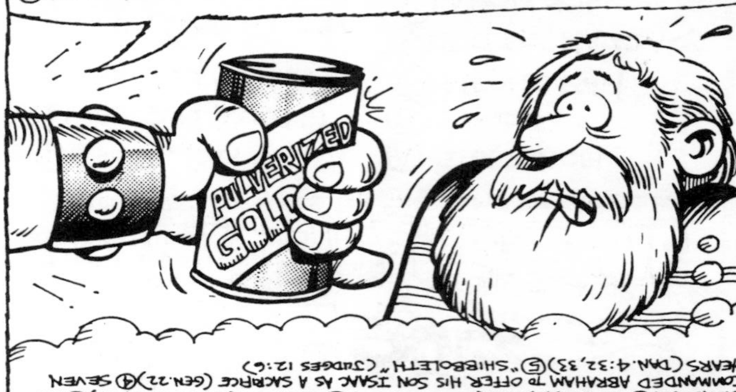
PULVERIZED GOLD

ANSWERS: ① THE ISRAELITES (EXOD. 32:20) ② ABSALOM (II SAM. 14:25, 26) ③ HE COMMANDED ABRAHAM TO OFFER HIS SON ISAAC AS A SACRIFICE (GEN. 22) ④ SEVEN YEARS (DAN. 4:32, 33) ⑤ "SHIBBOLETH" (JUDGES 12:6)

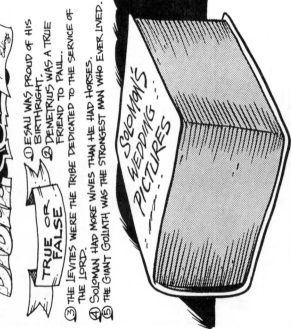

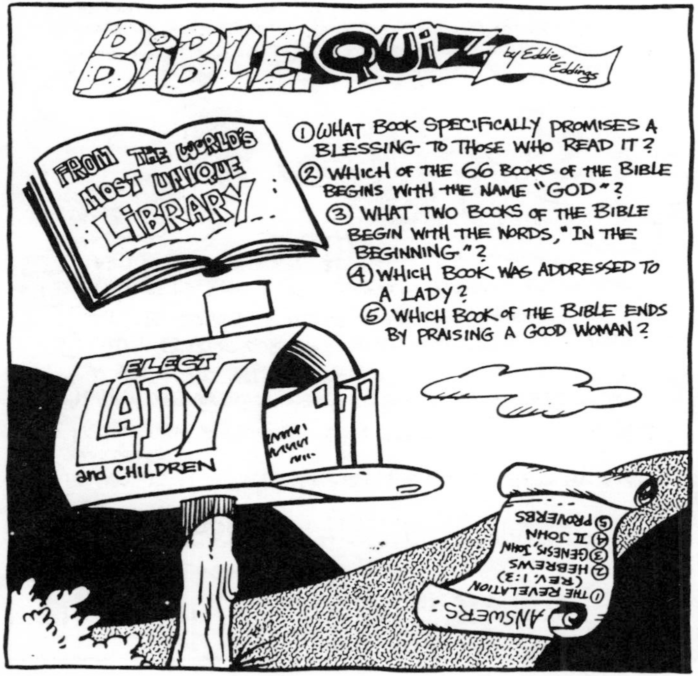
BIBLE QUIZ
by Eddie Eddings
FROM THE WORLD'S MOST UNIQUE LIBRARY...
① WHAT BOOK SPECIFICALLY PROMISES A BLESSING TO THOSE WHO READ IT?
② WHICH OF THE 66 BOOKS OF THE BIBLE BEGINS WITH THE NAME "GOD"?
③ WHAT TWO BOOKS OF THE BIBLE BEGIN WITH THE WORDS, "IN THE BEGINNING"?
④ WHICH BOOK WAS ADDRESSED TO A LADY?
⑤ WHICH BOOK OF THE BIBLE ENDS BY PRAISING A GOOD WOMAN?
ELECT LADY and CHILDREN
ANSWERS:
① THE REVELATION (REV. 1:3)
② HEBREWS
③ GENESIS, JOHN
④ II JOHN
⑤ PROVERBS

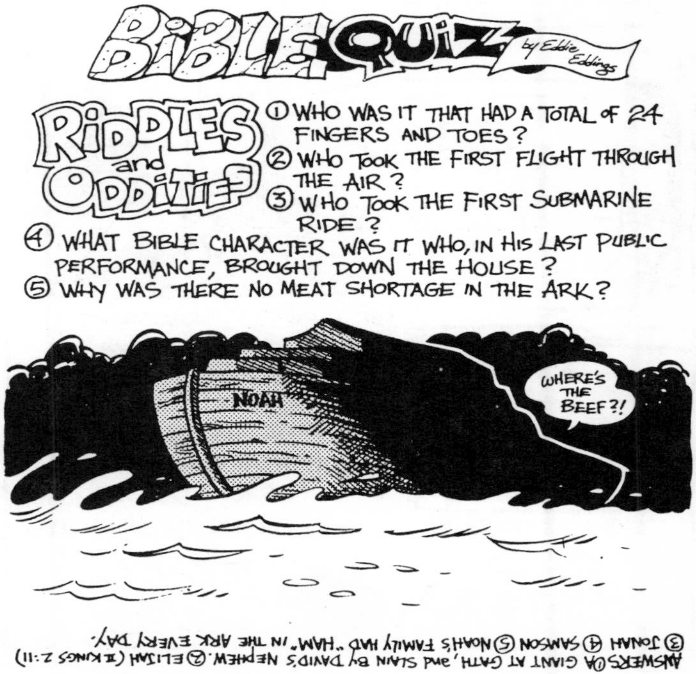
BIBLE QUIZ
by Eddie Eddings
RIDDLES and ODDITIES
① WHO WAS IT THAT HAD A TOTAL OF 24 FINGERS AND TOES?
② WHO TOOK THE FIRST FLIGHT THROUGH THE AIR?
③ WHO TOOK THE FIRST SUBMARINE RIDE?
④ WHAT BIBLE CHARACTER WAS IT WHO, IN HIS LAST PUBLIC PERFORMANCE, BROUGHT DOWN THE HOUSE?
⑤ WHY WAS THERE NO MEAT SHORTAGE IN THE ARK?
NOAH
WHERE'S THE BEEF?!
ANSWERS ① A GIANT AT GATH, and SLAIN BY DAVID'S NEPHEW. ② ELIJAH (II KINGS 2:11)
③ JONAH ④ SAMSON ⑤ NOAH'S FAMILY HAD "HAM" IN THE ARK EVERY DAY.

BIBLE QUIZ by Eddie Eddings

UNFORGETTABLE ROMANCES

1. WHAT IS IT THAT CANNOT BE QUENCHED BY MANY WATERS ?
2. WHO TOOK A HONEYMOON TRIP TO THE LAND of NOD ?
3. WHAT WOMAN GOT HER HUSBAND AS A RESULT OF A SORT OF BLIND DATE ?
4. WHAT BIBLE WRITER SAID THAT THE SMELL OF HIS BELOVED'S NOSE WAS LIKE APPLES ?
5. WHAT IS THE MOST FAMOUS ROMANCE OF THE NEW TESTAMENT ?

(1) LOVE (SONG of SOL. 8:7) (2) CAIN and WIFE (GEN. 4:16,17) (3) REBEKAH (GEN. 24) (4) SOLOMON (SONG of SOL. 7:8) (5) THAT of JOSEPH and MARY (MATT. 1; LUKE 1,2)

BIBLE QUIZ by Eddie Eddings

MATCH THE PERSON WITH WHAT HE WAS FOUND "UNDER".

1. MOSES (EX. 18:5-7)
2. ELIJAH (I KINGS 19:4)
3. SAMSON and PHILISTINES (JUDGES 16:29-30)
4. JEWS and GENTILES (ROMANS 3:9)
5. CHRISTIANS (ROMANS 6:15)

(A) GRACE
(B) SIN
(C) JUNIPER TREE
(D) PILLARS
(E) A TENT

MOSES SLEPT HERE

(1)-E (2)-C (3)-D (4)-B (5)-A

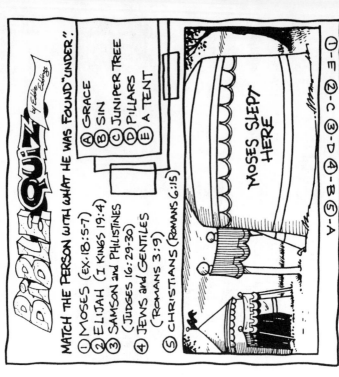

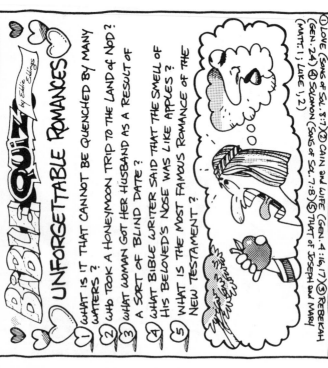

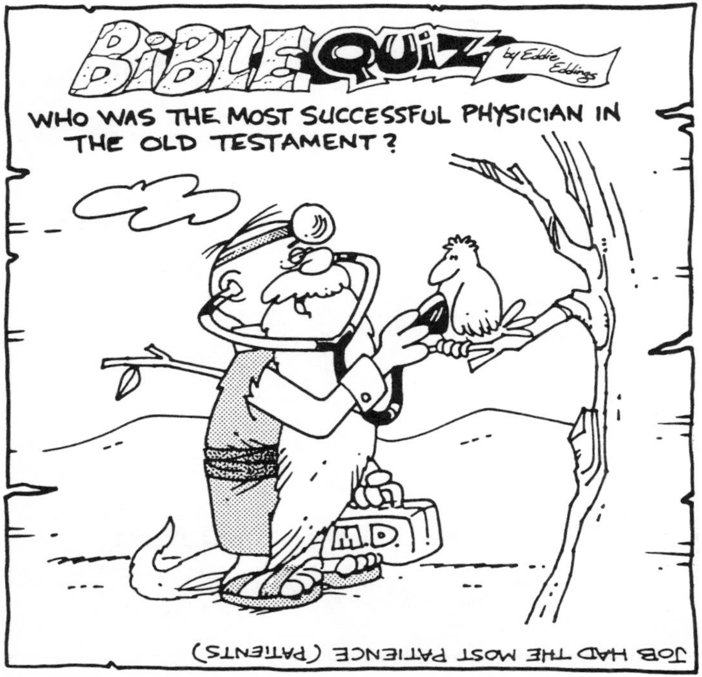
BIBLE QUIZ by Eddie Eddings
WHO WAS THE MOST SUCCESSFUL PHYSICIAN IN THE OLD TESTAMENT?
M.D.
JOB HAD THE MOST PATIENCE (PATIENTS)

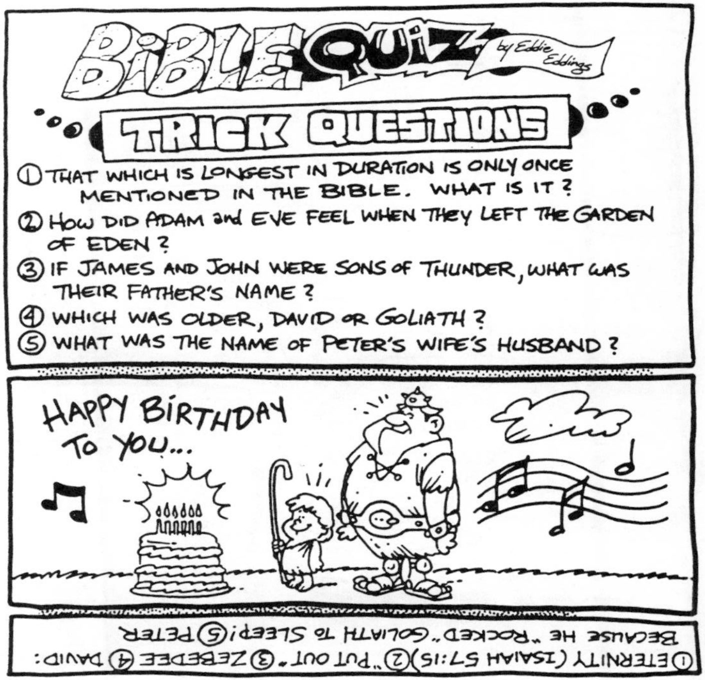
BIBLE QUIZ by Eddie Eddings
TRICK QUESTIONS
① THAT WHICH IS LONGEST IN DURATION IS ONLY ONCE MENTIONED IN THE BIBLE. WHAT IS IT?
② HOW DID ADAM and EVE FEEL WHEN THEY LEFT THE GARDEN OF EDEN?
③ IF JAMES AND JOHN WERE SONS OF THUNDER, WHAT WAS THEIR FATHER'S NAME?
④ WHICH WAS OLDER, DAVID OR GOLIATH?
⑤ WHAT WAS THE NAME OF PETER'S WIFE'S HUSBAND?
HAPPY BIRTHDAY TO YOU...
① ETERNITY (ISAIAH 57:15) ② "PUT OUT" ③ ZEBEDEE ④ DAVID: BECAUSE HE "ROCKED" GOLIATH TO SLEEP! ⑤ PETER

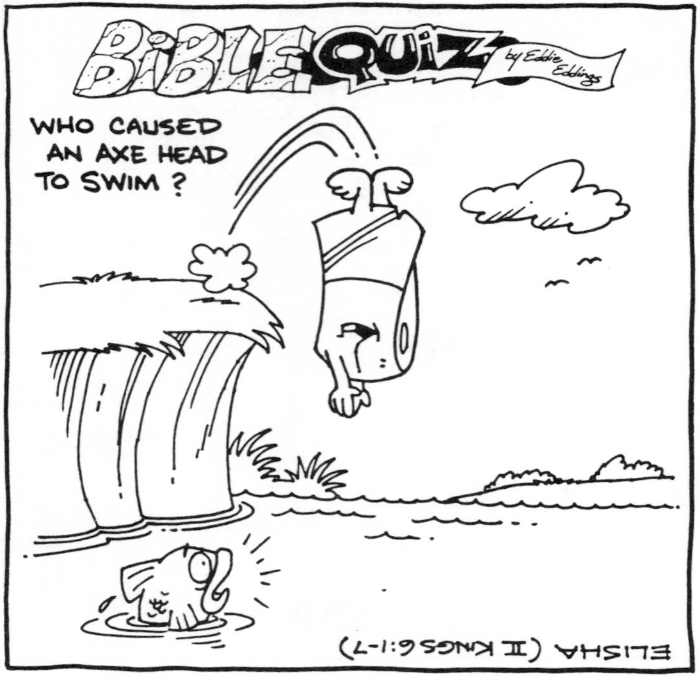
BIBLE QUIZ
by Eddie Eddings
WHO CAUSED AN AXE HEAD TO SWIM ?
ELISHA (II KINGS 6:1-7)

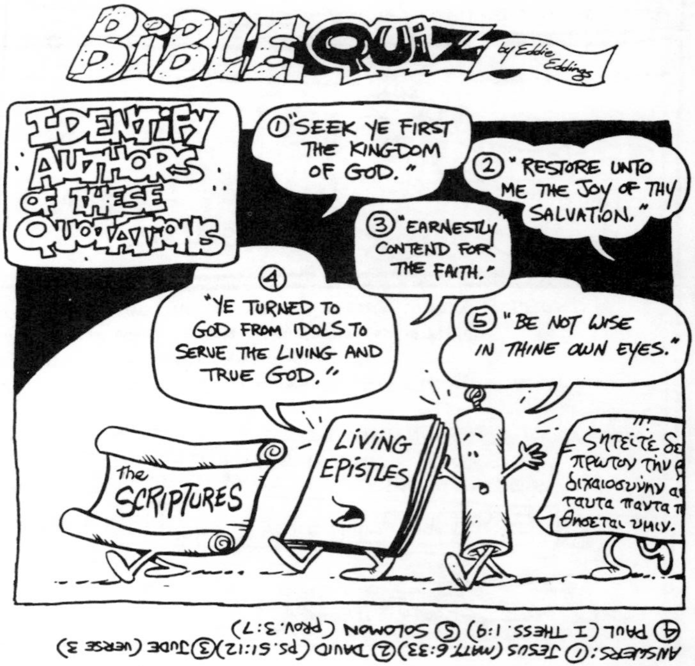
BIBLE QUIZ
by Eddie Eddings
IDENTIFY AUTHORS OF THESE QUOTATIONS
① "SEEK YE FIRST THE KINGDOM OF GOD."
② "RESTORE UNTO ME THE JOY OF THY SALVATION."
③ "EARNESTLY CONTEND FOR THE FAITH."
④ "YE TURNED TO GOD FROM IDOLS TO SERVE THE LIVING AND TRUE GOD."
⑤ "BE NOT WISE IN THINE OWN EYES."
The SCRIPTURES
LIVING EPISTLES
ANSWERS: ① JESUS (MATT. 6:33) ② DAVID (PS. 51:12) ③ JUDE (VERSE 3)
④ PAUL (I THESS. 1:9) ⑤ SOLOMON (PROV. 3:7)

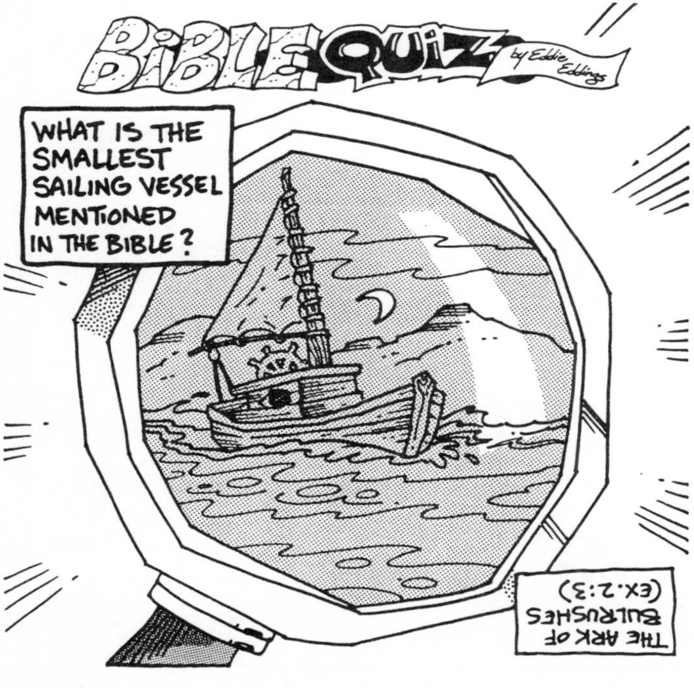
BIBLE QUIZ
by Eddie Eddings
WHAT IS THE SMALLEST SAILING VESSEL MENTIONED IN THE BIBLE?
THE ARK OF BULRUSHES (EX. 2:3)

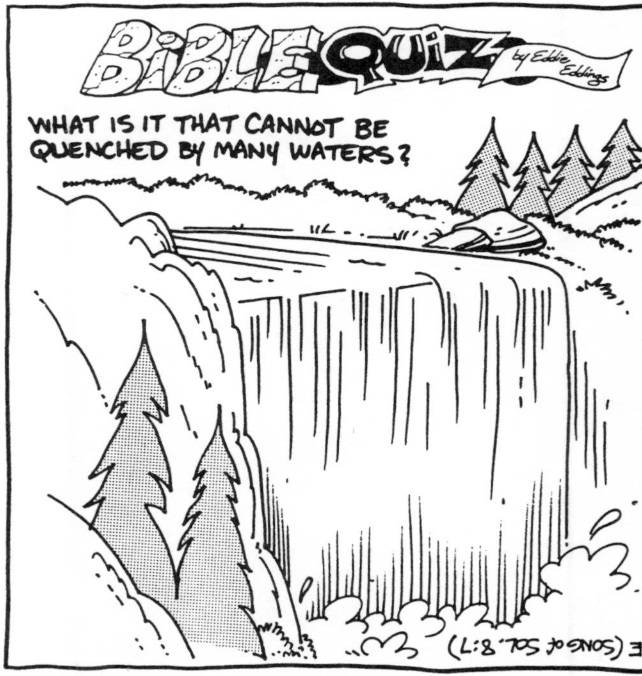
BIBLE QUIZ
by Eddie Eddings
WHAT IS IT THAT CANNOT BE QUENCHED BY MANY WATERS?
LOVE (SONG of SOL. 8:7)